Other books by Esta M. Rapoport

ADHD and Social Skills: A Step-by-Step Guide for Teachers and Parents

POSITIVE BEHAVIOR, SOCIAL SKILLS, AND SELF-ESTEEM

POSITIVE BEHAVIOR, SOCIAL SKILLS, AND SELF-ESTEEM

A Parent's Guide to Preschool ADHD

Esta M. Rapoport

ROWMAN & LITTLEFIELD
Lanham • Boulder • New York • London

Published by Rowman & Littlefield
An imprint of The Rowman & Littlefield Publishing Group, Inc.
4501 Forbes Boulevard, Suite 200, Lanham, Maryland 20706
www.rowman.com

6 Tinworth Street, London SE11 5AL

British Library Cataloguing in Publication Information Available

Library of Congress Cataloging-in-Publication Data

Names: Rapoport, Esta M., author
Title: Positive behavior, social skills, and self-esteem : a parent's guide to preschool ADHD / Esta M. Rapoport.
Description: Lanham, Maryland : Rowman & Littlefield, 2019. | Includes bibliographical references.
Identifiers: LCCN 2018060863| ISBN 9781475850406 (cloth : alk. paper) | ISBN 9781475850413 (electronic)
Subjects: LCSH: Attention-deficit disordered children--Education (Preschool) | Education, Preschool--Parent participation. | Behavior modification. | Social skills in children. | Self-esteem in children.
Classification: LCC LC4713.2 .R37 2019 | DDC 371.94--dc23
LC record available at https://lccn.loc.gov/2018060863

♾ ™ The paper used in this publication meets the minimum requirements of American National Standard for Information Sciences Permanence of Paper for Printed Library Materials, ANSI/NISO Z39.48-1992.

To my husband, Fred, my true love; my wonderful, loving children, Mimi, Ian, and Jake; their spouses, Kyle, Leah, and Candice; my grandchildren, Max, Jude, and Mac; and my devoted dogs, Ruby and Rocky, for all of their everlasting love, encouragement, pride, guidance, and support, without which I could not have written this book.

"If you're going through hell, keep going."

—Winston Churchill

CONTENTS

FOREWORD

Dr. Esta Rapoport has had extensive training and direct experiences of working with children with ADHD. Her individualized services to children with ADHD and families provide her with insightful and useful strategies to support this population.

In this book, *Positive Behavior, Social Skills, and Self-Esteem: A Parent's Guide to Preschool ADHD*, Dr. Rapoport offers the reader a practical tool that serves as a great resource for parents who encounter daily struggles of raising young children with challenging behaviors. From this book, parents will be able to find answers to the intriguing questions they have about their children they love and at the same time feel frustrated about. In order to understand their children who do not intentionally behave the way they do, knowing the needs of children, and understanding the functions and purposes of these behaviors will unlock the mystery and help parents interact with their children, and develop a positive and pleasant relationship with.

An important message this book sends is that the nurturing of social skills of young children from a young age, and building a nurturing environment and relationship is the key. Providing a predictable, consistent, and positive context is fundamental for young children to develop self-regulatory skills that will enable them to interact with peers and adults alike. The building of these foundations, the strategies parents need to learn to nurture these skills, and the examples that are laid out in this book will support the social and emotional development of all young children, especially young children with ADHD.

The details, the scenarios/cases, the suggestions, and ideas in her book represent common sense and special strategies that will enable and empower both young children and their families. The resources and tools from this book for parents will help them know their young children with ADHD, support their social and emotional development, and most importantly, prepare young children and parents to develop healthy, pleasant, and loving relationships.

Finally, this is a quite easy to read book. The language is user-friendly and straight-forward. Parents who read this book, practice the strategies, and develop the skills for promoting the self-regulatory and social skills of young children with ADHD will find that the ideas will help them work with their children with different needs, and will help them be better parents.

—Chun Zhang, PhD
Professor and Chair, Division of Curriculum and Teaching
Graduate School of Education
Fordham University

PREFACE

A five-year-old girl, Zoe, who had a diagnosis of ADHD, told me, "It's okay for the girls to tease me and laugh at me. It's just for fun. I laugh too."[1]

I told her that the girls' behavior was not amusing and certainly was not fun. As I am writing this book, I am thinking about the plight of several preschool children with ADHD who were treated in an unsympathetic and disparaging way.

One of these children was a cute little four-year-old boy whose name was Sam who had a diagnosis of ADHD. Sam told me that one boy in his class, Billy (whom I was told also had a diagnosis of ADHD), was constantly told by his classmates, "Billy just cannot control himself. He just never controls himself. We just laugh at him." His teacher said that when Billy's mom told her about these comments, her sadness was pervasive.

I asked Sam if he knew what it meant not to be able to control himself. We talked about it for a while and he really did have some understanding of what that meant. I then asked him if he had said the same thing to Billy as well. He admitted that he had done so. When I heard that he was also involved in this teasing, we had a conversation about it. I explained to Sam that it was not nice to tease someone. He then said, "But he laughs too!"

I then explained that Billy probably laughs because he is embarrassed, and does not know what else to do. I then had to explain what "embarrassed" meant, but after I did, he began to understand. At that point, I saw on his face the actual comprehension of the hurt that another child might feel. I asked him how he would feel if someone said to him that he could not control himself. He said, "I would not like that."

Justin, a five-year-old boy who had a diagnosis of ADHD, told me about how he thought that his teacher felt about him. He said that, "The teacher does not like me. She says that I just run around. She says I don't listen." Justin's mom had spent countless hours talking to Justin's teacher and explaining about the symptoms of his ADHD. Additionally, she tried to explain to the teacher that hyperactivity was one of the paramount symptoms of his ADHD and that Justin did not mean to purposely run around.

Justin's mom felt that it was true that the teacher did not like her son because she could not get him to sit at his table as the other children had done. Justin's noncompliance made the teacher's classroom difficult for her to manage. According to Justin's mom, the teacher's image of Justin as well as the teacher's perception of Justin's behavior had been predetermined. Additionally, in consideration of the fact that Justin's behavior was not going to change anytime soon, his teacher's negative perception of Justin would just linger.

Finally, four-and-one-half-year-old Eloise, who also had a diagnosis of ADHD, appeared to her teacher, as her mom told me, to be "in a fog. She just does not listen to my instructions. Sometimes I think that she is behaving in this way purposely." It is hard for me to believe that a teacher would think that a young child with ADHD would intentionally behave in this way. Her mom talked to the teacher about giving her daughter both verbal and nonverbal cues to get her to focus. According to Eloise's mom, the teacher declined. She apparently felt that Eloise would remain inattentive despite the implementation of any interventions.

It is very hard to alter someone's perceptions about a child who exhibits the symptoms of ADHD. I certainly understand that teachers (I have been one myself!) have many children in a classroom, even in a preschool, and that it might be difficult for them to design interventions for just a few children. However, I guarantee that if these interventions were implemented, the teacher would spend far less time managing a preschool child with ADHD's behavior than she would have if she had not used these methods. How many times can a child be criticized and berated for behavior that he cannot control?[2] Well, apparently many times indeed, which always makes me very sad for these preschool children with ADHD.

The upsetting stories go on and on, and at some point both teachers and parents need to try to be more positive toward preschool children with ADHD, or their self-esteem may be permanently impacted in a negative way. None of the preschool children with ADHD whom I have known have had good self-esteem, which was evident from the moment that I met them. Why did these children have such poor self-esteem?

I believe that the reason for these children's poor self-esteem is due to the lifelong negative reactions of others toward their behavior. A constant barrage of "Don't do that" and "Don't say that" and "No!" have a negative impact that is long lasting. A perfect example of this damaging verbiage may occur when you are pressured getting your child ready for school in the morning while at the same time you are getting yourself ready to go to work. During that time, do you find yourself feeling frustrated with having to manage your preschool child with ADHD's inappropriate behavior, and thus behave in a negative way toward him?

For a parent of a preschool child with ADHD, it is very difficult not to become aggravated when you are trying to get all of your children ready for school and yourself ready for work. However, if you reprimand your preschool child with ADHD, he will feel very badly about himself, even though he may not voice these feelings. Feelings of lack of self-worth are frequently internalized over time and are embedded into who the preschool child with ADHD becomes as a person.

Positive self-esteem is also built upon the feeling of being liked by one's peers. The cycle of the preschool child with ADHD exhibiting socially inappropriate behavior, to the teacher reprimanding him, and/or his peers slighting him, leads to these children feeling vulnerable, and results in poor self-esteem. In fact, these preschool children with ADHD often realize as they become older preschoolers that they were disliked by their peers. They are also quite cognizant of the fact that they did not have friends, but just did not understand why this was so. How did they know?

Well, when a child does not get invited to play dates or especially when he does not get invited to birthday parties, he gets the idea very quickly that the other children do not like him. Upon listening to many preschool children with ADHD over the years, my heart still breaks when I think about these children being rejected and rebuffed by their peers and then, in turn, how poorly they feel about themselves. I am repeating for emphasis here that the cycle of the vulnerable preschool child with ADHD exhibiting socially inappropriate behavior, to the teacher reprimanding him or his peers slighting him, may result in these children developing poor self-esteem.

Positive self-esteem, in contrast, results when these preschool children with ADHD feel accepted for themselves despite their symptoms and their diagnosis. That being said, some individuals shun children with ADHD and think that it is shameful to have that diagnosis.

I received a call from Benji's dad who asked me if I would come to see and possibly work with his son. I will always remember Benji, a sweet five-year-old boy who had a diagnosis of ADHD. I taught social skills to him for over a year. On the first day that I met Benji and his mom, I drove into his driveway and stepped out of my car. Benji's mom introduced me to him quickly and then whisked me into their house through the basement door. I certainly felt strange being rushed into their house through the basement and then having to climb a couple of flights to the room where we would be working. I realized that Benji's mom did not want anyone to see me.

Apparently, everyone who lived in their close-knit neighborhood knew who was coming and who was leaving each of their houses on a minute-by-minute basis. Each and every person in that neighborhood knew everything that occurred throughout the day.

One day, after I had been working with Benji for just about a year, as I was being hurried into the basement to then make the trek upstairs, a man quickly walked up the driveway and spoke in an agitated way to Benji's mom. He left as quickly as he had come. Apparently, that man was her brother. She told me at that point that the family and the neighbors had found out who I was and why I was working with Benji (I remember saying to myself, "How, and so what?"). Benji's mom then said in a matter-of-fact tone that I had to leave immediately.

I was simply stunned. In their community, apparently, people with ADHD were shunned. It was shameful and embarrassing to have a diagnosis of ADHD. Additionally, it certainly was something that was never discussed, nor was hiring someone to help this child learn how to diminish his socially inappropriate behavior and learn positive social skills. This was a sad day for this little boy who had learned so much about social skills in our time together. Benji had grown so much in his ability to control his behavior, especially at such a young age, and because of the stigma attributed to his ADHD, he could no longer get the help that he so badly needed.

How did shunning this child who had ADHD affect him? Did either his mom or his dad not tell his teacher about any of his behavioral difficulties? His hyperactive symptoms were quite apparent to anyone observing him, and in fact, were apparent to him as well! How could his teacher not notice Benji's hyperactive behavior?

Before I leave this conversation about Benji, let me tell you about another incident that happened with him a few weeks before I had to discontinue working with him. This is interesting because it shows how some behavior can be misunderstood. One day when his mom and he came home from school, and I was waiting to work with him, his mom told me that he had just had a huge temper tantrum. She did not understand why. When he had gotten out of the car, he went to look for one of his trucks but he could not find it. At first when he saw me, he started screaming at me and accused me of taking his truck away from where he had placed it before he had left for school. (As it turned out, their housekeeper had moved his truck . . . always a big mistake. Children with ADHD like the predictable and when he saw that his truck was not where he had left it, he had become unreachably upset. He had had a major temper tantrum.)

He was absolutely hysterical. His mother took him on her lap and tried to say, "Oh, my baby, did something happen at school to upset you?" All she saw were more tantrums. After several minutes, I asked his mom if I might try to talk to him. She left him with me and when I saw that he had calmed down a bit, I spoke with him about why he was so upset.

He then told me that the previous day his class had had a class trip to the Build-A-Bear Workshop. He said that his mom had promised him that she would buy his bear clothes after school today. When he asked her if she was going to take him to buy his bear clothes, she just said, "No" and then continued to talk on her cell phone the entire ride back from school. He said, "She always talks on her phone. She never talks to me." It would be nice to know that that was not true, but *his* perception was that she always talked on her phone instead of talking to him. In contrast, a typical[3] four-and-one-half-year-old boy told me in reference to wanting something specific and not getting that particular thing, "You get what you get and you don't throw a fit!"

Benji's mom ignored him, so his perception was correct. The important point is that whatever he thought to be true was ever-present in his mind. It was more than his mom promising him that she would buy his bear clothes for him on that day and not doing so. He felt ignored because she was talking on her phone instead of speaking to him.

> Young children can tell when their parents' heads are always in their cells . . . when parents are constantly distracted by their phones . . . it can make children less likely to follow rules . . . or at the very least, make "kids' levels of irritable behavior worse" (Chassiakos, Y. R., March, 2017, *ADDitude*, np).

If she had not been on the phone the entire car ride, for example, perhaps she would have explained to Benji that she had to attend a parent meeting at his school. So therefore, she had to get home quickly instead of going to the Build-A-Bear Workshop. All he heard was a cryptic "No," which he did not understand. The word "No" sent him into a spiral of frustration, disappointment, and anger. All he could do at that point was to become distressed, which got the best of him and ended up in him having multiple temper tantrums.

No one likes to be ignored. Parents do whatever they deem necessary and certainly are allowed to say "No," but preschool children with ADHD need to understand the reason for that "No." It is the feeling of being ignored and/or disliked that may add to a preschool child with ADHD's low self-esteem.

So now you can understand the reason for Benji's temper tantrum to some extent. Preschool children with ADHD are typically inattentive and vulnerable. They need to have *everything* explained to them. In that way and only in that way, they will understand exactly the reason as to why some things do not go as planned. I know that you may be curious to hear that these children need to understand the intricacies of changes in their lives, but they certainly do. When they do not comprehend someone's behavior and feel ignored and frustrated, their self-esteem may be negatively impacted, and behavior such as temper tantrums may occur.

Clearly, one of my major concerns for preschool children with ADHD is their self-esteem. We, as parents, need to examine our own behavior toward our children and change it from negative, critical, and harsh to positive, supportive, and understanding. Let me be clear here. I am not blaming parents for a preschool child with ADHD's low self-esteem. There are many variables including genetics that form the pieces of a very large puzzle that affects a preschool child with ADHD's self-esteem.

When a child has poor self-esteem, he comes across as vulnerable, which incurs more negativity on the part of others, as well as bullying. Self-esteem issues begin when a child is very young, when the symptoms and the behavior of preschool children with ADHD cause these children typically to appear as if they are different. These self-esteem issues must be treated as being serious as soon as possible.

No one likes to be treated as if they are annoying, different, and less important than others. However, the symptoms that preschool children with ADHD exhibit make it very difficult for the child's parents to manage. It is definitely difficult to go through day after day trying to run a household, do your work, raise your children, and interact with your spouse in a positive way when you feel that there is a roadblock in your way: the symptoms of your preschool child's ADHD.

Here are a few tidbits of advice and recommendations that I can offer you to try to accomplish in your day-to-day existence. I hope that this information is helpful to you in terms of intersecting with the interventions and the information that you will access from this book.

- Monitor your behavior and see if you can work on diminishing any reprimanding and criticizing of your preschool child with ADHD that you find yourself exhibiting.
- Try to treat your preschool child with ADHD in a positive manner and most importantly, throw some humor into the mix!
- Find support groups (through Children and Adults with Attention-Deficit/Hyperactivity Disorder [CHADD]) for the parents of preschool children with ADHD, so you are not so alone in your plight.
- Inform your child's teachers so that they know what behavior management techniques that you are using. If you do so, you will find that there will be a better consistency in the two settings where your child inhabits most of the time: home and school.
- Take some time out for yourself and relax and/or refresh yourself from time to time.

I hope that my book is helpful to many parents of preschool children with ADHD. Even though I will focus on preschool children with ADHD in this book, I will concentrate on young children who are four- or five-years-old specifically, because these are the ages that it is possible to differentiate their behavior from the more variable behaviors they exhibit before they are four-years-old. As the *Diagnostic and Statistical Manual of Mental Disorders* (DSM-5) states, "Many parents first observe excessive motor activity when the child is a toddler, but symptoms are difficult to distinguish from highly variable normative behaviors before age 4 years" (APA, 2013, p. 62). However, if your child is younger than four-years-old, my interventions will definitely help your child anyway!

Let us continue on . . .

NOTES

1. The names used in this book are pseudonyms in order to protect the privacy of all individuals discussed.

2. For clarity purposes, I am referring to a child with ADHD as "he" instead of "she" in this book, even though clearly there are many girls who have ADHD as well. Additionally, I refer to parents and teachers as "she" when many parents and teachers are men.

3. Throughout this book, I will use the term "typical" to refer to those children who do not have a diagnosis of ADHD.

ACKNOWLEDGMENTS

To all of the children with ADHD who struggle each and every day to make and to keep friends and to feel good about themselves.

To all of the children who have ADHD with whom I have worked.

To Tom Koerner at Rowman & Littlefield, who granted me permission to travel down this road to help parents of preschool children with ADHD.

To J. J. Ignotz who made me look beautiful in my cover photo, after I'd spent more than three exhausting years writing this book.

To Blanche Rapoport, my mother-in-law, who along with my father-in-law, Murray, always supported me in my effort to write, and constantly told me that I would be successful at it.

To my parents, Lilyan and Irving Milchman, and to my brother, Hartley, whom I wish had known that I had written this book, so they could have read it.

To my true love, Fred, "F":
   After almost 49 years of marriage, you always know the right thing to say to me when you see me trying to reach a new challenge and asking myself whether or not I will be able to get there. Thank you so much for your consistent and constant encouragement and support, which began

when I wrote the proposal for this book, then continued on as I wrote each and every chapter, handed in my final manuscript to Rowman & Littlefield, and has endured throughout this whole process! How can I thank you enough for coming home from a long, long day at work after many hours of driving, and then editing my chapters as you ate your dinner? You then helped me with my final revisions again and again and again, after having already done so much! I could not have sent in a well-written, completed book without all of your incredible assistance. And thank you so much for all of your stellar help with my usage of commas. I hope that you are happy with my use of them here! Your constant "Don't worry! Your book will be great!" and endless valuable suggestions along the way, motivated me, and prevented me from getting frustrated when I thought that I had no more words left in me to write! When you told me after reading some of my chapters, "I think this is a great job. I am really proud of you," it made my heart swell with pride! I love you today more deeply today than I have ever loved you and I cherish our relationship. You are my true love! Love, Esta, "E"

To my wonderful children, Mimi, Ian, and Jake and their spouses, Kyle, Leah and Candice, respectively, who were always telling me that I can and will finish this book!

Mimi: Thank you so much for such insightful advice from you, a true special education expert on a myriad of topics. Learning from you was imperative so that I could be sure that my statements about preschool children with ADHD were accurate. It was thrilling for me that you, a current special educator, told me, a retired special educator, vital facts for parents to know such as the approximate amount of time that parents must wait for an answer to a question that they ask their preschool child with ADHD. You knew how essential it was for me to get every fact right, and I appreciate so much that you understood my desire to do so. Additionally, thank you so much for your help in finding me the best ABC chart for me and explaining it! You showed me that you were so proud to have an author as your mom, and especially one who wrote about a similar population of children with whom you have worked your entire 14 year career! Thank you so much for having your sweet and special Mac tell me, "Good luck," on my final night of revisions. I needed his support! You always said, "Go do it, Mom," so I did, as you are doing now! Meems, you are so incredibly tough and my heroine! I emulate your amazing spirit of resilience and optimism!

Ian: Thanks for the "five pages" each day reminder and for encouraging me by saying, "You are almost done, Mom!" As busy as you were with your work, you always managed to ask me how my book was going and I really appreciated that attention to my job of writing my book. I always felt your encouragement, pride, and trust in my writing—from one writer to another! You kept pushing me to finish, which I really appreciated. You gave me a great perspective when you said, "Don't worry about the little things, Mom, like the prepositions. Just send it in!" However, in reality you knew that it was very hard for me to not worry about the small corrections. When I was completing my final revisions, you said, "Go, Mom, go!" So, I just had to go! It was always clear that you had my best interests at heart and understood my level of precision in terms of getting every word and every sentence correct. Additionally, I knew that you had a real understanding of how much this book meant to me; you always made me feel that the job of an author was very important. When those lovable boys, Max and Jude asked, "What does Gramma do for work," you always proudly told them that I wrote books and that I was an author, which meant so much to me!

Jake: Thank you for doing such a stellar job editing the technology chapter and for your unplanned editing of another chapter, as well. Your insight on the science of apps was invaluable to me. When I was anxious about analyzing such complex technology, hearing your confidence in my ability to do so really energized me, and helped me to believe that I could really succeed. Thank you so much for answering multiple editing questions, a responsibility for which you did not sign up and which added up exponentially when I was completing my revisions! In fact, right before I handed in my final manuscript, late at night, you still answered my questions and helped me until the very last revision was completed! More importantly, thank you so much for constantly telling me to "keep going," when I was exhausted, frustrated and losing faith in my ability to finish this book. You clearly cared so deeply, Jake that I would do a good job and you appreciated the importance to me of writing a book that might help parents, which motivated me more than you will ever know! Jake, it was just extraordinary that were so cognizant of how important writing this book was for me and how proud of me you were for working so hard to finish it! Additionally, it just thrilled me that you were so proud to have a mom who was an author!

To my three adorable and endearing grandsons, Max, Jude, and Mac:

To my "five in change" grandson, Max: At five years old, you made me feel that my book was so important to you, so I just had to finish it! Your constant, precocious interest in what my book was about helped me to tailor it in ways that I might not have done. Your insightful questions and comments energized me and made me think about my answers to you. You kept asking me when I would have to send my book into the publisher. So, when I called you before bed on March 1, 2018, and said that I was not quite ready to send the book into the publisher, you asked me, "Why Gramma? Why?" You seemed so upset, which motivated me to send it into the publisher at 11:58 P.M, which was two minutes before my deadline! Our conversations about my book have been truly remarkable, Max, especially the one when you told me that you did not want me to "mess up the book" because I had so many other responsibilities. I then explained to you the ramifications of having priorities, which somehow, you clearly understood! You simply astounded me with the depth of your thinking. I love you so much for caring so deeply and especially that in your words, "I remember everything that you say, Gramma!" Additionally, as someone who knows the importance of social skills, it just thrills me to see you being so social with teachers, friends and family. You love to talk and I love to listen to you! You are incredibly endearing, lovable, and special Max, and I am so lucky to learn from you!

To my grandson, Jude: Thank you so much for reminding me of the authenticity and the sweetness of a preschool child because you are so authentic and so sweet, which has made it easy for you to be social and to make friends at your new school. Your teachers love you too! You have taught me to understand the joy, and the energy of a preschool child, while at the same time, having focus and concentration. Importantly, your insightful, intelligent and honest answers to my questions about sharing really illuminated my understanding of how a preschool child truthfully feels about it, and I am so appreciative of that lesson. Since I know social skills so well, watching you interact with your big brother Max, and trying to stand up for your own independent needs was vital to my understanding of the social interaction of siblings. You are now standing up for yourself more and more every day, which has been so much fun to watch!

Jude, you are also such a free spirit! You have encouraged me to not be afraid when you are jumping from the slide to a big pillow on the floor or watching you do somersaults on my couch and hoping that you do not fall! That lesson has played a large part in my understanding of preschool children's behavior. Jude, you are such a lovable child and I treasure each and every hug that you give me and so does everyone else!

To my grandson, Mac: Thank you so much for being such an incredibly funny little guy! Your hilarious behavior has kept me laughing amidst the stress that I have endured writing this book. Additionally, you are also always so inquisitive. When I say something and you respond by saying, "Why, Gramma?" I have to quickly think of an answer to satisfy your curiosity. Watching your language development ascend into such deep and intelligent thinking has taught me so much about a preschool child's thinking and development. Additionally, you have taught me to remain calm while you insisted on speeding your scooter down the streets of Brooklyn, which gave me a good understanding of other preschool children's behavior. Go, Mac! Thanks to you, as well, I have learned the fine line between stubbornness and independence. I have also learned, however, about how lovable and endearing a preschool child can be to everyone who loves him, Mac, because everyone loves you, other children, your teachers and your family. Wherever you go, Mac, you make friends, which make me so happy. You are truly a social being. You have the gift of joy, Mac and give the very best hugs, which I always need! Additionally, you have taught me about the resiliency of preschool children because of the way you have dealt with a difficult year for a four-year-old, by giving mommy lots of hugs and kisses which has made her very happy and strong!

To my special girl, Ruby: You are my tough little girl, persevering through so many health issues, including an ACL tear, followed by surgery; osteomyelitis, which resulted in a toe amputation; kidney issues; allergies; and this past September, an undiagnosed 105 degree fever, that caused you to spend ten days in the hospital, while I was revising my book. You have a relentless spirit, which enabled you to come home and help me to finish this book. Despite your increased arthritis due to your ACL tear and surgery, you try to run for the sheer joy of running. You have taught me to complain less and instead to be more appreciative. I so loved you hanging out with me as I wrote this book, either on your towel at the pool, on your blanket in the family room, or right next to me on the rug in the dining room. Your constant devotion to me made writing every day so much easier! I love your hugs through my legs and your kisses at your discretion! You are truly the sweetest girl, and I love you so much!

To my special boy, Rocky: Thank you so much for making me get up from my computer as I was writing this book, so that you could constantly go outside to get your exercise! You made me do the same! Your crazy energy kept me alert as I was writing. Even though you would rather be outside every minute of the day, you decided to hang out with me as well, especially at the pool with Ruby, which made me so happy. You also have had some health issues, first with displaced hips and then rupturing your disk last April, having surgery, and then having to remain in the hospital for eleven days! You came home with great difficulty walking and somehow through your strength and stoicism, learned to walk again, which gave me strength to continue to write this book. Now you are running again and back to being a silly, lovable and energetic guy. You are truly the sweetest guy, and I love you so much!

Since my forte is social skills, I am just so thrilled that you guys, Ruby and Rocky are such great friends and siblings. You truly love each other, as you prove each and every day by kissing each other as we take our walk! I love you guys so much!

INTRODUCTION

As parents of a preschool child with ADHD who have to manage their child's behavior on a daily basis, you certainly know how behavioral and social skills difficulties affect the lives of your child. Preschool children with ADHD frequently have poor social skills, which causes them to have difficulty interacting with their siblings and their friends as well. For example, sharing and taking turns may just not be in their repertoire.

Your preschool child with ADHD may exhibit temper tantrums when he reaches a frustration point that he just cannot tolerate. His peers may rebuff and reject him (yes, even in preschool!) for touching and pushing them and invading their space. In fact, preschool children with ADHD may be targets for bullies as well (yes, even in preschool!). Additionally, transitions may be a difficult challenge for these children.

Preschool children with ADHD may also have problems interacting with their own family, which may lead to a stressful family life dynamic. These children typically do not have intact, positive social skills. The effects of social skills problems upon preschool children with ADHD are far-reaching and may generalize to many aspects of their lives. In fact, if a preschool child with ADHD does not achieve social success, he will most likely be characterized by low self-esteem.

Why don't these children have intact positive social skills? Don't they internalize them from the modeling of these skills by their parents? No, they typically do not learn social skills from their parents, while their siblings do learn these social skills. Why? Preschool children with ADHD experience more difficulty learning social skills from their parents than do typical children because they are often distracted. Their attention to learning social skills may be interrupted by anxiety, temper tantrums and/ or by merely paying attention to something else, while their parents are trying to teach them social skills.

There *is* room for optimism, however. These children *can* learn social skills. However, it will just be more work intensive for the parents as well as for the children. The teaching of these positive social skills can be embedded into their natural environment and may be taught as preschool children with ADHD interact with their siblings. These social skills may also be taught in conversations between you and your child, among other ways that will be explained here.

Preschool children with ADHD present with socially inappropriate behavior that is reflective of their ADHD. Their parents are not typically trained to manage this behavior which is often exhibited as impulsivity in their actions or verbiage or both. This impulsive behavior causes these children to act without thinking about the consequences of their behavior.

The most common characteristic among preschool children with ADHD, however, is hyperactivity. Parents should know from the start that they will not be able to magically erase all of the hyperactivity out of their child. They will learn here, however, how to manage their child's hyperactivity by permitting it to flourish in certain safe circumstances that their child will learn to accept.

Preschool children with ADHD may have difficulties with motor skills and motor control. Consequently, they may incur more accidents than typical preschool children probably due to their poor coordination as well as their increased activity. In fact, they also change activities more frequently as well, therefore, spending less time in each activity as compared to their peers. Additionally, these children may be characterized by language deficiency and poor early academic skills. When I talk about preschool, to which ages am I referring?

Even though I will focus on preschool children with ADHD in this book, I will concentrate on young children who are four- and five-years-old only, because these are the ages that it is possible to differentiate their behavior from the more variable behaviors they exhibit before they are four years old. As the DSM-5 states, "Many parents first observe excessive motor activity when the child is a toddler, but symptoms are difficult to distinguish from highly variable normative behaviors before age 4 years" (American Psychiatric Association, 2013, p. 62). However, if your child is younger than four-years-old, these interventions will definitely help your child anyway! How can the experience of parents who have a preschool child with ADHD be described?

Parents of preschool children who have ADHD typically travel a very frustrating journey. However, that being said, they react instead of respond to their child's socially inappropriate behavior and immediately punish him. Frequently, their child is reprimanded for behavior that he cannot control, which increases his inappropriate behavior.

That reasoning may appear to be circular, but socially inappropriate behavior may occur as a result of being treated in a negative and harsh way. I am repeating for emphasis here that parents of preschool children with ADHD's behavior is frequently reactive instead of responsive, for which parents should not be blamed, because they simply may not know what to do.

What do I mean by behaving in a reactive way? These parents do not think beforehand about how they will rationally or intentionally respond to their child behaving in an inappropriate way. When a person reacts, they behave in a quick way to a situation. Frequently, these parents react to their child's socially inappropriate behavior in a negative way. Sadly, their adverse behavior may affect their child's self-image and self-esteem in a deleterious manner.

Why do parents need a book such as mine to help them to manage the behavior of their preschool child with ADHD? Raising a preschool child with ADHD, who will grow into a school-age child with ADHD and then into an adolescent with ADHD, may be a daunting experience.

The only way to get through these challenging times in a successful way is for the entire family to try to diminish their child's inattentive behaviors in the home environment. They need to follow simple, step-by-step methods to facilitate positive behavior in their child. Consequently, the parent's affirmative responses to their child's appropriate behavior will help to impact his self-esteem in a positive way.

These parents will need to learn methods of positive and constructive parenting, which will lead to successful outcomes in their child's lives. They will learn these approaches in my book, so they can then try to intentionally respond to their child's socially inappropriate behavior instead of merely reacting to it.

What is the recommended treatment for preschool children with ADHD? The American Academy of Pediatrics (AAP) has recommended that behavioral interventions should be the first line of treatment for preschool children with ADHD. The type of treatment that works, according to the AAP, is focused on parent training as compared to therapy for the child.

> The evidence suggests that what works is not therapy that focuses on the child—such as play therapy—but coaching and training for the parents. That does not mean that the parents were the problem in the first place, it means that the parents have been dealt a particularly difficult assignment, and the standard strategies that the rest of us use with our children are not going to be sufficient (Klass, 2016, np).

Parent training is critical especially because research has found that a combination of critical, harsh parenting and child negativity is associated with an increase in demonstrated socially inappropriate behavior in preschool children with ADHD, as I have discussed previously. Additionally, these negative responses maintain these children's impulsive behavior. "Studies show that the average child with ADHD has one to two negative interactions per minute with parents, peers, and teachers," says William Pelham, director of the Center for Children and Families at the State University of New York. "If you extrapolate, that's half a million negative interactions a year. Either you sit back and let your child have those negative experiences, or you intervene early and do something to stop them." (McCarthy, L. F., *ADDitude*, 2008, np).

In this book, parents of preschool children with ADHD will learn that instead of reacting in a disapproving way, they should selectively ignore some of their child's socially inappropriate behavior, as long it is not harmful to the child or to others. Concurrently, they should pay positive attention to their child's acceptable behavior and compliance.

Due to the typical impulsive behavior of preschool children with ADHD and their parent's frequent reactive responses, these parents will be offered methods and interventions for managing their child's socially inappropriate behavior.

According to Wolraich (2016), "If your child does have ADHD, then you have to be a lot more consistent than most parents need to be in managing your child" (as cited in Klass, M., 2016, np). Hopefully, the lessons of maintaining an organized home routine, controlling your own behavior, selectively ignoring certain socially inappropriate behavior, positive reinforcement, social skills training, among other interventions found in this book, will encourage parents to build positive self-esteem in their preschool child with ADHD.

HOW DO I KNOW IF MY PRESCHOOL CHILD HAS A DIAGNOSIS OF ADHD?

Parents who have a child of the preschool age who suspect that he has ADHD typically know from a young age that their child's behavior looks different from another child's behavior of the same age. Even though we try not to label a child and try to look at his behavioral symptoms instead of a diagnosis, many preschool children exhibit behaviors that resemble the symptoms of ADHD. The difference in these children's behavior is the degree to which they exhibit hyperactive or inattentive behaviors. I have seen many children who are jumping off of the couch one minute seemingly out of control, who are sitting looking at a book with focus and concentration the next minute.

This inconsistency of behavior also makes it somewhat difficult to make a clear diagnosis of ADHD in preschool children. However, the correct diagnosis is based upon the intensity and the persistence of these symptoms, as well as how their behavior impacts their interactions with other people in their lives. In addition, a diagnosis of ADHD may not be determined unless the child exhibits socially inappropriate behavior in at least two settings.

WHAT WILL YOU LEARN FROM THIS BOOK?

This book will offer suggestions for parents of preschool children with ADHD on how to build and maintain positive interactions with their children. I will appropriately apply some of the social skills discussed in my first book to preschool children with ADHD such as joining ongoing activities, cooperating with peers, listening to all instructions without interrupting, and having good manners, among others. I will also instruct parents in how to teach their preschool child with ADHD to problem-solve successfully, which is a very difficult skill for them to learn.

Due to the typical impulsive behavior of preschool children with ADHD, both verbally and physically, and their parent's reactive behavior, I will offer parents methods and interventions for managing their child's behavior. Additionally, methods will be offered as related to how to diminish a child's inattentive behavior by teaching him in simple, sequential steps.

Parents will also learn the following:

- The definition of ADHD according to the *Diagnostic and Statistical Manual of Mental Disorders, 5th Edition* (DSM-5). We cannot assume that every parent has knowledge of that definition and its specifics. From there, I detail the number and/or percentage of preschool children who have ADHD so that the parents of these children will feel less alone in their plight. I then offer a list of some examples of the social skills difficulties that these children exhibit, such as difficulty compromising and cooperating, and therefore, problems making friends, among others. This section concludes with a discussion of the *American Academy of Pediatrics Guideline for the Diagnosis, Evaluation and Treatment of Attention-Deficit/ Hyperactivity Disorder in Children and Adolescents.* It is essential for parents of preschool children with ADHD to become familiar with these guidelines. If they do so, they will know what to expect from their physician when he diagnoses their child as well as when he gives them treatment options for their child.
- The importance of parental observations and judgments. Parents are the first line of recognition of issues related to their child's behavior. By noting that their child's behavior may be more extreme in degree when compared to another child's behavior at the same age, they provide an invaluable resource in order to take the child quickly to a professional for diagnosis and treatment. Additionally, these parents supervise play dates and so are aware of how their child interacts while playing. They are specifically cognizant of how socially inappropriate behavior becomes evident in certain elements and types of play. Parents will learn which behaviors are typically seen in preschool children with ADHD. They will also be taught to be insightful observers, so that they will be able to determine as to whether or not their child should be taken to a professional for a possible diagnosis.
- The possible feelings of stress, anxiety, and guilt that parents of preschool children with ADHD might experience. Few parents are

trained to deal with children who exhibit impulsive, unpredictable, and inconsistent behavior—as do preschool children with ADHD. A discussion is offered to explain the stress that may be expected when parents try to manage the behavior of their preschool child with ADHD. That being said, I will assist parents in knowing when and how to begin to manage their child's behavior. Before they try to manage their preschool child with ADHD's behavior, it is suggested that they should collaboratively design house rules with their child. In that way, he will feel ownership. Continuing on, I suggest that once the rules are established, you can begin to teach your preschool child with ADHD to follow instructions more effectively. Examples of morning and bedtime instructions are offered along with suggestions of visual prompts. A conversation ensues as to the three sources of guilt that a parent of a preschool child with ADHD may experience. The first source of guilt is related to the parent's perception that she may be ignoring her typical child's needs. The second source of guilt is related to the parent's concern that her preschool child's ADHD is her fault. The third source of guilt is related to the parent's concern that her preschool child's ADHD may be related to her parenting skills. Continuing on, I discuss the dilemma of whether or not parents of preschool children with ADHD should use discipline and punish a child with ADHD who cannot control his own behavior. What should these parents expect in terms of their child's behavior? What should both parents do if they do not agree on disciplinary decisions? I will offer parents of preschool children with ADHD answers to these questions, so that they will be able to help to build positive self-esteem in their child. These answers will also help them to anticipate their child's socially inappropriate behavior so that they will be able to diminish it and replace that negative behavior with positive behavior.

- Social skills deficits, which after all are at the crux of the difficulties that preschool children with ADHD exhibit. The definition of social skills as well as the types of social skills deficits are examined, as was discussed in my first book. A further conversation will include how preschoolers with ADHD exhibit difficulties with social skills because it is imperative that parents know and/or learn how their child's social skills problems interfere with his interactions with his peers, as well as with his family. I will then offer

parents a list of social skills that preschool children with ADHD
need to learn. A discussion will be begun to help parents who are
not teachers to teach social skills intentionally to their child with
ADHD. Certain challenging topics for preschool children with
ADHD such as sharing, taking turns, and transitions will be delineated and explained.

- The recommended treatment for preschool children with ADHD,
  which is essentially behavioral interventions. Before we begin with
  that treatment, however, a discussion will be started as how to help
  these parents to model positive behavior for their child. Children
  typically imitate their parents in affect and actions, so modeling
  appropriate behavior is an important start. That discussion is a little
  tricky, however, due to the distractibility of children with ADHD.
  How can parents succeed in getting their preschool child with
  ADHD to imitate their behavior if they are inattentive themselves? I
  continue on to offer the parents a list of detailed behavioral interventions. Picture charts will be described delineating the order of
  the activities that preschool children with ADHD can follow, so that
  they can perform their morning, afternoon, and evening activities
  more easily. These picture charts delineate activities such as brushing their teeth, and getting dressed, among others. Various positive
  reinforcements and their implementation are discussed.

- Some general interventions, such as those of organization and executive function. These interventions will help preschool children
  with ADHD to remember their responsibilities by planning and
  following through on their actions. These children must learn how
  to self-regulate not only their behavior, but their verbiage as well.
  Their parents, their first teachers, will teach them how to inhibit
  their socially inappropriate behavior by implementing these interventions. Parents can model good planning as well as executive
  function skills for their child, which will help him to follow through
  while managing his own activities.

- The role of technology for preschool children with ADHD. In consideration of the fact that children with ADHD become hyperfocused while using apps, playing video games and other computer
  games, is it a good idea to involve preschool children with ADHD
  with technology? How do you introduce technology to preschool
  children with ADHD? What are the advantages and what are the

drawbacks of these children using screens and technology? Should the use of technology be used as an incentive to build positive behavior? How can parents of these preschool children with ADHD monitor their child's time on these devices? Are there guidelines for how much time should be spent on screens for these children?

- Various types of technological devices will be discussed and reviewed for this population of children. Some of these include the Time Timer for both iPhones, iPads, and Android devices, as well as apps that are seemingly effective for preschool children with ADHD who have behavior and distractibility issues. A detailed description, analysis, and review of these apps will be included for both the Apple and the Android Platforms.
- Preschool children with ADHD have difficulty understanding and managing changes that occur in life, both planned and unplanned. Some examples of these events might include moving to a new neighborhood, having a new baby in the house, and a grandparent dying, among other changes. Included here are some questions that parents can ask themselves to help them to respond to a life change, rather than reacting to a life change. In that way, parents can intentionally help their child to manage his emotions when changes occur. Parents will also have access to suggestions of books they can read to their child to encourage conversations about these topics.
- Bullying in preschool children with ADHD. I will delineate the research data, so that parents will be able to understand the fact that preschool children with ADHD are indeed bullied. You will learn some signs that will help you to discover if your preschool child with ADHD is being bullied. Also offered are some techniques that parents can try, so that they can diminish or stop their child from being bullied. A discussion will be started as well regarding preschool children with ADHD being bullies themselves. You will learn signs that will alert you as to whether or not your preschool child with ADHD is a bully, as well as how to stop your child from bullying other children. You will be given suggested books to read to your preschool child with ADHD to start a positive dialogue about bullying.

In addition, I include a bibliography and suggested resource list that includes books, materials and resources that may assist parents along their journey to help their preschool child with ADHD in many challenging areas, such as learning how to share, listening and learning, following the rules, and learning about his emotions, among many other topics. These materials will incorporate books that parents can read to their child that address the issues of confidence and low self-esteem, which interferes with his ability to make friends and interact successfully with adults. Also included are books that focus on changes that occur in these children's lives such as, having a new baby, a friend who has moved away, the death of a grandparent, moving to a new neighborhood or city, and being bullied, among other topics. It will also include suggestions for materials as related to the role of using positive reinforcement in terms of managing these children's behavior. Finally, the list will incorporate informational books, so that parents can learn more about ADHD.

SOME GENERAL TIPS TO START YOUR JOURNEY OFF IN A POSITIVE DIRECTION

Let us be honest here. It is difficult to manage a preschool child with ADHD's behavior. Think about the behavior that your preschool child with ADHD has exhibited. He can be stubborn and rigid sometimes and at other times be malleable, funny, and flexible. He can also be unfocused at one moment and not respond to you when you give them an instruction, and the next moment, poof! He can also be hyperfocused upon building a tower!

When a child has a diagnosis of ADHD, the symptoms of this disorder may cause the entire family's life to seemingly spiral out of control exponentially. In order to manage these symptoms, you might find yourself screaming at your child one moment and desperately bribing him to behave the next moment. Who could blame you? Certainly not me!

As I will discuss later in this book, I am sure that at times you have difficulty managing your own emotions and behavior. Therefore, here is a guide that is similar to the one we all receive whenever we buy a new piece of technology. Think about this as your quick guide for managing your preschool child with ADHD's behavior:

- Keep your home routine as structured and as organized as possible. In that way, your preschool child with ADHD will know precisely what to expect at all times. He may not know how to tell time as of yet, but he will certainly know (when aided by a picture to remind him) that after he plays outside in the grass, you require him to wash his hands before he eats his dinner. For example, you might set up a routine so that each and every time that your child sees you cleaning up the table and the dishes, he goes to his reading area to look at books. The more structured your routine, the better behavior you can expect your child to exhibit.

- When you tell instructions to your preschool child with ADHD, make sure that he is looking at you directly in your eyes. Additionally (this is *so* important!) give him a single, simple instruction. Preschool children with ADHD or those children at risk for ADHD can be easily overwhelmed by too many directives. The instructions such as "Wash your hands, brush your teeth, and find a book for me to read to you", all become jumbled as he is trying to listen to them.

- Always give one, single instruction at a time, such as, "Go wash your hands." When you notice that he has accomplished that task, praise him and state the next instruction. Now, "Find your pajamas." Praise him and give him the next instruction. "Put your pajamas on your body." Praise that accomplishment and then offer the last instruction. "Bring a book to me to read to you." Then if he has successfully accomplished the last task, say to your child, "Good job!" or "Good listening!" By giving a single instruction, your preschool child with ADHD will feel more successful and realize a new level of positive self-esteem after he has successfully completed the designated task. In addition, you will feel less frustrated, because you will not have to tell him what to do more than once.

- One of the most important things that you can do (just so you know, this is not my original idea!) is the phrase catch your child being good. I find myself trying to do so every single time that I am with a preschool child with ADHD, or one who is at risk of having a diagnosis of ADHD. What should you do? When you see a preschool child with ADHD behaving in a positive way, praise him for behaving in that way, such as saying, "Matt, I love the way that you are sitting in your chair waiting for me to bring you your dinner." Your child will begin developing positive self-esteem as a reflection of the fact that he pleased you and exhibited the appropriate behavior that you requested of him.

- Along the same line of thinking, but becoming a little more creative, try (I know that it is very difficult!) to ignore your preschool child with ADHD's negative and inappropriate behavior and positively reinforce his positive behavior. I will talk in more depth about how to execute this strategy later on in this book. When we pay attention to our child's negative behavior, we frequently see that behavior increasing. I hope that you do not think that I am communicating a message to you here that ignoring your preschool child with ADHD's socially inappropriate behavior is easy! On the contrary, it is a very difficult thing to do! It is imperative to do so, because then and only then will your child learn that certain of his specific behaviors make you happy and some do not! One would hope that if you continue to emphasize your preschool child with ADHD's socially appropriate behavior to him amidst all of his socially inappropriate behavior, he will somehow learn to exhibit appropriate behavior.
- One suggestion which sometimes gets lost in the transmission of ideas is to make sure that your preschool child with ADHD gets enough sleep and goes to bed early. Fatigue only increases temper tantrums. Seemingly, it may be an easy problem to avoid!
- I am suggesting that you try to model positive behavior for your preschool child with ADHD, while at the same time, I know that it is very difficult for children with distractibility issues to do so. However, your preschool child with ADHD also picks up on your emotional state of being, even though he may not be able to express it to you. If you have an argument with your husband or with a neighbor, and you become frustrated and angry, your preschool child with ADHD may model that behavior without even realizing it! It is imperative (as we will discuss later), that you learn how to control your own behavior. You may observe your preschool child with ADHD becoming angry when you become irate. Additionally, when you scream, you may observe your preschool child yelling as well.
- One last suggestion for each parent is to try to become aware of the time in the day or evening when you become anxious and pressured yourself. What would you do if you find yourself unable to modulate your own behavior? Next time, think about what you could do to better control your behavior, so that you can intentionally behave

appropriately yourself! Try deep breathing. Play the kind of music that makes you happy, so that you can play it continuously until you calm down.

A FEW SUGGESTIONS FOR HOW TO READ THIS BOOK

How do you begin reading this book? You might try to read it as you would read any cookbook. Look for a recipe that interests you, or in this case, what you are curious about in the table of contents. I would then recommend skimming all of the chapters, so that you can decide which chapter to read first. You certainly do not want to miss reading about any of the topics included, so browsing them may be your answer.

If you have not as yet read anything about preschool ADHD, you just might want to start with the preface and read each chapter consecutively. If you are already well-versed in the definition of ADHD, you might want to skip the first part of chapter 1. However, do not skip over the treatment guidelines in the latter part of the chapter!

Certainly, use your judgment in terms of how much time you have to read. Chapter 5 is a very comprehensive look at how to manage your preschool child with ADHD's behavior and social skills. Take your time with this chapter. Additionally, make sure to investigate and peruse the interventions that correspond with the various social skills that preschool children with ADHD need to learn, one at a time, among other included topics.

However, if you travel past one chapter quickly, do not forget to read through the bibliography and suggested resources, where I list some really good books that you can read to your preschool child with ADHD on various pertinent topics. Finally, if you want to introduce your child to technology, specifically apps on both the Apple and the Android platform, go to chapter 6, where I review many apps in terms of their use for children of the preschool age.

I have so many ideas, information, and interventions that will help your preschool child with ADHD, so read on!

I

ATTENTION-DEFICIT/HYPERACTIVITY DISORDER (ADHD)

The Definition and the Symptoms

THE DEFINITION OF ATTENTION-DEFICIT/ HYPERACTIVITY DISORDER

Even though as parents, you are acutely aware of your child's behavior, it is imperative to know the accepted definition of ADHD, as stated in the *Diagnostic and Statistical Manual of Mental Disorders (DSM-5)*. Here is the well-accepted and current definition:

> A persistent pattern of inattention and/or hyperactivity-impulsivity that interferes with functioning or development as characterized by (1) and/ or (2):
>
> Inattention: Six (or more) of the following symptoms have persisted for at least 6 months to a degree that is inconsistent with developmental level and that negatively impacts directly on social and academic/ occupational activities:
>
> > Often fails to give close attention to details or makes careless mistakes in schoolwork, at work, or during other activities
> > often has difficulty sustaining attention in tasks or play activities
> > often does not seem to listen when spoken to directly
> > often does not follow through on instructions and fails to finish schoolwork, chores, or duties in the workplace
> > often has difficulty organizing tasks and activities

often avoids, dislikes, or is reluctant to engage in tasks that require
  sustained mental effort
often loses things necessary for tasks or activities
is often easily distracted by extraneous stimuli
is often forgetful in daily activities

Hyperactivity and impulsivity: Six (or more) of the following symptoms have persisted for at least 6 months to a degree that is inconsistent with and that negatively impacts directly on social and academic/
occupational activities

often fidgets with or taps hands or feet or squirms in seat
often leaves seat in situations when remaining seated is expected
often runs about or climbs in situations where it is inappropriate
often unable to play or engage in leisure activities quietly
is often "on the go," as if "driven by a motor"
often talks excessively
often blurts out an answer before a question has been completed
often has difficulty waiting his or her turn
often interrupts or intrudes on others

Several inattentive or hyperactive-impulsive symptoms were present
prior to age 12 years.
Several inattentive or hyperactive-impulsive symptoms are present in
two or more settings.
There is clear evidence that the symptoms interfere with, or reduce the
quality of, social, academic, or occupational functioning.
Specify whether:

314.01 (F90.2) Combined presentation: If both Criterion A1 (inattention) and Criterion A2 (hyperactivity-impulsivity) are met
  for the past 6 months.
314.00 (F90.0) Predominantly inattentive presentation: If Criterion
  A1 (inattention) is met but Criterion A2 (hyperactivity-impulsivity) is not met for the past 6 months.
314.01 (F90.1) Predominantly hyperactive/impulsive presentation:
  If Criterion A2 (hyperactivity-impulsivity is met and Criterion
  A1 (inattention) is not met for the past 6 months (American
  Psychiatric Association, 2013, pp. 59–60).

THE DIAGNOSTIC FEATURES

According to the American Psychiatric Association (AAP),

> The essential feature of attention-deficit/hyperactivity disorder (ADHD) is a persistent pattern of inattention and/or hyperactivity-impulsivity that interferes with functioning or development. Inattention manifests behaviorally in ADHD as wandering off task, lacking persistence, having difficulty sustaining focus, and being disorganized and is not due to defiance or lack of comprehension. Hyperactivity refers to excessive motor activity (such as a child running about) when it is not appropriate, or excessive fidgeting, tapping, or talkativeness. . . . Impulsivity refers to hasty actions that occur in the moment without forethought and that have high potential for harm to the individual . . . Impulsivity may reflect a desire for immediate rewards or an inability to delay gratification. Impulsive behaviors may manifest as social intrusiveness (e.g., interrupting others excessively) and/or as making important decisions without consideration of long-term consequences (American Psychiatric Association, 2013, p. 61).

The persistent inattention that was delineated in the *DSM-5* as a paramount characteristic of ADHD was exemplified by Bess when she told me about her young child with ADHD's difficulty with focus. She also explains how using a manipulative helps him to concentrate.

> He's just really bright and has difficulty shifting his focus from one thing that is interesting to anything else. He always has something in his hand, always plays with something in his mouth too, but yet it's not distracting. It helps him to concentrate.

All the words in the above definition from the *DSM-5* may seemingly be overwhelming. I would like to offer what I consider is a good suggestion. It is important to establish a diagnosis for your child in terms of obtaining services. However, please realize that the most important thing for you as parents is to begin trying to help your child to diminish his symptoms. If he does so, he will achieve more success in terms of making and keeping friends, as well as realizing eventual accomplishment in school. Your child's behavior is obstructing his interactions with his friends, his family, and his teachers. I know that it is very difficult, but if you remain positive, it is more likely that your child will feel positive.

ADHD has a long history. If you are interested in reading about the history of ADHD, please take a look at appendix A, where you can read all about it.

WHAT ARE THE NUMBERS?

As of 2011, The Centers for Disease Control (CDC) reported that 6.4 million children in the United States aged four to seventeen, were diagnosed with ADHD. Two million, or one-third, of these children were diagnosed before age six, between two and five years old. Among the children characterized by their parents as having severe ADHD, one-half of these cases were diagnosed before age four. The *Diagnostic and Statistical Manual of Mental Disorders (DSM-5)* claims that 5% of children have ADHD, with higher rates in community samples. In 2012, the CDC found that 1.7% of children three to four years old were diagnosed with ADHD as compared to 9.5% of children who were five to eleven years old.

HOW DO THE SYMPTOMS OF ADHD PRESENT THEMSELVES IN PRESCHOOL CHILDREN?

The Diagnostic and Statistical Manual for Mental Disorders- (*DSM-5)* states that "In preschool, the main manifestation (of ADHD) is hyperactivity" (American Psychiatric Association, 2013, p. 62). The CDC also found that the most typical and paramount symptom of ADHD in preschool is hyperactivity (www.CDC.gov, np). It does not mean that preschool children with ADHD are not inattentive and unfocused because many are characterized by these symptoms as well. The Children and Adults with Attention-Deficit/Hyperactivity Disorder (CHADD) states that preschoolers with ADHD are more likely to have difficulty in daycare, including problems with peer relationships, and learning, as well as a higher risk of injuries than preschool children without ADHD. Frequently, these children are suspended or expelled from preschool for their behavior, which I know sounds extreme, but it does happen.

Preschool children with ADHD experience difficulty in their relationships with their parents, as well as struggles in their social interactions.

Why do these things happen? These children do not have intact positive social skills. They either do not have knowledge of effective social skills or they have knowledge of the appropriate social skills, yet do not perform them. How does the fact that these children do not have intact positive social skills, affect their ability to change in their routines?

Preschool children with ADHD are less able to change in terms of their routine. In terms of their time with their parents, they are typically less compliant than preschool children without ADHD, as well as being more demanding. These children's behavior may be more aggressive. Their inappropriate behavior is the reason why early intervention is critical to helping these children to learn as much positive behavior as early as possible.

Perhaps if parents are trained to manage their child's behavior at an early age, the likelihood that these children will be rejected by peers for their inappropriate behavior might be diminished or even prevented altogether. Oftentimes, parents of preschool children with ADHD interact with their child in a negative and harsh way, for which they cannot be blamed.

It is very challenging to deal with a child's behavior that is so frustrating. These parents react to the symptoms of their preschool child with ADHD's behavior often with frustration and intolerance, especially if the preschool child with ADHD is not their only child. When parents produce negative verbiage, their preschool child with ADHD often reacts by exhibiting socially inappropriate behavior, or by maintaining the socially inappropriate behavior they previously displayed. Low self-esteem is often seen in preschool children with ADHD due, among other reasons, to hearing constant negative criticism and comments.

In fact, children with ADHD, no matter how young, hear too many negative and critical comments that may affect their self-esteem. If parents are trained in behavior management techniques and are taught to focus on positive reinforcement, perhaps they will respond to their child with ADHD in less negative ways. Preschool children with ADHD desperately need to hear positive comments. Parent behavioral training might very well impact parenting techniques which will encourage more positive parent-child interactions.

Additionally, parents need to be trained in social skills training. Once parents learn how to teach their child positive social skills, they could possibly serve as the conduit between the social skills that their child performs at home, in the classroom, as well as in other contexts. Social skills training is not considered successful unless the child displays the positive social skills that he has just learned in at least two settings for generalization. You might be wondering how parents can possibly teach social skills to children who are so distractible. We will discuss that issue later on in this book.

Before you check to see if the child in question has social skills deficits, let me give you some specific behaviors that may occur if a child has these deficits.

- Difficulties in social perception: A child walks up to two children who are disagreeing and asks, "Can I play?" Even though the child clearly sees the ongoing argument between the two children, he seemingly is unaware that they may be so involved with disagreeing that they may not consider including him at that moment. Additionally, they may become annoyed with him if he intercedes.
- Lack of consequential thinking: A child walks up to another child and pulls the chair out from under him. The child who pulled the chair out does not realize that the child who was sitting on the chair will fall down on the floor, possibly hurting himself.
- Difficulty expressing feelings: A child pushes another one down and cannot say he was sorry.
- Difficulty delaying gratification: A child walks up to another child who is using a shovel at a sand table. Instead of asking to use the shovel, he grabs it and knocks the child down. The first child did not have the patience to wait until the second child finished with the shovel. Instead, he acted on impulse.
- Failure to understand and fulfill the role of listener: In conversations with peers or adults, the child talks incessantly and continuously interrupts. He does not understand that when one person talks the other person listens.
- Inability to take the perspective of another: One child is upset because the other children did not permit him to play. The preschool child with ADHD does not understand why that child is upset.
- Less time spent looking and smiling at a conversational partner: As a child is playing with another child, the preschool child with ADHD does not look or smile frequently at the other child.

- Unwillingness to act in a social situation to influence the outcome: A child is playing by himself on the playground while watching the others play together. He is unwilling to go over to these children to ask them to play.
- Less likely to request clarification when given ambiguous or incomplete information: A teacher hands out permission slips and tells the children in her class to return them to school signed by their parents. She does not tell the children when they have to return them. The child with social skills deficits does not ask the teacher when to return the permission slip. He then forgets to hand it in to his teacher.
- Tendency to talk more or less: A child either talks too little or excessively to peers and adults.
- More likely to approach teacher and ask inappropriate questions: A teacher gives instructions on speaking out in class. She instructs the children to raise their hands when they have something important to ask her or to tell the class. The child with ADHD raises his hand and asks, "Can we stand up in our seats and shout out our questions?"
- Less proficient in interpersonal problem solving: A child feels rejected by another child. He has not actually been rejected but does not understand how to go about trying to be friends (Vaughn et al., 2007, p. 255; Rapoport, 2009, pp. 28–30).

Does your preschool child with ADHD children have problems with social skills? Among others, some of the social skills difficulties that they exhibit are:

- He either has difficulty making friends or does not have any friends.
- He does not understand other children's body language.
- He has problems with responsibility; he does not understand how to behave responsibly.
- He has difficulty listening to others without interrupting.
- He has difficulty listening to and interpreting other children's social cues.
- He appears vulnerable and is often bullied or may be a bully himself.
- He has difficulty with self-control.

• He has problems cooperating and compromising with peers.

How do you know if your child has social skills problems? Of course, you could check the list of positive social skills that I have listed in chapter 4. You can also ask yourself, "Why doesn't my child behave in a socially appropriate manner as do other children?" (Rapoport, 2009, p. 31). Additionally, you could observe your preschool child with ADHD as he engages in activities with other children and make a judgment as to how typical children interact as compared to how your child interacts.

BE CAREFUL NOT TO ASSUME THAT A SPECIFIC PRESCHOOL CHILD HAS ADHD

I was sitting in temple this year for the High Holy Days services and the Rabbi was giving a sermon about having a sense of humor when one is dealing with certain problems in their lives. He continued on, speaking about various types of humor. He said that in his own personal life he certainly needed some humor because there was an "interrupter" in his family. He then began his actual sermon and began to talk about making decisions. He began to talk about how one of the prophets could not make up his mind so he vacillated back and forth and back and forth indecisively when he was trying to make a decision.

Somewhere from the congregation, a voice shouted out, "Why couldn't he just decide once?" The Rabbi tried to explain to the voice that the prophet wanted to make sure that he had made the correct decision. A few moments passed, and the same voice rang out again and said, "Even a T-Rex would decide once!" Of course, everyone laughed in sort of an uneasy way. I was wondering who was the one who was interrupting and shouting out in the middle of the service.

The Rabbi, who also clearly felt ill at ease, said, "Oh, that was my five-year-old, in case you were wondering. That was my interrupter." He nonverbally sent his wife immediately over to quiet his son down. From my seat, my thoughts went quickly to wondering if the Rabbi's son had ADHD and if he had been taught social skills. If he had indeed been taught social skills, then why was he shouting out in the middle of the service in front of the whole congregation?

After the service, I was talking to the Cantor, who had recently opened a preschool. She and I were talking about whether or not she had come across preschool children with ADHD in her school. She then asked me whether or not I thought that the child who had shouted out had ADHD. Before I could answer her question (which I actually would not have answered without seeing him for an evaluation!), she answered her own question. She said, "That is Rabbi Kid Syndrome."

I asked her to explain to me what she was talking about. She told me that her father is a Rabbi and when Rabbis give sermons and their children are in the congregation they are speaking to other people and not to their own children. So therefore, the Rabbi's children feel ignored and act out in the way that the Rabbi's son had acted out on that evening. She then told me that she used to behave in that way as well! I was shocked because I had never heard that explanation before that night. It actually made a lot of sense. If you were a five-year-old child and your father was talking to two hundred people and not to you, people might see that same sort of behavior from you!

Even though there are many preschool age children who have a diagnosis of ADHD, be very careful before you think in a certain way and label one of them as having ADHD. After all, he just might have "Rabbi Kid Syndrome!"

THE TREATMENT GUIDELINES

It is very important to offer interventions for preschoolers who are displaying early signs of the symptoms of ADHD but are not yet diagnosed as well as for preschoolers who have been diagnosed to have ADHD. Who should be the first individuals to work on trying to diminish the socially inappropriate behavior that these children exhibit? These children's parents spend the most time with them and know them better than anyone else, so they are the first individuals who should try to help them. The American Academy of Pediatrics (2011) states that behavioral training, which includes parent training should be the very first line of treatment for preschoolers with ADHD.

Additionally, evaluations for preschoolers to determine if they have a diagnosis of ADHD should clearly be thorough and follow the guidelines outlined by the American Academy of Pediatrics (AAP) as well as the

American Academy of Child and Adolescent Psychiatry (AACAP). Parents who have preschool children with ADHD need training in behavior management. In fact, a number of studies have been done on children who are five years old and younger who have ADHD and found that parent training is more effective than medication for these children.

The AAP has published clinical guidelines for the diagnosis and evaluation of ADHD in children. You will find the citation for these guidelines in the bibliography and suggested resources chapter. You will also find the actual guidelines in appendix B. These recommendations are a great resource for parents, so that they will know the primary doctor's responsibility in terms of diagnosing their child. There are basically five action statements. You should pay particular attention, however, to action statement 5 and 5a.

> Action Statement 1: The primary care clinician should initiate an evaluation for ADHD for any child 4 through 18 years of age who presents with academic or behavioral problems and symptoms of inattention, hyperactivity, or impulsivity
>
> Action Statement 2: To make a diagnosis of ADHD, the primary care clinician should determine that *Diagnostic and Statistical Manual of Mental Disorders, Fourth Edition (DSM-IV-TR)* criteria have been met (including documentation of impairment in more than one major setting) and information should be obtained primarily from reports from parents or guardians, teachers and other school and mental health clinicians involved in the child's care. The primary care physician should also rule out any alterative cause.
>
> Action Statement 3: In the evaluation of a child for ADHD, the primary care clinician should include assessment for other conditions that might coexist with ADHD, including emotional or behavioral (e.g., anxiety, depressive, oppositional defiant, and conduct disorders) developmental (e.g., learning and language disorders or other neurodevelopmental disorders) and physical (e.g., tics, sleep apnea) conditions.
>
> Action Statement 4: The primary care clinician should recognize ADHD as a chronic condition and, therefore, consider children and adolescents with ADHD as children and youth with special health care needs. Management of children and youth with special health care needs should follow the principles of the chronic care model and the medical home.

Action Statement 5: Recommendations for the treatment of children and youth with ADHD vary depending on the patient's age.

Action Statement 5a: For preschool-aged children (4–5 years of age), the primary care physician should prescribe evidence-based parent and/or teacher-administered behavior therapy as the first line of treatment . . . and may prescribe methylphenidate if the behavioral interventions do not provide significant improvement and there is moderate-to-severe continuing disturbance in the child's function. In areas in which evidence-based behavioral treatments are not available, the clinician needs to weigh the risks of starting medication at an early age against the harm of delaying diagnosis and treatment (American Academy of Pediatrics, 2011, 128, 1007–1022).

RESEARCH SUPPORTED GROUP BEHAVIORAL TRAINING PROGRAMS

The following are parent behavioral training programs for parents of preschool-aged children with ADHD. These programs have enough research evidence to be described as effective:

- Helping the Noncompliant Child
- Incredible Years Parenting Program
- New Forest Parenting Programme
- Parent-Child Interaction Therapy
- Triple P (Positive Parenting Program)
- Be-Prox Program

These are group programs that you may want to investigate. They teach parents how to use praise or positive reinforcement to encourage their children to exhibit more positive behavior.

In chapter 2, you will learn how important the parent's input is in terms of determining if she should bring her child to professionals for a possible diagnosis. Parents must act as observers and detectives in terms of recognizing behavior that may not be typical for their child's age. They are the individuals with whom their child primarily interacts along with siblings and other family members. Therefore, parents are an invaluable

source of information about their preschool child who exhibits the symptoms that may correspond to a possible diagnosis of ADHD.

2

PARENTS AS OBSERVERS

I cannot overstate the importance of being observant and vigilant parents in term of helping to alert professionals that your child might be exhibiting symptoms of ADHD. The child's first teachers and most influential supporters are his parents. These same parents, therefore, are vital when it comes to observing their child's behavior and determining whether or not his behavior is the same as or is significantly different from another child's behavior. It is essential to find out as well to what degree that behavior varies from another child's behavior of the same age. Is your child's behavior, according to you, more extreme than another child's behavior of the same age? Do you see the same behavior in more than one setting? If you answered yes to these questions, then you probably will want to see a doctor for a diagnosis. I am a firm believer in the mantra that is better to be safe than to be sorry.

What is the worst thing that can happen if you take your child to a physician? He will evaluate your child's behavior and you will know if you need to follow a specific treatment regimen or not. If the doctor does not think that any treatment is warranted, well then, off you go. If the doctor does think that a treatment regimen is indicated, then both you and your child will have benefited from the evaluation.

THE DETECTIVE WORK

How should you begin your detective work? First of all, you need to know what behaviors are most prominent in preschool children with ADHD. Certainly, much of the behavior of preschool children with ADHD is characterized by inattention. However, the most prominent behavioral symptom of preschool children with ADHD is hyperactivity, according to the Centers for Disease Control. (www.CDC.gov).

Parents might see the following behavior in their preschool child with ADHD:

- climbing on furniture
- difficulty staying seated at meals
- intruding on their sibling's space or toys
- being fidgety
- difficulty transitioning (i.e., from dinner to the time when he puts his pajamas on, to brushing his teeth, to getting ready to have a book read to him, to going to potty before bed, to going to bed, etc.)
- multiple temper tantrums
- not listening to parental instructions and instead, running around the room
- not listening to parental instructions and instead, playing by himself in his own world
- on play dates, not wanting to share or not wanting to take turns
- frequently being frustrated, which leads to pushing and hitting

Dr. Mark Mahone of the Department of Neuropsychology at the Kennedy Institute in Baltimore, Maryland, recommends that parents look for the following signs that are associated with an ADHD diagnosis when children reach school age.

- dislikes or avoids activities that require paying attention for more than one or two minutes
- loses interest and starts doing something else after engaging in an activity for a few moments
- talks a lot more and makes more noise than other children of the same age
- climbs on things when instructed not to do so
- cannot hop on one foot by age 4

- is nearly always restless—wants to constantly kick or jiggle feet or twist around in his/her seat. Insists that he/she "must" get up after being seated for more than a few minutes
- gets into dangerous situations because of fearlessness
- warms up too quickly to strangers
- is frequently aggressive with playmates; has been removed from preschool/daycare for aggression
- has been injured (e.g., received stitches) because of moving too fast or running when instructed not to do so (www.kennedykrieger.org/overview/news/it-adhd-or-typical-toddler-behavior-ten-early-signs-adhd-risk-preschool-age-children)

You need to recognize and understand your own perceptions about your child's behavior. It is very easy to develop negative feelings about your preschool child with ADHD's behavior. Nothing is seemingly easy, whether it is brushing his teeth, getting dressed for school, eating his breakfast, or getting into his car seat. Every single action that you ask your child to do and, needless to say, expect him to do, he does not want to do.

What behavior occurs instead? In addition to the behaviors listed above, your child might be looking at a book, looking out of a window, playing with the water in the sink, or, perhaps, just generally fooling around. He might be taking all of his socks out of his dresser and throwing them on the floor or taking the baby's diapers from the box just to do it. He might also be taking each of his books out of his bookcase one by one until they are strewn all over the floor.

ACT AS AN OBSERVER

How do you act as an observer? Begin by keeping a running list of your preschool child with ADHD's behavior on a iPad, in a book, or on your phone. This data collection does not have be formal, but rather informal. Alternatively, you can create a journal on your computer or a spreadsheet of your child's behaviors. You can buy a spiral notebook and write your observations in there. In fact, in addition to creating a list, you can also write lengthier descriptions of how your child has behaved.

I am sure that as you read the previous list of behaviors, you were thinking of all the inappropriate behavior that your child exhibits that are not the behaviors that you want him to display. Please do not write down *only* the hyperactive behavior that your child exhibits. It is essential that you observe and then write down your child's inattentive behaviors as well. Additionally, make sure that you write down the appropriate behavior that he is exhibitting, so that you can gather the whole picture of what your child is like.

Your observations will make each and every one of your child's behaviors rich and complex. Observations are powerful. Take advantage of that power by putting down your phones and your iPads. How important are your texts, Facebook entries, Instagram pictures and chats on Snapchat, when it compares to really delving into what makes your child function? In order to observe your child's behavior, you will need a quiet setting away from all of your technological devices.

As you are observing your preschool child with ADHD, you need to ask open-ended questions "that allow the child to take an idea and build on it from his or her own experience, knowledge, and interests" (Christakis, 2016, pp. 55–56). As you watch your child build a structure, ask him to simply tell you about his building. In answering your question, your preschool child with ADHD can be insightful and give you some idea as to what are his needs. As you observe your child at play, try to build a way of conversing with him, so that he shares his creative thoughts with you.

Well, you are probably asking, "How can I observe my child's behavior?" Thankfully, due to the types of activities in which preschool children are engaged, it is actually quite easy. Before you observe, however, you have to try to rid yourself of at least part of the negative perception of your child's behavior in your mind. Most parents, including myself, of course, only see what they choose to see when evaluating their own child's behavior.

> This is the art of suspending preconceived expectations and assumptions about a person in order to understand where he is coming from, what he is thinking, and what he is feeling. . . . When we suspend our memories and desires, we're better able to observe the child in the moment, and we see things we otherwise were not able to see: a child who is unfocused and sloppy when getting out the door every morning

becomes the child who can hold a fragile newborn with the utmost concentration (Christakis, 2016, p. 56).

If we readily accept our child's socially inappropriate behavior as accurate and as evidence, then whom might we blame for that inappropriate behavior? Ourselves, of course . . . our preschool child typically spends much of his time with us, his parents, who constantly try to teach him about how to behave and how to successfully socially interact. However, be assured that due to your child's symptoms of his possible diagnosis of ADHD, even though you have taught your child social skills, for instance, he has not been able to focus and pay accurate attention to the details of your lessons, due to the symptoms of his ADHD. So now you can please stop blaming yourself!

When I work with teachers, who also quietly admit a type of bias either for or against preschool children with ADHD, I give them a visual image about which to think before they work with these children. I tell them to imagine that they are a pitcher on the mound who is getting ready to throw a pitch. Then, pretend that the ball is a paper ball and simply throw it away (and all of your personal biases with it) over your shoulder. After you have done so, begin to observe your preschool child with ADHD's behavior with a clear mind and an uncluttered, unbiased heart.

Observation 1: A Play date

There are several moments in time when you can facilitate your child's social interactions. At the same time, make some rather astute observations about your child's behavior and/or his social skills. One such opportunity is a play date. Here are some questions that you may attempt to answer as you are observing your child's play date.

- How did your child greet his play date?
- Whose decision was it as to what to play? If your child made that decision, how did he make it?
- If the other child decided what to play, to what degree was your child agreeable to that decision?
- If he was not agreeable to that decision, how did he behave?
- Describe how your child played. Did your child play with the other child or did he play in a parallel manner next to the child?

- Who initiated the social interaction, your child or the other child? If your child initiated the social interaction, describe his behavior.
- Did the child who initiated the social interaction take on the role of the leader or the follower? Describe his behavior.
- If your child took on the role of the follower, did he play in an agreeable way, listening and acting upon the other child's instructions? Describe his behavior.
- If he did not play in an agreeable way, how did he play?
- If there was a disagreement, what occurred that triggered the disagreement?
- During the disagreement, how did your child behave?
- What behaviors did your child exhibit?
- What happened between the children after the disagreement to maintain your child's behavior?
- How did your child solve issues that came up with the other child without your help?
- Did you have to intercede into your child's social interaction or did he manage his own behavior? If he managed his own behavior, how did he do so?
- If you helped to diffuse a difference of opinion, how did your child return to play without becoming involved in any more altercations?
- Was your child able to continue the play date after the alteration was over? If he did, how did he do so?
- If your child apologized for his behavior, how did he do so? What did he say to the other child?
- How was your child able to change his socially inappropriate behavior after the altercation was over? If he did so, describe his behavior.
- How did your child maintain focus to play with the other child throughout the play date? Describe his focus.
- Did your child play in a specific activity, such as block play, or did he go from activity to activity? Describe how he played.
- What was the style of your child's talking? Did your child exhibit excessive talking or display behavior that annoyed the other child? If so, describe that behavior.
- If your child's behavior was socially inappropriate, how was that behavior resolved?
- If you interceded, what did you do?

- How did your child realize that his behavior was inappropriate? When you asked him about his behavior, what did he say?
- How did you apply the consequences for your child's inappropriate behavior after the play date was over?

Observation 2: A Class or an Activity

Another situation where you can observe your child's behavior is at a class or an activity, such as soccer, a gym class, an art class or a martial arts class. Sometimes, parents are told that the child must attend the class by himself, but at other times, the parent is asked to remain or is able to observe through a window. This class or activity would be a good opportunity to see how well your child follows instructions and directions. Here are some questions to try to answer as you are watching your child, either in person or through a viewing window.

- What did your child do in terms of immediately following the teacher's instructions or did he go off on his own?
- If he did not follow instructions after the teacher reminded him to do so, what did he do?
- Do you think that your child behaved in an independent manner? Describe his behavior.
- Did he transition away from you and become involved with the activity? How did he transition? If he did not do so, then what did he do?
- If you were in the room while your child did the activity, how did he follow through on the instructions? Describe if and how he followed the teacher's instructions or went off on his own. How was he redirected to the appropriate activity?
- Once he understood the directions, how did he comply with what was expected of him during the rest of the class? If he complied with the instructions, explain how he complied.
- If he did not comply, how did he behave?
- How did he behave in terms of intruding upon another child's space or going out of turn? Describe his behavior. Explain if he was in fact able to wait for his turn or not.
- When your child was told to sit quietly and wait, what did he do?

- Did he become involved in any physical altercation with the other children? If so, describe his behavior.
- When the teacher/coach interceded, was he able to return to the activities in which he was involved? Describe his behavior.
- How did your child respond to praise from the teacher/coach when he complied?

Each and every observation should be personal and pertinent to your family situation. There is no right and wrong in the way that you observe your child's behavior. Remember, the reason for the observations is so you will know if your child needs to see a pediatrician, a pediatric neurologist, or a pediatric psychiatrist for a possible diagnosis.

Observation 3: Your House

As you are observing, take advantage of the natural setting of your house. Observe your child in typical, daily situations during the day and night, such as:

Getting Dressed to Go to School

- Does your child get dressed himself or does he stall in terms of getting his clothes on? Describe his behavior.
- When you try to help him, does he run away and act silly? Describe his behavior.
- How does your child respond to any expeditious methods that you employ, such as a countdown or a reminder of a consequence?

Getting in His Chair for Meals

- Does your child get into his chair for meals or does he crawl around the floor or run around instead? Describe his behavior.
- How does your child respond to any expeditious methods or a reminder of a countdown or does he have to be put in his seat by you? Describe his behavior.
- Does he stay in his seat throughout the meal or does he either try to get up or actually get up several times during the meal? Describe his behavior.

Going to the Supermarket

- Does your child hold your hand in the parking lot or does he pull away and run off so that you have to run after him? Describe his behavior.
- Once he is in the supermarket, does he sit in the shopping cart or cry and fuss to get out? Describe his behavior.
- Does your child actually try to climb out of the shopping cart, and if so, how does he do it?
- As you are shopping can he sit quietly talking to you in the shopping cart or does he constantly whine and ask for things? Describe his behavior.

Putting His Pajamas On at Night to Get Ready for Bed

- Does your child put on his own pajamas or does he let you help him put them on?
- Does he understand the nighttime routine or does he run around so you have to chase him down in order to put on his pajamas? Describe his behavior.
- Do you have time to read a book to your child or is that time used up by negotiating? Describe the situation.

Behaving Appropriately When Company Is at Your House

- Is he polite when guests arrive? Describe his behavior.
- Does your child say hello, or does he start running around in circles? Describe his behavior.
- Does he go up and talk to the guests incessantly, interrupting the adult conversation? When you tell him that the adults are talking, does he withdraw or continue talking? Describe his behavior.
- When you tell your child again not to interrupt and that the adults are talking, how does he behave?

Behaving Appropriately When He Visits Someone Else's House

- How does your child play when he is at another child's house? Does he play with toys fairly and share and/or take turns? Describe his behavior.

- When the other child takes a turn with his own toys, is your child aware that those are the child's toys? How does he behave when he is waiting for the other child to share his toys?
- When he is directed to share and take turns is he compliant, or does he become angry and refuse to share?

Behaving Appropriately When You Have a Phone Call

- How does your child behave when you have a phone call? Does he play by himself until you are done or does he interrupt your conversation? Describe his behavior.
- When you tell him that you are on the phone, how does he behave? Does he talk incessantly and continue to interrupt or wait quietly?
- When you tell your child again not to interrupt, how does he behave?

Behaving Appropriately When You Are on Facetime with His Grandparents or Other Family Members

- How does your child behave towards whomever is on Facetime? Does he say hello and is polite, or is he rude and does not say hello? Describe his behavior.
- How does he converse with the people who are on Facetime? Is he interactive, or does he act as if he in his own world? Describe his behavior.
- Does your child remain quiet so that you can speak, or does he make continuous noises? Describe his behavior.

Putting Away His Toys

- How does your child play with his toys? Does he play with his toys, or throw them around or both? Describe his behavior.
- Who puts his toys away? Is he able to put his toys away by himself? Describe his behavior.
- When he is directed to put his toys away does he do so, or does he ignore you telling him to do so? Describe his behavior.
- When you help your child to put away his toys, does he help you to put them away, or does he remain in his own world or throw the toys around again? Describe his behavior.

Playing with a Peer

- How does your child play with a peer? Does your child play fairly, or is he unwilling to share and take turns? Describe his behavior.
- Does he hit or push the child when he wants a turn playing with a toy with which your child is playing? Describe his behavior.
- When it is pointed out to him that his turn is up, does he walk away in anger or refuse to give up the toy? Describe his behavior.
- How does your child respond when time limits are employed? Does he wait calmly for the other child's turn to be up, or is he still resistant to share? Describe his behavior.

Exhibiting Immature or Inappropriate Social Skills

- Is your child able to control his frustrations when he is interacting with his peers or does he have difficulty with self-control? Describe his behavior.
- Does he understand another child's body language, or does he have difficulty doing so? Describe his behavior.
- How does your child listen to others? Does he have difficulty listening to others and instead of listening, interrupts their conversation? Describe his behavior.
- How does your child compromise? Does he compromise easily and cooperate with peers, or does he have difficulty doing so? Describe his behavior.
- Is he able to interpret another child's social cues, or does he misinterpret these cues? Describe his behavior.

Difficulty with Transitions

- Is your child able to change from one activity to another smoothly, or does he exhibit inappropriate behavior as he is doing so? Describe his behavior.
- When he is transitioning from dinner to putting his pajamas on, how does he behave? Does he go with you to do so, or does he begin to play with his toys and seemingly ignore what you are saying? Describe his behavior.

- When you tell your child that he cannot do another activity until he puts on his pajamas, does he do so or does he continue to do whatever he was doing? Describe his behavior.

THE BEHAVIOR OF A PRESCHOOL CHILD WITH ADHD AS COMPARED TO A TYPICAL CHILD'S BEHAVIOR

I have listed here many behaviors for you to observe and check off, so that you will have a fairly accurate list of the behaviors that your child exhibits that *might possibly* mean that a professional might diagnose him as having ADHD. That being said, I also realize that it is very problematic to separate out which behaviors one would deem different in an extreme sense to the ones that are exhibited by typical preschool children. Developmentally, it is quite possible that preschool children and preschool children with ADHD might behave in similar ways.

The difference is that the behavior that the preschool child who is suspected of having ADHD demonstrates is different in an extreme sense. "A child with ADHD is much more extreme than the average three-year-old," says Alan Rosenblatt, MD, a specialist in neurodevelopmental pediatrics." (Schusteff, 2007, np). Additionally, as I have said before, his socially inappropriate behavior must appear in two settings instead of just one (*The Diagnostic and Statistical Manual of Mental Disorders, 5th Edition, DSM-5*, 2013, p. 61).

It may be problematic and difficult to be honest with yourself about your child's behavior. Who would want to imply negative things about their child? No one. However, it is imperative that you, as your child's parent is honest about your child's behavior, so that you can get him the help that he requires, so that he will make friends more easily and develop positive self-esteem.

ADHD is a lifelong disorder which is manageable if one is vigilant, constant, and consistent in their approach. Your child has the right to an accurate diagnosis, and frequently, his parents are the best vehicle to facilitate that process and get him to the right professional. Since ADHD is an enduring disorder, however, it is difficult for parents to manage it without experiencing stress, anxiety, and guilt, as you will find out in the next chapter.

PARENTING A CHILD WITH ADHD: THE STRESS, THE ANXIETY, AND THE GUILT

THE STRESS AND THE ANXIETY

If you observe parents waving good-bye to their child as the school bus arrives to take him to his first day of school for the year, each of his parents appears to be smiling and relaxed. What you see may not necessarily be what the parents are actually feeling at that moment in time.

These same parents of a preschool child with ADHD most probably will sigh immediately after their child rolls away on the yellow school bus. Why might you observe this parental behavior? The parents might respond in this way because they actually got their child to the school bus, despite his dawdling and arguing.

The following is an example of the stress that one of the parents might have endured that first morning that school began: "Please get dressed. The bus is coming in five minutes. Are you coming yet? You are sitting on your bed staring off in the distance and not dressed yet! I have a doctor's appointment, so I just cannot drive you to school today, so come on. Let's go!"

Here is a possible scenario of what the child is thinking or saying: "I am coming! I am almost ready! I'm tired! Don't rush me! You always rush me! Please! Please drive me to school like you did yesterday! I'm coming! I'm coming! I cannot find my other shoe. Where is it?"

The parent's stress was most likely derived from what actually happened that morning. However, her stress might also have been caused by her anticipation of and anxiety over what may have occurred in school after her child arrived there. She almost felt that what may have happened on that morning was out of her control, which added exponentially to her level of stress.

Additionally, these parents are continuously worn down by the arguing, haggling, and/or bribing that occurs each and every day in terms of their interaction with their preschool child with ADHD. In a study of preschool children with ADHD, DuPaul et al. (2001) report that "parents of children with ADHD report higher levels of stress associated with child behavior and dysfunctional interactions than control parents" (p. 514). The level of your stress and anxiety just keeps building and building as the morning continues on, wondering if you will be able to get to work on time. If you do make it to your job on time, at what cost is it to you? Additionally, after you were so pressured and stressed in the morning, how will you be able to settle down to do your own work?

Each and every day parents who have preschool children with ADHD or those who exhibit similar behavior get up in the morning and realize immediately that they will have a challenging day. The symptoms of ADHD are chronic, constant, and consistent, unfortunately.

In addition to the struggles that the parents of a preschool child with ADHD experience, the life of a preschool child with ADHD is a difficult one as well, in large part due to his challenges with transitions. Some of these transitions may appear to be easy (but are definitely not simple for these children), such as going to school and coming home. Other such changes in the structure of the family, such as those brought on by a new sibling, for example, frequently are tumultuous to a child who as yet does not have the sophisticated language or perception to understand the nuances of these transitions. For more changes that preschool children with ADHD experience, go to chapter 7.

Bess reported about Aaron's difficulties with transitions:

For Aaron, there was the emotional part, which manifested itself very early on, and he had great difficulty in transitions. And I didn't realize at first what that meant, what was going on in his head. From the time that he was big enough that I couldn't physically strap him into his car seat, that I needed his cooperation, there was trouble. He was never a child to just "go with the flow." He's not the kind of kid to just do what everybody else is doing just because that's what everybody else is doing (Rapoport, 2009, pp. 34–35).

The consequences of how a preschool child with ADHD deals with these changes clearly affects his parents as well. It is very easy to become frustrated. The general feelings of frustration that parents feel are indicated by the following quotes from actual parents. Preschool children with ADHD have difficulty interacting with others.

> I can remember when he was four and he talked back to his grandfather. I said nothing, because it was like, you know what the situation was with the grandfather. I don't want to say he asked for it, but the tone and attitude and the behavior was such that Aaron was "back at ya," you know. I did correct him. I told him, Aaron that was not right, even though my thinking was, I'd have done the same thing as an adult. You're a child, you don't behave that way. So, it's always been a very tricky situation. I talked to him at that point. I did say to him, Aaron, you know, you need to apologize; that was wrong. To let him know that it was unacceptable, but at that same point in time I knew that what he said was something that anyone, any adult would have said in the same situation. But the problem was that he wasn't an adult. He was a child. He didn't know he wasn't supposed to say that. That was how he felt, so that's how he handled it.

These children exhibit social skills difficulties.

> As far as social skills go, I do think that kids with ADHD have significant issues with this. Sometimes it seems to be a matter of the fact that they do not notice their own behavior as being unusual or inappropriate in any way. Thus, they make no effort to control it. But, even when pointed out, they often seem unable to control odd or inappropriate behavior (Rapoport, 2009, p. 24).

They may be impulsive, as well, as one of the moms, Christen Saber, stated:

> Okay, so friends have been difficult, because he does have that impulsivity, eventually, the hyperactivity. Kids can go with the flow with the hyperactivity. The distractibility, they're distractible too. Impulsivity is tough. People, kids get scared of him, because he'll do; he'll beat [sic], he'll hit them, he'll poke them. He'll quickly become upset, and

run away, and so he's very unpredictable in other kids' eyes, and they don't like that. So, friends are hard (Rapoport, 2099, p. 37).

That impulsivity may be just plain annoying to other children.

> He has ADHD. . . . He's very impulsive, so he bops people in the head if he feels like bopping people in the head. When he feels like bopping people in the head, not out of meanness, just because, well, it looks like it was fun to do. Or because they had curly hair, and he wanted to touch it. Or he pushed somebody in front of him in line because he thought that he would be fun to see if it would be a domino effect. And so, he was getting in trouble for things like that (Rapoport, 2009, p. 33).

One of the frustrations that parents feel occurs when they try to point out to their child that she is behaving in an inappropriate way, hoping that she will.

> Well, I call her on it, and explain to her that that's not appropriate. Sometimes she'll act out, I mean act inappropriate just because she can, act inappropriate in this environment. But if she continues to act inappropriate, then we'll talk to her about it. I would say, Kristen, please don't do that or Kristen please. And usually, she'll try to respond and be good for twenty minutes or ten or twenty minutes or something and then she'll forget (Rapoport, 2009, p. 37).

In addition to the parent of a preschool child with ADHD feeling a sense of frustration due to her child's social skills and impulsivity problems, the misinterpretation of social cues that characterizes her child makes it very difficult for her to manage him on a play date. Typically, preschool children learn how to interpret social cues from their parents, and therefore, behave appropriately by observing them. Their parents teach them how to behave in a social situation and specifically how to learn the meaning of what another child is saying to them.

However, preschool children with ADHD cannot pay attention to their parent's words or actions because they are paying attention to something else. Their focus is also inconsistent, so they may hear only a part of what their parent is saying to them. The result of this inconsistent focus is that these children behave in a socially inappropriate way, leaving the other children to look at them in a strange way, not understanding their peer's inappropriate behavior.

Children may look at the preschool child with ADHD as different. They may ask themselves why their peer does not understand how to behave. These children appear vulnerable, which may lead to them bullying others and to be bullied themselves even at a preschool age! (check out chapter 8). They may misunderstand other children's social cues as well.

Here is an actual parent explaining one example of her young child misinterpreting social cues:

> Like he took it away, and I didn't know what to do, and I took it back, then he started hitting me. The poor kid has a lot of instances of that sort of thing happening, because he'll misinterpret what is going on. And then when some kid does something, he'll think he, Aaron, is innocent in the eyes of the other, and won't understand why the other did something that seems mean. And then Aaron will react in a mean way to respond.

Here is one more actual parent giving an example of her child misinterpreting social cues:

> Three children are playing a hide-and-seek game on the playground. Jimmy wants to play with them. Instead of waiting to see if the children in question ask him to play, he tries to get involved in their game, which has already started. He goes up to one child who is hiding and says, "I see you." The children rebuff Jimmy and make mean faces at him while continuing their play. Jimmy does not pick up their cues that they do not want him to play.
>
> Misinterpreting social cues in a school setting may be among many reasons that children with ADHD do not pay attention to another child's actions or words (Rapoport, 2009, pp. 38–39).

The misinterpretation of social cues often results in preschool children with ADHD being characterized by inconsistent behavior. Even though Timmy learned and understood how to play kickball, he misinterpreted a child trying to throw him out at home. One moment, he was exhilarated, running around the bases, while the next moment, he became aggressive.

As noted on one of the days that I worked with Timmy, the inconsistency of these children's behavior is very frustrating to teachers who work with them.

> One of the most difficult things about Timmy's behavior is that it is evidenced by inconsistency. This is the first year that the school has allowed him to have gym. Last year, the teacher did not feel that she could run the gym class successfully because she constantly had to manage Timmy's behavior. I believe that one of the reasons, among others, that he exhibited socially inappropriate behavior in gym class was that he did not know how to play many of the games that the teacher played. Therefore, I taught him many games this year that he had never been taught how to play. For example, I taught him how to play soccer and kickball.
>
> Today, I talked the gym teacher into permitting him to participate in the kickball game that she was facilitating in gym class. After teaching him how to kick the ball properly, and run around the bases according to the rules, he made a big kick that enabled him to get two children "home," as well as himself. Timmy ran "home" at the same time as a child threw the ball in an attempt to get him out before he crossed the plate.
>
> Timmy then took the ball and threw it at the child's face, hurting him. When he saw the child cry, he felt very badly. I made him apologize. I also had him sit out of the game for a few minutes. There was clearly no "rhyme or reason" for his behavior. He finally had athletic success yet behaved in a destructive manner.
>
> On the same day that Timmy had displayed the socially inappropriate behavior I just described, he also exhibited socially appropriate behavior. I simply could not explain Timmy's enigmatic, inconsistent behavior.

Again, my notes:

> The social studies teacher finished her lesson earlier than expected and allowed the children some free time. Timmy played a clever variation of a hang-man game with Hebrew letters for thirty minutes with three other boys and one girl. He was clearly the leader at this game and set up the rules. He was able to negotiate with all of the children who were playing hang-man with him. I have witnessed this positive interactive behavior before. This was not parallel playing as with Legos but inter-

active behavior, where Timmy was laughing and having a good time. He was an equal member of the group, in terms of social interaction.

On that day, Timmy exhibited both socially inappropriate behavior and socially appropriate behavior. When children with ADHD behave in such an inconsistent way, the people around them often misperceive their behavior. These outsiders, as I call them, view these children's behavior as representing the child. They view ADHD as a disease.

That is why you will hear me referring to children who are diagnosed with ADHD as children with ADHD or children who have ADHD rather than ADHD children. These children, our children, have a disorder that affects their behavior. Children with ADHD and their behavior must be viewed as two separate entities, even though these children are ultimately responsible and accountable for their behavior (Rapoport, 2009, pp. 9–10).

Does it seem that a child's inconsistent behavior might cause his parents stress? Absolutely! It is easy to imagine that parents of preschool children with ADHD become stressed when they are trying to manage their preschool child with ADHD's behavior. In fact, DuPaul et al. (2001) found that "families of young children with ADHD report less adaptive coping styles in response to stressful situations" (p. 514). It arguably becomes exponentially more difficult when these parents have more children than just the child with ADHD. What would you do?

There seems to be no choice but to try to deal with the socially inappropriate behavior initially, because it is obstructive to the entire family dynamic. There you are trying to find some positive behavior that you can praise in your child with ADHD while so many other socially inappropriate behaviors pop up that entangle you in a maze of stress. Seemingly, you hope that your other children will rise up to the occasion and get themselves dressed!

WHAT STRESS SHOULD I ANTICIPATE IN TRYING TO MANAGE THE BEHAVIOR OF MY PRESCHOOL CHILD WITH ADHD?

The amount of stress that you experience depends to a large extent on what kinds of events cause you to become anxious. Some people become frazzled in their work environment and not in their home environment.

For others, the opposite is true. How each person deals with the impact of stress is also individual. Perhaps stress and how each person responds to it may be related to whether or not these individuals have other successes in their lives. Perhaps it is related to whether or not they have friends. Perhaps it is related to whether or not they have a successful relationship with a significant other. Perhaps a person's stress is related to something out of their control and of which they are not aware.

So, it appears that stress and how it affects each person is related to an intersection of many variables in their lives. It is also important how long that a person permits stress to affect them. Do you have stress at work and let it affect your interaction with your child? If your child spills a cup of juice on your wood floor, do you start yelling at him instead of realizing that these types of things happen and have him help you to clean it up? As has been stated previously, none of us are perfect. Therefore, if you have had a stressful day at work, on that day, it just may happen that you reprimand your child more harshly than he deserves.

Just remember, however, that preschool children with ADHD react differently than children who do not have ADHD. Their self-esteem may not be formed yet and in fact may be negatively impacted by their ADHD, so they may become more upset than a typical child. These children certainly do not mean to behave in an inappropriate way. Therefore, they are *not* exhibiting socially inappropriate behavior on purpose!

As I have stated previously, these children are somehow reprimanded and yelled at all too frequently, so if you have done so, just try not to let it happen all of the time. If it does happen, explain to your child that you have had a rough day at work and that you did not mean to yell at him for whatever he did.

A child's socially inappropriate behavior may result in harsh parental reactions which may, in turn, increase the preschool child with ADHD's socially inappropriate behaviors even more. It is possible that if you intercede by talking to your child about the negative behavior that you feel he should not have exhibited, you may have interrupted the child's socially inappropriate behavior just enough to stop it for that moment.

Back to stress. . . . The reality of raising a preschool child with ADHD is that you will be dealing with stress as related to the behaviors that your child exhibits, the reactions of people who witness your child's behavior, the attitudes of teachers toward your child, and the responses of your family to seeing behavior that is in all likelihood dissimilar to their own child's behavior. Additionally, and even more important is that trying to manage your child with ADHD's behavior every minute of every day, as a preschool child said, is "super" stressful.

It is imperative that you work on trying to control your own stress, (and clearly that is not easy), so that your child does not pick up negative signs from your behavior. You almost have to develop a turtle shell so that you are not constantly upset. Acting as if other people's negative responses to your child's behavior does not affect you is very difficult, but it is essential to try to do so.

The situation that is one of the most difficult is that every simple request that you ask your child to do may result in him behaving in a socially inappropriate way. That is arguably the most stressful part. The only way to diminish your stress (because you will in all likelihood not erase it) is to think intentionally and ahead of time about all of the possible socially inappropriate behaviors that your child might exhibit. In that way, when and if these socially inappropriate behaviors occur, you will have a plan of action as well as a barometer of your own stress.

Make a list of the socially inappropriate behaviors that you have observed over a five-day period of time. Next to each behavior, write a possible response for yourself. The use of the word "response" here instead of the word "react" should indicate to you that your behavior must be well thought out and planned. In the introduction to this book, you will find a discussion of this predetermined way of thinking. A reaction is a quick and uncontrolled behavior. A response is well thought out and strategic. The discussion of this thought process is stated again here to emphasize how important your behavior is to your child's behavior. If you are organized and intentional in your mind ahead of time, you will respond (and *not* react) to your preschool child with ADHD's behavior in the best way possible, while experiencing as little stress as possible.

THE GUILT: IS MY PRESCHOOL CHILD WITH ADHD'S INATTENTION, IMPULSIVITY, AND SOCIALLY INAPPROPRIATE BEHAVIOR MY FAULT?

Here is where the guilt ensues. You may experience three sources of guilt. The first is related to your typical child. There is absolutely no time in the morning but to try to get everyone into the car to go to school.

Sometimes, you forget something that your typical child needs for school and are left running there to bring him that object. You are left with such sad feelings because you forgot about *his* needs! By the time 9:00 a.m. arrives, you are definitely ready for a nap. However, in all probability, you have to get ready for work and travel there yourself! Additionally, you may be upset that you spend so much energy managing your preschool child with ADHD's behavior, as compared to the time you spend with your typical child, but what can you do? Nothing!

The second is related to your concern that your preschool child's ADHD is your fault. It is not fair to you. ADHD does run in families, but the reality of the cause of ADHD is unclear. It is not fair to blame yourself because there are so many possible causes for your child's ADHD. As was stated previously, the reality of the cause of ADHD is not clear as of yet. "However, scientists have discovered a strong genetic link since ADHD can run in families. More than 20 genetic studies have shown evidence that ADHD is strongly inherited. Yet ADHD is a complex disorder, which is the result of multiple interacting genes" (https://chadd.org/about-adhd/overview/#sthash.Dmdenc1v.dpuf).   However, your preschool child's ADHD may or may not have a genetic basis.

The third is that you may be thinking that the cause of your preschool child's ADHD may be related to your parenting skills or techniques. Whereas parenting skills do interact with your child's behavior, they are not the *cause* of your preschool child's ADHD. So, can you or should you blame yourself? No! First of all, blaming yourself for your child's symptoms is not productive in terms of diminishing these symptoms. Second of all, condemning yourself for anything negative as related to your child is way too stressful.

In consideration of the fact that ADHD does run in families and you think that you have ADHD as well or have experienced the symptoms of ADHD in your lifetime, you are in a good position to help your preschool child with ADHD with his symptoms. If you did exhibit behavior similar to your child's conduct, retrace your behavior as a child and think about how you behaved and how your parents managed your conduct. Additionally, ask your parents and other family members how you behaved as a child so that you will know if they intervened in any way and how they tried to help you diminish your socially inappropriate behavior.

Similarly, if you were distractible as a child, ask your parents how they helped you to try to become more attentive, if they did so. Did they try to help you at home based on their own ideas, or did they interact with your teachers and work together with them? What did they do to effectively help you? Did they feel that they successfully assisted you?

Were you impulsive as a child, either physically or verbally? Are you impetuous now? If so, how do you manage your own impulsivity? If your child is rash, think about your own impulsivity. Did your parents intervene in any way to manage your impulsivity? What did they do? Were they successful? The more information that you gather, the easier it will be for you to try to manage your preschool child with ADHD's behavior.

WHAT SHOULD I DO TO BEGIN TO MANAGE MY PRESCHOOL CHILD WITH ADHD'S BEHAVIOR?

The very first thing that you should do is to talk to your preschool child with ADHD to help you to design some house rules. Explain to him why you need house rules, of course. Any rule that you design for your preschool child with ADHD will only benefit his typical sibling as well. Does this sound silly to do with a preschool child with ADHD? Not at all! You will quickly find out that your child thrives when he feels that he has some control of the workings of your house. You can discuss these rules in a collaborative manner, because if you do so, your child will feel a sense of ownership.

Of course, he will not realize that you are the final decision maker! For example: If your child puts on his pajamas, he will be permitted to watch a show. Here is another possible rule: If your child is dressed for school and is sitting in his chair at the breakfast table, he may choose what he wants to eat for breakfast. These rules may appear to be obvious, but children with ADHD typically run on their own motor and therefore, do not think of consequences.

What are these consequences? Well, as his parent, you know the stress that is involved with trying to get your child to do the simple things, such as those mentioned above, that typical children just easily do. You tell your child to put on his pajamas many, many times. You inevitably end up chasing him around and arguing instead of having a nice, quiet pre-bedtime. By the time you get him into his bed, you are ready to faint with the exhaustion that comes with the stress of trying to get your child to listen to you and comply with your requests. The stress and the frustration that you experience is the reason why it is imperative that you and your child set up rules together, so that there is no argument concerning what your child should be doing from moment to moment.

Rules may seem superfluous in your mind, but if you have a preschool child with ADHD, you will see that after you institute some rules and your child internalizes them, order will prevail with fewer socially inappropriate behaviors. In terms of rewards and praise, remember to keep in mind, however, that praise is more effective with preschool children with ADHD who are predominantly hyperactive than rewards. Rewards are effective if not overused, however. More later on rewards and praise.

Once you have successfully restored some order, you can begin to teach your preschool child with ADHD to follow instructions more effectively. It is a mistake to give these children several instructions at a time, because they will simply become overwhelmed. You can give your child one instruction and then tell him to come back to you after he has accomplished that one task. Make sure that your instructions are short and very clear. In fact, if you act out exactly how you want your child to execute your instruction, it may make it easier for him to follow it.

For example, if you want your child to pick up his clothes from the floor and put them into his hamper, show him how to do so. Do not assume that he is listening to your instructions. If you act out exactly what you want him to do, you are seeing that he actually observes and understands in real time what you are telling him to do. After you act out your instruction for him, ask him to repeat to you exactly what you want him to do, or better yet, have him carry out the instruction that you have stated and demonstrated. Doing so will in essence be a form of assessment, so that you will know whether or not he heard, understood, and then was able to carry out your instruction.

How will your child remember what to do? Make a long, vertical sign with pictures of what he has to do secured by Velcro. To begin, have him take the picture of the first thing that he needs to do along with him. As he completes each activity, he should Velcro back to the sign the picture of what he has just done and take the picture of the next instruction with him.

Once again, it is imperative to tell your child the instructions that you want him to follow in simple and precise terms. Preschool children with ADHD are less mature developmentally than preschool children without ADHD. They need to hear the directions that you want them to follow in basic terms by using as few words as possible. Here are some possible instructions that may work in your house, and all are based on doing them *one at a time*.

Morning Instructions

- Get out of your bed in the morning.
- Immediately go potty.
- Brush your teeth (with help).
- Go back to your room.
- Immediately begin to take your pajama pants off.
- Take your underpants off.
- Take your pajama shirt off.
- Put your pajamas and underpants in your hamper or a designated place.
- Put your socks on.
- Put your underpants on.
- Put your shirt on.
- Put your pants on.
- Give your mom or dad your sneakers so that they can help you to put them on, unless you can put them on by yourself.

You will want to design your own instructions based on your child's behavior. Only you know what behaviors you need to help your child to manage and what inappropriate behaviors you want him to work on to diminish. If you need help, check out the interventions that you will find in chapter 5.

What is the reward for accomplishing each task? A "high five" may be just enough to motivate him to go on to the next step until he finishes the task, along with the phrase "Good job!" Why does giving a high five or saying, "Good job!" work? These children seem to hear reprimands multiple times a day, whether from you, (in consideration of the inappropriate behavior that you manage, it is not surprising!) his preschool teacher, other children, as well as his immediate and extended family. "Don't do this" and "Don't do that" are so frequently said to the preschool child with ADHD that his self-esteem may well be impacted negatively at this young age. These children desperately want and need to hear that they did something good and worthy when they exhibit socially appropriate behavior, instead of always hearing negative comments upon exhibiting socially inappropriate behavior.

Bedtime Instructions

- Go to your room.
- Take off your shirt.
- Take off your pants.
- Take off your socks.
- Take off your shoes.
- Put on new socks.
- Put on new underpants.
- Put on your pajama pants.
- Put on your pajama shirt.
- Watch one show.
- Go potty.
- Brush your teeth (with help).
- Go to bed.

It is vital therefore to reorganize your home environment so that your child knows where to find his clothes as well as where to put his clothes. It is imperative that all of your children are required to adhere to the same rules. Children with ADHD need structure and consistency. That structure and consistency will not hurt your other children either, and in fact, will help them to thrive. Additionally, preschool children with ADHD also need to know what comes next in any scenario so that they will behave in an appropriate manner. Many more interventions will be discussed in a later chapter.

WHAT SHOULD I EXPECT AFTER I TRY TO IMPLEMENT THESE INSTRUCTIONS?

It is reasonable to expect that when you first design your own customized instructions, it will take time for you to succeed in getting your child to adhere to these directives. In order to truly accept these instructions, he has to see some yield in them for himself. For example, if he follows the bedtime instructions correctly, he will be permitted to watch a show. If he adheres to the morning instructions, he will be able to choose what he wants to eat for breakfast. In fact, it would behoove you to have some breakfast foods around that he loves as a way of encouraging him to comply. Once in a while it is okay to give your child foods that he likes, some of which you may not be such an avid fan. Being consistent is very important but being flexible is as well!

You can expect to hear some noncompliance until your child is somehow convinced that those are definite requirements that will not change. You must be firm when introducing the rules and/or the instructions (even though there was some collaboration with your child in terms of designing them) or he will not accept them as something that you are requiring him to do.

Another incentive may be that the Velcro strip that lists each step of every instruction should be a color and, in some way, related to his interest area. If he likes red, then design the strip in red. If he likes trucks, then design the strip with a truck that labels each step. One preschool child whom I know loves trains so I would design a strip with a different train for each step.

WHAT IF I MAKE A MISTAKE?

No one is perfect, and your child should see that certainly you are not either. If you forget the steps yourself, or for example, you are in a real hurry to get to work and you skip a step, then just explain to your child why you did so. No mistake is too big to explain. In fact, making a mistake should not cause you to be embarrassed at all!

Additionally, it is good for your child to see that he is not the only one who forgets, which is a paramount symptom of ADHD. Even though you may not have ADHD, you still may forget to do something. Tell him precisely the mistake that you made, how it happened, and how you feel because you made that error. The important lesson for your child to see is to observe how you pick yourself up and recover after you make a mistake. (You can even tell him that fact!) In that way, he will learn how to conduct himself in the same way as you do. When he makes a mistake, you should encourage him to use his words and explain to you about the error. It is far better for him to explain to you about how he forgot, instead of letting him cry in frustration.

SHOULD I TALK TO MY FAMILY AND FRIENDS ABOUT MY PRESCHOOL CHILD'S ADHD?

I certainly understand that you might want to be private about your family's health concerns, especially any health issue that affects your child. However, unfortunately, ADHD is not a quiet, dormant, or invisible disorder. Your child's behavior will be visible to everyone.

Just to emphasize as you read in the preface, I worked with a preschool child whose entire community thought that having ADHD was shameful. His parents knew that he had that diagnosis and the socially inappropriate behavior that went along with it. They also knew that he really needed help to learn to behave in a socially appropriate manner. Therefore, they hired me to teach him positive social skills.

One day, after I had been working with Benji for just about a year, as I was being hurried into the basement to then make the trek upstairs, a man quickly walked up the driveway and spoke in an agitated way to Benji's mom. He left as quickly as he had come. Apparently, that man was her brother. She told me at that point that the family and the neighbors had found out who I was and why I was working with Benji. I remember saying to myself, "How?" and "So what?" but Benji's mom then said in a matter-of-fact tone that I had to leave immediately. Did they really think that even though the family might not know that the child had ADHD, that his behavior was the same as the other children in the family? How could she hide her son's behavior?

You certainly do not want anyone, certainly not your family or friends, to think poorly of your child or to develop a prejudice against your child. You want to enjoy being with your friends and family without worrying about whether or not they are criticizing your child. Additionally, if people who are not familiar with ADHD are not told about the symptoms of your child's ADHD, they might just think that your child's behavior is your fault.

Perhaps you are permitting your child to behave in a wild way; perhaps you have not taught your child the acceptable behavior of sitting quietly at dinner; perhaps you have not taught him good manners; perhaps you let your preschool child control you; (What? Yes, some individuals *do* think in this way!) perhaps you are afraid to discipline your child for fear that he will have a temper tantrum in public.

Somehow, many people blame parents for their child's socially inappropriate behavior. Well, in this case, this child's socially inappropriate behavior was manifested due to the symptoms of Attention-Deficit/Hyperactivity Disorder (ADHD). In addition to exhibiting hyperactivity, children with ADHD may exhibit behaviors that are often impulsive. This impulsivity is a signal to others, as one parent, Mary Ann, told me below, that, "that child is so annoying." Have you had an experience similar to Mary Ann, who told me about her son Robert? (I will repeat this quote because it precisely describes impulsivity.)

> He has ADHD. . . . He's very impulsive, so he bops people in the head if he feels like bopping people in the head. When he feels like bopping people in the head, not out of meanness, just because, well, it looks like it was fun to do. Or because they had curly hair, and he wanted to touch it. Or he pushed somebody in front of him in line because he thought that he would be fun to see if it would be a domino effect. And so, he was getting in trouble for things like that.

You certainly want to hope for the best when you are with family and friends, but that being said, you will need to make a choice as to whether or not you tell them that your child has a diagnosis of ADHD. They might find your child irritating and/or annoying but that is something with which you will always sadly have to grapple.

What happens when a parent of a preschool child with ADHD looks to a friend to talk about her struggles with her child? Typically, the parent soon realizes that her friend has little patience for her problem with her preschool child with ADHD. Additionally, she is not compassionate in any way about the parent's plight because she has not had a similar experience in any way. What happens next?

The parent of the preschool child with ADHD feels isolated and alone in trying to diminish the difficulties that she experiences with her preschool child with ADHD.

Therefore, you may choose to decide about telling your friends and family based upon one of two hypothetical scenarios:

Scenario One: You do not mention anything to your friends or family about your child's ADHD. When you are together with your family and/or friends, your child's hyperactivity and/or impulsivity takes over as everyone is just sitting around and relaxing. Everyone just watches your child and wonders why he is behaving in that manner. Perhaps they might hesitate the next time they ask your family over for dinner. It is possible that because they do not understand why your child is behaving in that way, they look upon him as strange, accompanied by behavior that is out of control.

Scenario Two: You mention to your family and friends that your son was just diagnosed to have ADHD. They ask you how it presents itself. You explain that sometimes he is unfocused and behaves in a hyperactive way, or in an impulsive way, which you are working on with him to try to manage. When everyone is sitting around and relaxing, your child becomes hyperactive and runs around in circles. Your family sees you trying to manage his behavior, and because they were aware of his diagnosis, they just continue to relax and have conversations without being judgmental about his behavior.

Whatever you decide, make sure that you are definite in your decision and are consistent in how you respond to others when they comment upon your child's behavior. Your friends and family will take cues from you as to how they will respond to your child's hyperactivity and/or impulsivity.

IF I DO DISCUSS MY PRESCHOOL CHILD WITH ADHD'S DIAGNOSIS WITH MY FRIENDS, WILL THEY PERMIT THEIR CHILD TO PLAY WITH MINE?

If your friends are *real* friends, then they will be enthused to hear about your child in any way you choose to tell them. They will also be happy to understand how you are trying to manage your child's behavior, as well as how the diagnosis of ADHD is impacting your family.

If your friend is not a *real* friend, but just an acquaintance, then she will show you in some way, probably by her critical remarks, that she is not really interested in anything to do with your child's ADHD.

This parent will appear annoyed and rebuff your efforts to have a play date with both of your children. So, this is how you will know whom to trust, as well as who are your real friends! However, she might agree to have her child get together for a play date with your child until some socially inappropriate behavior occurs, at which point she will decide not to have another play date. Neither you nor your child (and especially your child), should to rebuffed in that way.

However, now that you have figured out if your friend is a loyal and a supportive person, be careful as to where you decide that your child's play date will be located. It is true that a child with ADHD's behavior may be annoying as well as a challenge to manage. You cannot blame people, however, or better said, please try *not* to blame people if they become impatient with your child's behavior, especially if it affects their child.

To repeat for emphasis, one of the many difficult issues that parents have to manage with a child with ADHD's behavior is that it is so unpredictable. One moment your preschool child with ADHD is complying with the rules of your home, and the next moment he is not sharing, not taking turns, and hitting and pushing. In these preschool children with ADHD, a temper tantrum might erupt as well. However, on the contrary, your child's behavior might be perfectly fine, with him playing nicely with his friend and not accompanied by any difficulties.

Due to the challenges that preschool children with ADHD have with changes and transitions, your child with ADHD's first play date should take place at your house. Why? You want to guarantee social success if at all possible. Success builds on success, and positive self-esteem begins to grow with successful social interactions. Your child will be more likely to behave appropriately in his own house, where he knows where his toys are located and where there are few changes. However, there *is* a possibility that he will be less likely to share his toys in his own house, but if he is learning to comply with your house rules, then he should be getting better at sharing.

As related to your preschool child with ADHD having play dates, you may also feel stress and/or anxiety as associated with whether or not the other child in the play date likes your child. What should parents do when their preschool child with ADHD behaves inappropriately toward his peer at his play date? These parents need to anticipate feelings of stress when they are trying to manage their preschool child with ADHD's behavior. In that way, any decision about discipline will be intentional.

DO I DISCIPLINE MY PRESCHOOL CHILD WITH ADHD WHEN HE CANNOT CONTROL HIS OWN BEHAVIOR?

Should preschool children with ADHD be disciplined when it is known that they cannot control their own behavior? Clearly, they do not willfully misbehave. As delineated in the diagnostic criteria that describe ADHD, these children are impulsive, hyperactive, and inattentive. Certainly, I would implement all of the interventions that you will read about or have read about in my first book, *ADHD and Social Skills: A Step-by-Step Guide for Teachers and Parents*. Sometimes, however, you may feel that your child needs something more.

Do you believe in time out? If you do, here is a caveat: By giving a preschool child with ADHD time out, you may be punishing him for behavior that he cannot control. When you tell a preschool child with ADHD that he has to go to time out, you take the chance of embarrassing him and making him feel poorly about himself. These children already have poor self-esteem. Why make them feel worse about themselves? When time outs are used with these children, they may just be counter-productive. "Unfortunately, using a time-out as a punitive method with kids diagnosed with ADHD may turn out to be counterproductive" (Arm-strong, 2018, np).

In fact, there is every reason to believe that preschool children with ADHD will just be more active when they are in a place where they are alone. They will, in all likelihood, stimulate themselves. What is the alternative? What these preschool children with ADHD need is a place where they can try to achieve some quiet and relaxation. Permit them to have control over the time that they spend in a place that they choose. In fact, give your child a *Time Timer*[1] and tell him to make a decision on the length of time that he will spend there.

You can call it "the quiet place," "the relaxation place," or whatever your child wants to call it. There is no reason to make your child feel worse about himself than he already does by making him go to a typical time out. You can instead help your child to realize that he needs some time to unwind. What can he do in his quiet time? He can look at a book, listen to a book, draw a picture, listen to music, or do something else that he enjoys, such as a puzzle.

Because you're changing the purpose of a time-out from passive punishment to working out problems, suggest activities that your child can do in the time-out area to help him gain control and feel better. Possibilities include

- Visualizing an image that helps him cope (a special place in nature, a favorite trip, or an imaginary journey).
- Meditating (focus attention on the inflow and outflow of breath, notice distractions that pop up, and return to focus on the breath).
- Doing physical relaxation exercises (the yoga pose called the Cat) or imagining that you're in a cozy elevator. As you feel it slowly descend, you feel more relaxed.
- Thinking about, writing down, or drawing the solutions to his or her problem (Armstrong, 2018, np).

One other activity that your child can do when he is in his quiet place is for him to use a Me Reader. These are electronic readers that typically come with eight books. When you push the button, a voice reads a story to your child. One example is *The World of Eric Carle*. The instructions are located on the back of the book cover. These Me Readers are really quite entertaining because in addition to a pleasant voice reading your child a story, each story is accompanied by pleasant sounds. Each picture has a color-coded button that corresponds to the text box border on the page that your child is reading. When it is time to turn the page, your child will hear a pleasant chime.

What should you do if you and your husband do not agree on this behavioral procedure among other ways to manage your preschool child with ADHD's behavior? Read on, please . . .

WHAT DO I DO IF MY HUSBAND AND I DO NOT AGREE ON HOW TO MANAGE OUR PRESCHOOL CHILD WITH ADHD'S BEHAVIOR?

This question is a vital and a difficult one. Preschool children with ADHD require structure and consistency in order to behave in the most optimal way possible. Therefore, when it comes to discipline, these children need to know the consequences of their behavior. If a child's mother invokes one consequence upon him for his behavior and then his father implements another consequence for that same behavior, the preschool child with ADHD may in all likelihood be left confused.

Clearly, mothers and fathers may disagree as related to the significance of their child's socially inappropriate behavior. They may also disagree on when to reply in the affirmative to their child's requests. It is likely that most of you have had your preschool child ask you for a snack. You may say no because it is close to dinner, while your significant other may say yes.

This difference in approaches and answers to your child's requests may lead to negotiating, which is less than ideal. Your child needs an even playing field with both parents responding in the same way. In that way, your child will know what to expect in terms of consequences. Additionally, he will know his boundaries, which is imperative for a preschool child with ADHD to know.

THE UNCERTAINTY OF MANAGING YOUR PRESCHOOL CHILD WITH ADHD'S BEHAVIOR WHEN *YOU* HAVE ADHD

"About one-third of children with ADHD continue to meet the criteria for an ADHD diagnosis as adults . . . about 10 million adults have attention-deficit/hyperactivity disorder" (CHADD, 2019, np). Even though hyperactivity tends to diminish when children become adults, these individuals may still be inattentive.

So how can you manage your child's hyperactivity and distractibility if you are also inattentive? You must manage your child's behavior because you have no choice. Your responsibility as a parent is to help your child in any manner that you can. Therefore, you must manage your own inattentiveness first, before you manage your child's hyperactivity and distractibility.

For example, you certainly cannot let your child run around in circles and not put his pajamas on! As you have previously read, hyperactivity does not just disappear. However, you can keep your child in situations where when he is hyperactive, he can be safe. It may not be easy, however. You will undoubtedly have to manage your own distractibility first before you help your preschool child with ADHD to focus better. That will be quite a challenge, but you can do it!

The key concept here is vigilance. I use the word "vigilance" because it is *you* who needs to be observant and watchful that your child's inattentiveness is modulated, and diminished if at all possible so that he can feel successful in whatever he is trying to accomplish. Remain determined that whatever you have experienced will be easier for your child, with your help, of course. Now, you are not only helping yourself to live a more stress-free and a more organized life but additionally, you are responsible for helping your child do so as well!

However, the preschool age is difficult because these children frequently are not aware of the chaos that surrounds them. Additionally, they may not have the understanding that they need to diminish that "noise." The lessons that you impart to your preschool child with ADHD at this young age will encourage him to have better self-esteem and improved self-confidence. So what can you do? First, determine how confident you feel in terms of your own self-esteem. Use self-talk to help you to activate your own level of self-assurance that will enable you to help your child to feel good about himself. What is self-talk? It is, simply put, talking to yourself, either verbally or nonverbally. It is imperative, however to use *positive* self-talk.

Say to yourself, "I can convince my child to follow all of the steps he needs to take when going to bed" or "When he interrupts me, I will give him a method to wait, until it is his turn to talk" or "When he does not have the patience to put a puzzle together and becomes frustrated, I will help him to relax and try to help him to finish the puzzle."

Somehow, self-talk will hopefully help *you* to relax and develop an organized way to help your child achieve his goal. If you are successful in terms of organizing yourself, which will help you to feel more stress-free, your child will then internalize the feelings that you have expressed and, hopefully, will feel that same sense of satisfaction.

Just make sure that you are not negative in your self-talk. Most certainly you think that you cannot fool yourself. However, the adverse thoughts that you say in your self-talk are not productive. If you think negatively, you will find yourself devoid of energy to do whatever it is that you want to do. All of your drive will be used up quickly by paying attention to these damaging thoughts.

The essence of self-talk is really no different than how you talk to your child. When he is leaning over in his chair at dinner and is almost falling down, what do you say? Do you say, "Don't lean over in your chair" or

"What are you doing leaning over?" or "You will fall!" Instead you should say "Try to sit up in your chair when you eat" or "I really like the way that you are sitting up in your chair so that you can eat your dinner." Positive talk leads to affirmative behavior. Positive self-talk leads to constructive actions and positive self-esteem as well.

Second, look into your skill set and determine honestly how *you* are succeeding in terms of organizing your life. Make sure that you are using a planner, as well as organizing your child's events in the same way. Find a method for helping your child to arrange his activities even in his house. There are certain responsibilities that your child must accomplish each day. Some of these are putting his pajamas on, brushing his teeth, and many other activities that have been delineated earlier in this chapter.

Remember: Each and every activity that your preschool child with ADHD accomplished himself (albeit with a little help from you) will add to his positive feelings about himself. In other words, all of these affirmative feelings will incur positive self-esteem. You have most certainly placed a high value on affirmative self-esteem for yourself. Therefore, you must also teach your child to value positive self-esteem as well. Always talk to yourself in the same way that you would talk to others, including your child.

Here are some examples of self-talk that you may try as you are managing your child's behavior.

- I will walk into my child's room and convince him to put his pajamas on.
- I will give my child choices as to which pajamas he wants to wear so that he will be able to make his own decision.
- I will focus so that I will be able to read my child a book.
- I have so many thoughts in my mind, so I will go to take a walk downstairs before I read to my child.
- When I get the children ready for school, I will retain my sense of humor.
- I will tell my child to do one activity at a time.
- I can do this.

Remember to only employ positive self-talk. Negative self-talk is destructive to your own self-esteem.

Should you tell your preschool child with ADHD that you have ADHD? At this young age, it is likely that your child will not have an accurate understanding of his ADHD, even though you have the same diagnosis. Instead, you might say to your child that you sometimes have difficulty concentrating on a book, but you say to yourself: "Yes, I can. Yes, I can." When you are swimming in a pool with your child and he is learning to swim, have him shout out "Yes, I can. Yes, I can." That message is powerful and will impact your child in a positive, energetic way.

Much of the difficulty that the preschool child with ADHD experiences is based upon his lack of knowledge of social skills, or his difficulty performing social skills. Due to these children's distractibility, they do not readily learn positive social skills, which you will read about in the next chapter.

NOTE

1. The Time Timer is a visual timer that is useful for children who cannot tell time. It has a flag that winds down as the time decreases. It is available at www.timetimer.com as well as www.amazon.com.

4

SOCIAL SKILLS

"A four-year-old brother should take care of his three-year-old brother at his birthday party" (Anonymous, four and change). This statement was made to me by a typical four-year-old child immediately after his brother's third birthday party.

Would a preschool child with ADHD exhibit this type of nurturing behavior as well and be aware of the positive social skills that are expected of him? Probably not. Preschool children with ADHD need to learn the social skills that a typical preschool child has already learned.

THE DEFINITION OF SOCIAL SKILLS

What are social skills? "Social skills may be defined as socially acceptable learned behaviors that enable a person to interact with others in ways that elicit positive responses and assist in avoiding negative responses" (Elliott and Gresham, 1993, p. 287).

THE IMPORTANCE OF PARENTAL KNOWLEDGE OF THEIR PRESCHOOL CHILD WITH ADHD'S SOCIAL SKILLS

Why do parents of preschool children with ADHD need to know the importance of learning social skills? Typically, preschool children with ADHD have poorly developed social skills. They have difficulty following instructions, they do not listen well, and therefore interrupt others, among other negative behaviors.

Since these children generally do not have positive social skills, they are in danger of being bullied, which we will talk about in chapter 8. When a child appears to be vulnerable as these preschool children with ADHD often appear to be, they are at risk for negative and difficult social experiences. Social situations which typical children find easy to manage may be treacherous for preschool children with ADHD. They may have difficulty making friends and even their families may find them annoy-ing, which is very sad!

Here is what one mom told me about her son: "He has this behavior that really pisses people off. Some ADD or ADHD is either manageable or they're so charming or sometimes it passes. We have one. His person-ality makes people really upset. And that was pretty evident early on."

I was troubled by her statement about her son because I knew that his life and his parent's life had to be very difficult. I was especially heart-broken hearing any mother talk about her child in such negative terms. How do preschool children with ADHD who have social skills deficits behave? They either talk excessively without realizing that they are doing so, or they may talk so infrequently that their parents hardly know that they are in the same room. Additionally, they may not understand social cues that other children are expressing in conversations.

Social cues are signals, either verbal or nonverbal, that help to com-municate behavior. Some of these social cues may be facial expressions or body language. Preschool children with ADHD typically misinterpret social cues, as we will discuss later on in this chapter. If they do so in their activities, this miscommunication may be very confusing for them.

> Gymnastics has been a problem, like other activities that we have gotten him involved at one time or another (mom laughs, nervously), because he has trouble going with the flow. And he gets distracted from what he's supposed to do very easily, and that can turn into behavior problems with, you know, goofing off with other kids, also sometimes misinterpreting social cues because he gets so focused on one way of doing things.

Let us return to social skills. There are many other examples of poor social skills, including touching another child, pushing, hitting, etc. I am sure that we all know the definition of social skills. However, in terms of accuracy, Elliott and Gresham (1993) stated that "social skills may be defined as socially acceptable learned behaviors that enable a person to interact with others in ways that elicit positive responses and assist in avoiding negative responses" (p. 287). You can see from the previous parent's statements that preschool children with ADHD need to learn and exhibit positive social skills in order to make friends, get along with their family, and build positive self-esteem.

These children have experienced rejection and criticism constantly because of their inappropriate behavior and their lack of social skills. If they live in the same house as their siblings, why do they do not learn the same social skills as them?

DO PRESCHOOL CHILDREN WITH ADHD LEARN THE SAME SOCIAL SKILLS AS THEIR SIBLINGS?

If you look at the previously stated definition, preschool children with ADHD have difficulty learning social skills. How can that be? Aren't they being brought up in the same house as their siblings who exhibit positive social skills? We will find out the answer to that question in a moment. If you are a parent of one of these children, you know very well that your child has immature social skills. In fact, due to the point that they do not have a complete repertoire of intact, positive social skills, they are not only difficult to manage but sadly, annoy many people (as I have said before, but will emphasize again here), due to their excessive verbiage and socially inappropriate behavior.

One of the parents with whom I worked described her child's behavior this way:

> I can remember when he was four and he talked back to his grand-father. I said nothing, because it was like, you know what the situation was with the grandfather. I don't want to say he asked for it, but the tone and attitude and the behavior was such that Aaron was "back at ya," you know. I did correct him. I told him, Aaron that was not right, even though my thinking was, I'd have done the same thing as an adult. You're a child, you don't behave that way. So, it's always been a very tricky situation. I talked to him at that point. I did say to him, Aaron, you know, you need to apologize; that was wrong. To let him know that it was unacceptable, but at that same point in time I knew

that what he said was something that anyone, any adult would have said in the same situation. But the problem was that he wasn't an adult. He was a child. He didn't know he wasn't supposed to say that. That was how he felt, so that's how he handled it (Rapoport, 2009, p. 23).

Another parent described her son's inability to control his own behavior:

> As far as social skills go, I do think that kids with ADHD have significant issues with this. Sometimes it seems to be a matter of the fact that they do not notice their own behavior as being unusual or inappropriate in any way. Thus, they make no effort to control it. But, even when pointed out, they often seem unable to control odd or inappropriate behavior. (Rapoport, 2009, p. 24).

Okay, so let's get to the bottom of these children's social skills difficulties. Preschool children with ADHD of all types may have social skills problems, even though their behavior may be varied. Why? They have social skills deficits. These deficits typically have been described as either "can't do" or "won't do" (Gresham, Sugai, and Horner, 2001, p. 33). They either do not have the knowledge to behave in a socially appropriate manner or they know how to behave in a socially appropriate manner but do not do so (p. 33). Social skills deficits prevent these children from learning positive social skills. They typically do not pick up and internalize positive social skills that are modeled by their parents at home in the same way as preschool children without ADHD do.

THE ANSWER TO OUR QUESTION

So, why don't preschool children with ADHD learn the same social skills as their siblings who live in the same house? In fact, if these siblings do not have ADHD, you are probably asking yourself a very pertinent question. How can it be that your other children just picked up these social skills from your modeling of pro-social behavior while your preschool child with ADHD did not pick up these skills?

Preschool children with ADHD exhibit behaviors that interfere with their parent's teaching of social skills. Some of these behaviors are temper tantrums, distractibility, impulsivity, anxiety, and arguing (Elliott and Gresham, 1993, p. 295). These are behaviors that compete with what the parent is teaching her child in terms of social skills. Can you imagine a child listening to his parent teaching him to exhibit positive social skills like not interrupting when he is having a temper tantrum or when he is unfocused and/or looking at something else?

Immature social skills or absent social skills are one of the most prominent symptoms of ADHD and very often causes these children to have difficulty making and keeping friends and therefore interacting in a productive way. In fact, social skills difficulties frequently arise, as I stated previously, because these children are inattentive to social communication, especially to social cues that all children communicate. Additionally, these children perseverate on specific parts of the conversation and do not move on to the next topic (Brown, 2002, p. 35).

Elliott and Gresham (1991) state that there are five reasons why children do not learn positive social skills.

- lack of knowledge
- lack of practice of feedback
- lack of cues or opportunities
- lack of reinforcement
- presence of interfering problem behaviors (pp. 28–29)

Therefore, if a child is inattentive, unfocused and/or anxious, which are interfering behaviors, they simply do not learn social skills in the same way and as easily as do children who do not have ADHD. Therefore, these children do not behave appropriately when they are interacting with their peers, and often get rejected by their peers who do not have ADHD. What happens next? Very quickly, the preschool child with ADHD becomes rebuffed and marginalized, so that they predominantly play by themselves.

Let us be honest . . . preschool children with ADHD may be abrasive and annoying due to their inappropriate behavior, which is caused by social skills deficits. These socially inappropriate behaviors cause their peers to mistreat them by either ignoring them or by refusing to play with them. Parents quickly become aware as to how their children are being treated, sadly. They realize that their preschool children with ADHD have to learn to interact in a more acceptable way. All social experiences begin with the initial interaction. (Rapoport, 2009, p. 32).

IS THERE ANY GOOD NEWS?

Yes, there is some good news! Even though preschool children with ADHD have difficulty paying attention to their parent's words and do not consistently model her behavior, they can still learn positive social skills in other ways. These social skills may be taught and embedded[1] through their natural home environment. For example, these children may be taught positive social interaction through altercations with their siblings as a way of learning how to cooperate. Additionally, they may also learn social skills such as sharing and taking turns through role playing with their siblings.

They can learn to respect their parent's judgment, for example, even though they may have disappointed them with a certain decision that they made. This pronouncement might have been not going to the playground when they counted on going there, for example. Finally, they can learn social skills through the vehicle of a book that is read to them by their parents, among other ways.

What is the first skill that preschool children with ADHD need to learn? Maintaining eye contact and communicating to their peers through their body language is the first step to learning social skills and achieving positive social interactions.

MAINTAINING EYE CONTACT AND COMMUNICATING WITH OTHER CHILDREN THROUGH BODY LANGUAGE

Preschool children with ADHD often do not know the body language they have to adopt when they meet someone for the first time. For instance, when Amelia walked into the dress-up center at preschool, she looked down at the ground, and did not make eye contact. How would the other children know that Amelia wanted to make friends and play with them? Making eye contact in an initial social interaction is a signal that says "I want to be friends." When a child does not maintain eye contact, the message might be, "I do not want to make friends." These children do not internalize these lessons and must be taught how to behave in a socially appropriate manner.

Not knowing how to greet another child is among many reasons why preschool children with ADHD have great difficulties making friends. In fact, problems making and keeping friends became a common thread among the children with whom I have worked over many years. Furthermore, when a child is characterized by impulsivity, other children tend to stay away from him.

> Okay, so friends have been difficult, because he does have that impulsivity, eventually, the hyperactivity. Kids can go with the flow with the hyperactivity. The distractibility, they're distractible too. Impulsivity is tough. People, kids get scared of him, because he'll do; he'll beat [sic], he'll hit them, he'll poke them. He'll quickly become upset, and run away, and so he's very unpredictable in other kids' eyes, and they don't like that. So, friends are hard (Rapoport, 2009, p. 330).

When I have discussed the social skills difficulties of preschool children with ADHD with their parents, they are all too familiar with these issues. However, frequently they do not know what to do to help their child to develop positive social skills. They are acutely aware that their child cannot control his own behavior, as we read in Mary Ann's words earlier:

> He has ADHD. . . . He's very impulsive, so he bops people in the head if he feels like bopping people in the head. When he feels like bopping people in the head, not out of meanness, just because, well, it looks like it was fun to do. Or because they had curly hair, and he wanted to touch it. Or he pushed somebody in front of him in line because he thought that he would be fun to see if it would be a domino effect. And so, he was getting in trouble for things like that.

Clearly, preschool children with ADHD are not aware that their behavior is inappropriate, even though it may be an obstacle to other children interacting with them. Their behavior is so unpredictable, that they receive varied responses to their behavior by other children, which has to be confusing for them. Certain social skills are very important for preschool children with ADHD to learn, so please keep reading!

LISTS OF SOCIAL SKILLS THAT PRESCHOOL CHILDREN WITH ADHD NEED TO LEARN

Social Skills List 1 is a list of some of the social skills created by Elliott and Gresham (1991) and included in their *Social Skills Intervention*

Guide. Social Skills List 2 is a list of social skills that I have designed. Many of these social skills are necessary for children with ADHD to have in their repertoire if they are going to experience successful social interactions. Clearly, however, some of the social skills from Social Skills List 1 are not developmentally appropriate for preschool children with ADHD to learn. Social Skills List 2 includes social skills which are all developmentally appropriate for preschool children with ADHD to learn.

Study the following two lists of social skills and determine which social skills are the ones that your preschool child with ADHD needs to learn.

Social Skills List I

Social Skill 1: "Maintaining Eye Contact" (Rapoport, 2009, pp. 73–74)

Social Skill 2: "Greeting Others Nonverbally" (Elliott and Gresham, 1991, p. 22)

Social Skill 3: "Greeting Others Verbally" (Rapoport, 2009, p. 46)

Social Skill 4: "Introducing Oneself" (Elliott and Gresham, 1991, p. 21)

Social Skill 5: "Initiating Conversations" (Elliott and Gresham, 1991, p. 21)

Social Skill 6: "Joining Ongoing Activities" (Elliott and Gresham, 1991, p. 21)

Social Skill 7: "Volunteering to Help Peers" (Elliott and Gresham, 1991, p. 21)

Social Skill 8: "Inviting Others to Join Activities" (Elliott and Gresham, 1991, p. 21)

Social Skill 9: "Asking an Adult for Help" (Elliott and Gresham, 1991, p. 21)

Social Skill 10: "Answering the Telephone" (Elliott and Gresham, 1991, p. 21)

Social Skill 11: "Asking Permission to Use Property" (Elliott and Gresham, 1991, p. 21)

Social Skill 12: "Reporting Accidents to Appropriate Persons" (Elliott and Gresham, 1991, p. 21)

Social Skill 13: "Questioning Rules That May Be Unfair" (Elliott and Gresham, 1991, p. 21)

Social Skill 14: "Giving a Compliment" (Elliott and Gresham, 1991, p. 21)

Social Skill 15: "Responding to a Compliment" (Elliott and Gresham, 1991, p. 21)

Social Skill 16: "Telling Adults When Something Is Appreciated" (Elliott and Gresham, 1991, p. 22)

Social Skill 17: "Accepting people Who Are Different" (Elliott and Gresham, 1991, p. 22)

Social Skill 18: "Accepting Peer Suggestions for Activities" (Elliott and Gresham, 1991, p. 22)

Social Skill 19: "Cooperating with Peers" (Elliott and Gresham, 1991, p. 22)

Social Skill 20: "Compromising by Reaching Agreement" (Elliott and Gresham, 1991, p. 22)

Social Skill 21: "Responding to Teasing Appropriately" (Elliott and Gresham, 1991, p. 22)

Social Skill 22: "Receiving Criticism Well" (Elliott and Gresham, 1991, p. 22)

Social Skill 23: "Controlling Temper in Conflicts with Adults" (Elliott and Gresham, 1991, p. 22)

Social Skill 24: "Responding Appropriately When Pushed or Hit" (Elliott and Gresham, 1991, p. 22)

Social Skill 25: "Controlling Temper When in Conflict with Peers" (Elliott and Gresham, 1991, p. 22)

The following are social skills that I will discuss throughout this book, some of which I created during my field research for my dissertation and others that were designed by Elliott and Gresham (1991). I then adapted all of these social skills to be implemented for preschool children with ADHD.

Social Skills List 2

Social Skill 1: "Maintaining Eye Contact" (Rapoport, 2009, pp. 73–74)

Social Skill 2: "Teaching Social Skills through Conversations with your Child" (Rapoport, 2007, p. 273)

Social Skill 3: "Behaving in a Polite Manner" (Rapoport, 2007, p. 274)

Social Skill 4: Arguing with Disciplinary Decisions

Social Skill 5: "Joining Ongoing Activities and Play" (Elliott and Gresham, 1991, p. 22)

Social Skill 6: "Volunteering to Help Other Children" (Elliott and Gresham, 1991, p. 21)

Social Skill 7: "Inviting Others to Join Activities" (Elliott and Gresham, 1991, p. 21)

Social Skill 8: "Cooperation" (Elliott and Gresham, 1991, p. 22)

Social Skill 9: "Compromise" (Elliott and Gresham, 1991, p. 22)

Social Skill 10: "Asking Permission to Use Others' Property" (Elliott and Gresham, 1991, p. 22)

Social Skill 11: Sharing and Taking Turns

Social Skill 12: Incessant or Excessive Talking

Social Skill 13: "Listening to All Instructions Without Interrupting" (Rapoport, 2007, p. 274)

Social Skill 14: Transitions

Social Skill 15: Staying in His Seat for Meals

Social Skill 16: Staying in One Place

HOW PRESCHOOLERS WITH ADHD EXHIBIT DIFFICULTIES WITH SOCIAL SKILLS: MISINTERPRETING SOCIAL CUES

As stated previously, the behavior of preschool children with ADHD is frequently inconsistent. They may be stubborn and inflexible one moment and malleable and funny the next moment. They may also be unfocused one moment as indicated when they do not respond to your instructions, and then concentrated and hyperfocused on building a Lego structure a few minutes later.

In addition to their unpredictable behavior, which they cannot control, these children misinterpret social cues, as mentioned earlier. It is not only that they do not make eye contact, which they often do not do as well, but they also misunderstand the meaning of what another child is saying. Here is an example, as told to me by a mother of a preschool child with ADHD:

Three children are playing a hide-and-seek game on the playground. Jimmy wants to play with them. Instead of waiting to see if the children in question ask him to play, he tries to get involved in their game, which has already started. He goes up to one child who is hiding and says, "I see you." The children rebuff Jimmy and make mean faces at him while continuing their play. Jimmy does not pick up their cues that they do not want him to play (Rapoport, 2009, p. 39).

If these children do not pay attention to another child's words, they also do not pay attention to what those words mean, which often leads to misunderstanding, miscommunication, and inappropriate behavior.

Bess spoke to me about Aaron misinterpreting other children's social cues. She explained:
Like he took it away, and I didn't know what to do, and I took it back, then he started hitting me. The poor kid has a lot of instances of that sort of thing happening, because he'll misinterpret what is going on. And then when some kid does something, he'll think he, Aaron, is innocent in the eyes of the other, and won't understand why the other did something that seems mean. And then Aaron will react in a mean way to respond (Rapoport, 2009, p. 39).

Preschool children with ADHD may take longer to process the words that are spoken to them either by another child or by their parents. Sometimes, they attend to social cues that are not pertinent or grab on to one word or part of a phrase that another child has said. It is possible that because preschool children with ADHD are so distractible, they may be thinking about all of the thoughts that are racing around in their heads. Because they are so involved with these thoughts, they may lose interest in what their peer is saying. Due to the fact that they do not focus on what their peer is saying, they often interrupt his talking as well as his play. Belinda also explained to me how difficult it was for Max to "read people":

And you need to realize and read, and that is something that is his most difficult part of life, is that he doesn't know how to read people. He just doesn't really care if they're getting upset, because he'll just get more upset (Rapoport, 2009, p. 39).

The following are other possible difficulties with social skills that may occur with preschool children with ADHD.

- moving from one activity to another with very little sustained involvement
- frequent need for teacher redirection and verbal warnings of punishment
- disorganized, nonconstructive, and non-goal-directed play activity
- difficulty sharing with peers and being able to wait for a turn
- mood swings and behavioral outbursts (Woodbury, 2007, np).

PARENTS TEACHING SOCIAL SKILLS TO THEIR PRESCHOOL CHILDREN WITH ADHD: I AM A PARENT! I AM NOT A TEACHER!

You may feel overwhelmed at the thought of teaching social skills to your preschool child with ADHD. Parents may not think that they are teachers. However, they are their child's first and most influential teachers. Therefore, they may make a real impact on the social skills that their child learns. When parents teach social skills to their child with ADHD, they typically teach what I call "on the spur of the moment," as I observed in my doctoral field research. It is a good effort, but it does not lead to long-term results. It is imperative, therefore, to do two things:

1. Think ahead of time as to how you would teach these specific social skills so that when you need to teach these social skills, you are teaching them in an intentional way.
2. Teach the social skill in at least two settings so that the learning of that skill will transfer across settings and endure.

Additionally, make sure that the child clearly understands precisely what is the behavior that he is exhibiting that is socially inappropriate and the reason that it is socially inappropriate. *It is imperative, however, to read below in terms of how the child should surmise which behavior is inappropriate and which is appropriate.* As I expressed before, much of the success of teaching social skills to preschool children with ADHD is ensuring that they understand exactly what is being taught to them and why it is being taught. If you teach social skills as explained, the child should learn the particular social skill and internalize the comprehension of it for future need.

You may need to use visuals to get the point of the lesson across to the child. Preschool children with ADHD may require visual cues to stimulate their learning of social skills. Visuals will stimulate them so that they will be able to remember how to exhibit a specific social skill the inappropriate as well as the appropriate way. (Later, I will discuss more information on visuals).

Preschool children with ADHD need to understand which of their behavior is socially inappropriate. However, the way that you need to teach them which behavior is inappropriate is *not* to point out that a certain behavior is inappropriate. Instead, point out and teach them which behavior is appropriate. In that way, they will be able to deduce which behaviors are inappropriate themselves.

You do *not* want to point out that these children are exhibiting inappropriate behavior because you do not want their self-esteem to be impacted negatively. You *do* want to affirmatively respond when they are interacting in a positive way, however. As I have said before, preschool children with ADHD hear far too many negative comments about their behavior. There is a lot of good that you can find in your preschool child with ADHD. Unfortunately, inappropriate behavior often pops up that masks the appropriate behavior.

As a parent, you need to look long and hard to find the appropriate behavior that your child is exhibiting. After you locate that positive behavior, reward that behavior by stating affirmative and complimentary comments. "You did such a good job" or "Good listening" goes a long way in terms of trying to build up your child's self-esteem who has previously been criticized too many times. Always reward the effort that your child makes. Even if he does not totally succeed in what he is trying to do, at least he will feel better about himself if he feels that his effort is recognized by you.

Let us continue on to more specific details about the difficulties that preschool children with ADHD experience. You will find suggestions here in this chapter for teaching your preschool child with ADHD to learn how to share, to learn how to take turns as well to learn how to successfully transition. However, more detailed interventions for learning these social skills and others will be found in chapter 5.

PROBLEM-SOLVING AREAS FOR PRESCHOOL CHILDREN WITH ADHD: SHARING, TAKING TURNS, AND TRANSITIONS

Sharing

All preschool children with or without ADHD must begin to learn to share. It is not always an easy task to convince these children that *it is fair to share*. I love that phrase, but do preschool children? Not so much! They are very egocentric and only want to play with a specific toy themselves. One of the preschool children I know says to me all of the time, "I do not want to share. I do not like to share." Let us talk about the issue of sharing as it relates to preschool children with ADHD.

Preschool children with ADHD often become upset very quickly . . . *Poof!* . . . and have absolutely no interest in sharing. What do they do, typically? They grab a toy and start to cry that it is their toy and they had it first, with a kind of a rigid, inflexible air about them. They give themselves absolutely no time to think of an alternate choice. They are compelled by the tiny time period in which they find themselves.

They then become obstinate. "It is mine! I had it first!" It actually does not matter who had the toy first. If both children want the same toy, then a problem will ensue here. If the object comes in many pieces such as colored blocks, you can figure out how the preschool child with ADHD and the other child can play with them together. The preschool child with ADHD can play with the red blocks, for example, while the other child can play with the blue blocks. Then, they can switch colors, hopefully. You can try to convince the preschool child with ADHD that if they play with both of the colored blocks together, it would look much nicer as well as being more fun.

If there is only one toy or object, then convincing the child to share is more difficult. If you try to redirect the child, that certainly does not teach the child to share. Here are two techniques that you could try when there is only one toy to share.

- Set up a timer. First, give the toy to one child for a prescribed amount of time. When the buzzer goes off, give the toy to the other child. (Even if this technique seems to be more like taking turns than sharing, it is better than arguing over one toy!)

- If neither child can cooperate, place the toy on a shelf, so that both children can see it. In that way, they are forced to play with something else for a very short time period while they constantly see the toy that they would not share.
- After a short period of time, take the toy down from the shelf and see if the children will share.

There are several books on sharing that you might want to purchase. One of them is just wonderful and is called *The Rainbow Fish* by Marcus Pfister (you will find the citations to the following books in the bibliography and suggested resources chapter). *The Rainbow Fish* is a story about a beautiful fish whose name is The Rainbow Fish, who thought that he was too beautiful to play with the other fish. When the other fish asked him for one of his shining scales, he said no, until one by one none of the fish wanted to be friends with him. Once he changed his mind and decided to give the other fish some of his scales, they decided to be friends with him. He was happy because the other fish were happy. What was the other reason that was he so delighted? He was also pleased because he shared and no longer dwelled on whether or not he was beautiful. What a great story line!

Another book that has a message of the advantages of sharing accompanied by vibrant illustrations is *Not Fair, Won't Share* by Sue Graves. This book actually is about sharing and taking turns. The teacher in the book made the classroom into a space station with levers and buttons and helmets. However, the three children who were told to share and take turns do not choose to do so. Everyone including the teacher becomes "mad" until the children and the teacher step away from the space station. They then think about how badly they felt that they had not adhered to the classroom rules of sharing and taking turns. They also experienced remorse that they were not nice to the other children in the class. So, lesson well learned!

Another book that I came across that has a very cute and important message about the significance of sharing is *Rex the Dinosaur and a New Bike* written by Ellie J. Woods. The story is about a dinosaur who has a new bike and refuses to share it with a neighbor. His mother then explains to him about being nice and kind instead of being greedy. The part of the lesson that I loved was when his mother said that, "The best lessons are learned from mistakes." If you are looking for this wonderful book, I only came upon this book accidentally, because it was self-published. There-fore, it was only listed on a few sites. It has an outstanding message.

One last book to read to your child is *Share and Take Turns* by Cheryl J. Meiners. This book includes bright and clear illustrations of diverse characters. The illustrations are colorful and vibrant, and the lesson is very clear and understandable for preschool children. The message is one that delineates what it means to share, how to share, as well as well as the advantages of learning to share.

Additionally, the book states that "taking turns is a way of sharing too" (Meiners, 2003, p. 10). It then goes on to explain how to take turns. There are sharing games at the end of the book, from which parents of preschool children with ADHD may benefit. Teaching the child to take turns may also help you to convince your child that if he wants to play with a specific toy, the only way to do so is to cooperate with another child.

Taking Turns

Before I discuss taking turns, I must point out the difficulty that sharing entails. Somehow, however, taking turns is not often in the preschool child with ADHD's repertoire of behavior. However, preschools current-ly seem to be leaning toward parents teaching their children how to take turns instead of teaching them how to share. Why is that? Sharing a toy requires a sophisticated understanding of a concept that these children may not have the verbal or nonverbal language to understand, especially preschool children with the symptoms of ADHD. How do two children share one toy?

Learning to share is a very complicated lesson, while learning to take turns may, in fact, be more specific and easier to understand. This is especially true if a timer is used so that each child knows who has a toy and for how long they each have had it. Preschool children, especially those with ADHD, seem to respond better when they know the rules in advance and can predict what happens. I will still be including interven-tions for sharing in chapter 5, however, because for many children it is a lesson worth learning.

Before I discuss taking turns, even though we touched upon it in the above paragraph, I need to remind everyone that teaching sharing or taking turns or really any skill will be much easier if certain rules have already been put in place. It is always best to design rules collaboratively. However, if your child does not understand how to do so, you can still design a set of rules and go over them with him.

If he does not read, and many preschool children do not read as of yet, design some visual cues so that he will understand each rule. If you have rules already written down accompanied by visual cues, as well as consequences for not adhering to the rules, executing taking turns will be so much easier. In that way, the meaning of the rules will remain after you have stated them. How do you find visual cues? An easy thing to do is to take digital pictures and glue them onto card stock. Then laminate the cards and place them at the child's eye level in the room in which he is playing. In that way, he will be reminded of what rules he must follow.

For example, you can take a picture of the following:

- the child's toy
- the child actually playing with his toy
- the timer
- the other child playing with the same toy (with permission from his parent, of course)
- the TV playing your child's favorite show

The implication is that he needs to take turns playing with his toy with his peer, if he wants to watch his favorite show or receive any other reward. Voila! At the young age of four or five, his peer will hopefully not be critical of the visual reminders that you have hung up for your child.

It is difficult for a preschool child with ADHD to permit another child to play with a toy because he may think that he will not be able to play with it again. He undoubtedly does not understand that in a short time period that he will definitely play with it again. It would behoove you to create a social story that relates to your child taking turns with one of his important possessions, such as a stuffed animal. If he does so, he then might understand what it means to take turns on a deeper level.

Transitions

In as much as preschool children with ADHD become overly focused on the moment in which they are playing with a toy, they also behave in the same way when the need arises for a transition. They become hyperfocused on what they are playing or doing, so changing to a new activity becomes difficult territory for them as well as their parents. These children are often simply in their own world. During the research for my dissertation, I found that some of the parents felt that their children were in their own world, as well.

Many times, Alex Stoller was "in his own world," and did not even respond to people speaking to him. This unresponsive behavior was not unique to Alex, however. Some of the other children in my sample behaved in this way also, specifically, Alex Saber, Larry Speer and Renee Vernon (Rapoport, 2007, p. 229).

In one way, these children have difficulty focusing and maintaining focus, while on the contrary, they hyperfocus and become stuck in a place from which they cannot go. So along that line of thinking, therefore, preschool children with ADHD, or those who exhibit the symptoms of ADHD, become fixated ironically on whatever they are doing at the moment. Because they are so focused on what they are doing, they do not pay attention to the instructions that their parent is giving them. What a conundrum!

How frustrating is it for a parent to try to transition a preschool child with symptoms of ADHD from activity to activity or from place to place? Very frustrating, indeed. Some parents have told me that they have become so infuriated that they have to tell themselves not to scream at their child. What may happen next? Well, here we go . . . all of a sudden, after they simply cannot get their child to move to another activity, the child races to another endeavor that he finds interesting! How maddening!

The symptoms of attention-deficit/hyperactivity disorder make children who have that diagnosis enigmatic. As I have said previously, they behave in ways that are puzzling, such as paying attention in one circumstance and being inattentive in another situation. It can be aggravating! It is so important above all, however, that you remain calm. In fact, those children do not listen to their parent's instructions, so they cannot remember them. Additionally, they do not realize that there may be consequences for their actions.

As is related to the preschool child with ADHD not remembering his parent's directions and/or instructions, Bess told me about Aaron's difficulties with transitions:

For Aaron, there was the emotional part, which manifested itself very early on, and he had great difficulty in transitions. And I didn't realize at first what that meant, what was going on in his head. From the time that he was big enough that I couldn't physically strap him into his car seat, that I needed his cooperation, there was trouble. He was never a child to just "go with the flow." He's not the kind of kid to just do what everybody else is doing just because that's what everybody else is doing.

One thing that you can do to make your life easier is to learn to expect the unexpected. Realize that the more that you organize your house and your schedule, the more positive behavior you can expect your child to exhibit. Try to plan as much as you can ahead of time so he can depend on uniformity more than the transitions and the changes. In that way, when transitions come, most of his life has been predictable, so one change may not disrupt him too much, hopefully.

If there are any changes that you know about, please tell him to expect that schedule modification and when to expect it. One five-year-old child I know, Matthew, was learning how to play the piano. He started his lessons at four years old, so by the time he was five years old, he had a recital. (I know, I felt that it was a bit early, but oh well!) He knew and understood where his recital would be held. It was in the same place where he took piano lessons. A few days before the recital, his teacher sent his mom a notice that said that the location of the recital was going to be changed.

The day of the recital Matthew's mom took him to the recital at the new location. When he saw that it was an unfamiliar place, he had an immediate temper tantrum, which turned into a very long temper tantrum. Matthew never got to play the piano in the recital. I am not blaming his mom! We do not know whether or not the child would have had a temper tantrum even if the recital was held at the previous location. However, the child would have felt better about himself if he had had a successful recital, rather than having had a temper tantrum.

To try to prevent this type of incident, the child should have been taken to the new recital location and permitted to see it as well as to play the piano there, if at all possible. As I have said, the child may have very well had a temper tantrum anyway. However, any insurance is valuable. Perhaps if he had already seen the new location, he might have been able to play the piano and avoid a temper tantrum.

One little bit of advice regarding changes for a preschool child with ADHD: When you know about a change, provide your child with some notice. However, do *not* say, "We will be leaving the house in five minutes," because most preschool children with ADHD do not understand a time frame as of yet. Instead, say "After you finish your puzzle, we will have to leave to pick up daddy at the train." In that way, he has a concrete visualization of exactly when he has to change his activity and get into the car, for example. It still may not be easy to affect that transition. However, at least you have tried your best by incorporating your child's developmental ability within his understanding of the transition.

JUST A FEW MORE SUGGESTIONS

As I have said, and I need to reiterate here, try if at all possible, to tell your child that a change is coming so that he is not surprised when a schedule modification happens. For example, you can tell him, "You may watch one show and then you will go right up to bed." You can also remind him that "In a few minutes, you will take a bath and then go to bed." If you feel that he does not have a real understanding of the meaning of a few minutes, set up a Time Timer. The Time Timer has a flag that disappears when the time passes. Therefore, when the flag disappears, it is time to go to bed.

When he is getting dressed, only give him two choices as to what to wear. You can tell him that today he can wear the blue shirt or the red shirt. In that way, he does not become overwhelmed by so many choices. Instead, he will feel that he is in control of his decision and not you. Predictability at all costs! Aha!

Additionally, repeat your instructions many times. Ask him to tell you the instructions that you have just told him. Do this exercise again until you are satisfied that he knows your instructions. You may observe your child stop talking and seem to nonverbally say, "Wait. I am thinking." Preschool children typically need approximately eight to ten seconds (that time lag is definitely approximate) to gather their thoughts together before they speak about a specific topic. They do not always need that time to think, but if they do, you must give it to them.

You may feel that repeating the instructions multiple times will annoy your child, but since preschool children with ADHD are so distractible, you never know what they are hearing and/or internalizing. Additionally, give reminders both visually and verbally when he least expects it, such as during breakfast and when you are in the car driving him to school.

I am also a big fan of keeping your preschool child with ADHD busy. Following along with your child having lots of activities, however, is getting from one activity to another. Remind him that after the difficult transition, he will get a reward. For example, "After we get dressed for soccer, I will give you two fruit snacks." Finally, and probably most importantly, as I have reiterated before, please try very hard to remain calm. Additionally, remember once again, please, that preschool children with ADHD are complicated. Even though they may not remember the instructions that you gave them about bedtime activities, if you become frustrated when they make that time difficult, they will observe your emotions and may be negatively influenced by them.

Your preschool child with ADHD may internalize your emotions into his own range of reactions. The consequential behavior might be a tantrum or a socially inappropriate behavior because all he is picking up on is your negativity. You also must learn that if you miss an appointment or if he is late for a play date, it is not the end of the world, but rather an "Oh well" sort of situation. You are doing the very best that you can do, I am sure. You have a very difficult task in your life managing the behavior of a preschool child with ADHD, so please give yourself some slack! Also, however, be vigilant in terms of making your life and your child's life easier by controlling as much as you possibly can.

Preschool children with ADHD thrive on consistency and routine, so that is why any change in the schedule may affect them in a negative way. If they are told about the expected change, they will be less anxious and more willing to go along with the transition. One of the preschool boys I know asks his mom each and every day what is going to happen on that day. He seems to need to know exactly what will happen, and if he knows the schedule he seems to feel more at ease and even excited about the upcoming day!

WHAT DOES YOUR PRESCHOOL CHILD WITH ADHD'S
BEHAVIOR LOOK LIKE DURING PLAY?

As you watch your preschool child with ADHD play with other children, you will see that when he plays in an unstructured way, he looks just about the same as other children do. However, you will also see that when he is involved in structured play, he looks very different. How does he look different?

In structured play, for example, a preschool child with ADHD might be less successful at remembering what he should do as he is playing. These children are more distractible in structured play, as well as less cooperative. They tend to resolve disagreements by exhibiting inappropriate, impulsive behavior, such as throwing things and pushing more often than the other typical child. Along with the child's impulsivity might be that the preschool child with ADHD violates the space of his peers.

He might also interrupt his peers while they are playing. Why does he interrupt his peers? Preschool children with ADHD often battle with the processing and organization of verbal and nonverbal information. As I have stated before, because they have difficulty understanding the meaning of what other children are saying, they take longer to process a conversation. At that point, they just start talking about whatever comes into their mind. This is very confusing of course to the typical child because the discussion that he is trying to have with the child with ADHD just does not make sense. How can children successfully play if they are not having the same conversation? Trust me, it is not easy.

The unfortunate outcome of the preschool child's inappropriate behavior during play might, if that behavior does not change, lead to your child's peers not wanting to be friends with him. Since preschool children with ADHD often become frustrated and aggressive during play, their peers may rebuff and reject him. What might be the result of this peer rejection? The preschool child with ADHD's self-esteem might be affected in a negative way.

If the children in your environment did not want to play with you, how would you feel? The answer is that you would most likely not feel very good. Preschool children have feelings in the same way as older children and adolescents have feelings. Younger children may not always be able to express how they feel, but they usually know when other children do not like them. I worked with a cute little boy who was diagnosed with ADHD in his classroom for one year.

> I walked into the school where I would be working for the next year and was stunned to see Timmy, an eight-year-old, curly haired, mop-topped imp sitting right outside of the principal's office. He had his head down and was not talking to anyone. I sat down next to him and after just a few minutes, tears began to flow gently down his cheek. He told me that he was trying to make himself invisible (Rapoport, 2009, p. xiii).

These are my notes:

> As hard as it is for me to admit it, you can see how a child like Timmy could be annoying for other children to have around. It was just about impossible for Timmy to get children to like him, let alone to make friends. Each time I entered the classroom, Timmy appeared to be happy.
>
> However, within a few moments, his face showed more and more sadness and hurt. Whenever he tried to talk to his classmates, they would ignore him or make insulting comments to him. His behavior would then suddenly become inappropriate. This was the cycle of Timmy's behavior: he would talk to his classmates; they would ignore him or make hurtful comments to him; and then he would exhibit socially inappropriate behavior that would irritate them. This cycle was prevalent during all of his classes as well as throughout lunch.
>
> No one wanted to sit next to him at lunch. Let us look at what typically happened. As Timmy ate his lunch, if the other children did not get up from their chairs immediately upon seeing him walking toward them and sit somewhere else, he would speak to them. They would say insulting comments to him, such as, "Oh no, here he is again, the talking monster," or "The jumping jack in a boy's body is sitting here, yuck." He would then exhibit inappropriate behavior, such as purposely chewing his food with his mouth open.
>
> The other children would then say to me, "He grosses us out." Since Timmy clearly did not understand how his behavior was causing his peers to respond to him in a negative way, he did not do anything to change his behavior. He just did not understand why his peers were rejecting him. He would speak to me about feeling rebuffed and un-wanted, but just did not understand the origin of his own socially inappropriate behavior (Rapoport, 2009, pp. xiv–xv).

In addition to the child knowing that his peers do not like him, clearly his parents know immediately that due to their child's inappropriate behavior during play, other children will all too quickly find out that he is abrasive and annoying. My job here is to help you, the parents, to diminish your child's socially inappropriate behavior, so that he is well-liked and develops positive self-esteem. Are you ready? Let's go!

NOTE

1. "Identifying times and activities when a child's goals and the instructional procedures for those goals can be inserted into children's ongoing activities, routines, and transitions in a way that relates to context. It involves distributing opportunities to learn goals and apply instructional procedures for those goals across different activities, routines, and transitions of the day" (Sandall et al., 2005, p. 300).

5

TREATMENT

As we have discussed in chapter 1, the American Academy of Pediatrics has recommended that behavioral interventions should be the first line of treatment for preschool children with ADHD.

> For preschool-aged children (4–5 years of age), the primary care physician should prescribe evidence-based parent and/or teacher-administered behavior therapy as the first line of treatment . . . and may prescribe methylphenidate if the behavioral interventions do not provide significant improvement and there is moderate-to-severe continuing disturbance in the child's function (American Academy of Pediatrics, 2011, 128, 1007–22).

Behavior therapy clearly has fewer side effects if any as compared to medication, so therefore it is much safer for your preschool children with ADHD. In fact, there have been several studies that have found that behavioral therapy yields more successful results than medication for children with ADHD who are five years old and younger.

CONTROLLING OUR OWN BEHAVIOR

Before we discuss behavior therapy, however, let us talk about the first step, which is trying to teach the child to model his parent's behavior. Many children observe their parent's behavior and imitate it. However, children with ADHD are distractible, which makes paying attention to their parent's behavior and modeling it difficult at best. So, what can parents do?

As I have stated before, it is a very difficult task to manage the behavior of a preschool child with ADHD, from many standpoints. They often do not pay attention to what their parents are telling them to do. Additionally, if they do listen and understand what their parents want them to do, they still do not exhibit the required behavior. Does your behavior affect your child's behavior?

Your negative behavior and demeanor absolutely affects your child's behavior, often exacerbating the more abrasive aspects of his behavior. Therefore, the best thing that you can do is to remain acutely aware of your own behavior, which is not so easy to do. Why not? The reason is that much of your conduct is reactive to your child's socially inappropriate behavior. Preschool children with ADHD do get a sense of their parent's behavior, however, even though they are distractible. They may not be able to model their parent's behavior. However, they nonetheless may internalize their parent's emotional state.

Therefore, learning to control your own negative behavior is imperative when you are interacting with your preschool child with ADHD. I have seen a preschool child with ADHD become angry at his mother when she became irate. Additionally, I have also seen a preschool child yelling at his sibling immediately after he experienced one of his parents screaming at him. What can you do to control your own negative behavior?

SOME SUGGESTIONS...

Try to become intuitive about the time of the day when you become anxious and stressed. Perhaps that time is getting your child ready for school. Perhaps that time is taking your child for a haircut or going to a birthday party. Undoubtedly, you are worried as to how your preschool child will behave, so your own anxious thoughts frequently prevent you from having control over your own behavior. Quite honestly, if you cannot control your own behavior, then how would you expect your child to control his behavior? In fact, how would you try to diminish your child's socially inappropriate behavior if you cannot control your own behavior?

Okay, so first, try to think of and write down the times recently when you have felt anxious as related to your own behavior as it related to your child's behavior. Second, write down what you could do if these feelings of anxiety occur again. If you intentionally think about how you will behave if your child acts in a certain way, chances are that you will be successful at modulating your own behavior. If your child does not see you exhibiting this negative behavior, chances are that he will exhibit fewer inappropriate behaviors. What can you do to try to regulate your behavior?

When you begin to become frustrated or outwardly angry or upset, if there is another adult in your house who can watch your child, walk out of the room and, perhaps, walk out of your house for a few minutes. If you are with your child alone, find some music that you like on your phone and play it until you calm down. Try to take a few deep breaths.

If there is another adult in your house from time to time, have them video you in a situation when you behave in a way that shows your child that you are angry. Then view the video and see exactly what triggered your negative behavior. If you can locate the spark that set your behavior off, the chances are that you will be able to learn to better control your behavior.

Lastly, make a list of what you decide will be the consequences of each of your child's socially inappropriate behaviors. If you have an intentional plan in terms of how to manage your child's behavior, there is a lower probability that you will feel out of control yourself.

IMPORTANT POINTS FOR EVERY PARENT TO REMEMBER

- Listen to your child.
- Tell him that you are proud of what he is doing right *before* you explain to him that what he did was wrong. In other words, find some positive behavior that he has exhibited. Even if what he has done that is affirmative is very small, the positive should always come before the negative.
- Teach him about the importance of other people's feelings so that he will feel a sense of accountability for his behavior when he is interacting with others.

- Through conversations with your preschool child with ADHD, teach him in a non-abrasive way about the frustrations that he may encounter. Additionally, tell him in a kind way about the behaviors that he exhibits that irritates and frustrates you. In that way, he will learn how to deal with his frustrations, because he will see that you did so as well.
- Try not to just say "No" after you observe that your child is not following your instructions. Once again, emphasize the positive. When you see that your child is drawing on his sister's paper, say, "Let us use the paper that I gave you. Your sister has her own paper." Preschool children with ADHD hear way too many "nos," so instead, try to encourage him. If he then exhibits positive behavior, then you can reward his behavior, which hopefully will build up his positive self-esteem.

What else do you think might affect your preschool child with ADHD's behavior? Do you think that your home routine affects your child's behavior as well?

YOUR HOME ROUTINE

Each and every person runs their home in a different way according to their own personality. Some people are very laid back and relaxed, so therefore, their child's behavior has to be very obstructive to bother them. Other people are much more affected by even a small evidence of their child exhibiting socially inappropriate behavior and feel compelled to act upon it immediately. However you respond, your house should run based upon a specific routine that will hopefully result in more agreeable and appropriate behavior on the part of your child.

Preschool children with ADHD crave order and a reliable routine so that they will know what is expected of them at all times. After an organized plan is executed, they will need some time to adjust to it, but in the long run, they will behave more appropriately in response to that predictable structure. This is true especially in consideration of the fact that the most typical characteristic of preschool children with ADHD is hyperactivity, which is anything but predictable.

Preschool children with ADHD who are hyperactive need some stimulation to lock them into behaving in an appropriate way or to hyperfocus. Perhaps, depending on the child, receiving rewards or praise may stimulate a child so that he will behave in a more socially appropriate manner. That stimulation may come in many forms, as you will see later. I know that you may not think that my paradoxical logic makes sense. However, children who are hyperactive need stimulation to become calmer.

I would, however, use selective praise so that the effect of the reward or praise does not lose its effect too quickly. Be careful about exactly which behavior you praise. Do not praise every behavior that your child exhibits that is positive. Try to praise effort as well. Preschool children with ADHD exhibit many annoying behaviors (as many parents have told me). What should you do when it comes to managing all of your preschool child with ADHD's aggravating behaviors?

DO I MANAGE ALL OF THE SOCIALLY INAPPROPRIATE BEHAVIORS THAT MY PRESCHOOL CHILD WITH ADHD EXHIBITS?

There are some behaviors that you will find more success at diminishing if you selectively ignore them instead of managing them. The main idea here is that children will often continue behaving in a certain way if they receive any attention of any kind, positive or negative. Therefore, if parents want to diminish certain specific behaviors, they should purposely and selectively ignore these behaviors.

An important concern here is your own stress. If you can successfully ignore your preschool child with ADHD's socially inappropriate behaviors, your own stress levels will decrease. If you are able to do so, you will have successfully eliminated some of the behaviors that your child exhibits that annoy you, as well the ones that give you the most stress.

There are two caveats here, however. The first caveat is that the use of selective ignoring must be consistent and correct. What does this mean? It is imperative that any adult who is observing her child's socially inappropriate behavior must not comment on that behavior. This means that neither parent should engage the child in discussing the socially inappropriate behavior that he is exhibiting. In fact, if either parent talks to the child about the socially inappropriate behavior that he has just exhibited, that behavior will most likely increase once again.

However, if the selective ignoring of socially inappropriate behavior is to work most effectively, it is vital that positive behaviors are recognized and praised. For example, if the child is continuously getting out of his chair at a meal, when he does sit as is required, the parents need to immediately say, "I love the way you are sitting and staying in your seat." The previous phrase or similar comments may not seem natural for you to say, but they will really work to diminish your child's socially inappropriate behavior.

The second caveat is that, in order for selective ignoring to be effective, there is some likelihood that the child's negative behavior will increase to a larger degree before it ceases immediately. Therefore, if you pay attention to the child's socially inappropriate behavior as it increases temporarily, your reaction will cause the child's behavior to remain and possibly even grow in intensity.

I cannot say that the child knows or even understands that when his parent attends to his socially inappropriate behavior that his behavior will escalate. However, it just happens that when parents reinforce a negative behavior, there will be an increase in the number of times that the child exhibits that behavior, as well as an increase in the intensity of that behavior.

Ignoring socially inappropriate behavior is challenging for parents, however. Parents must learn to respond instead of to react. The reactive response would be to say to the child who is bouncing up and down in his chair at a meal, "Stop that now. Do not do that or you will have to go to time out." Instead, responding is a much more effective tool than reacting, because it is behavior on the parent's part that is intentional instead of unpredictable. The responsive behavior would be to say, "I really like the way you are using your napkin to wipe your face when it gets dirty" while ignoring the inappropriate behavior of bouncing up and down in his chair.

What are some examples of behaviors that are not very serious (yet parents may find extremely annoying!) but nevertheless need to diminish, so that the preschool child with ADHD can interact successfully?

- bouncing up and down in his chair at a meal
- continuously using repetitive language
- banging his silverware on the table at meals (unless the table is glass and may break or become damaged)
- whining
- interrupting

- name calling
- making strange noises
- getting in and out of his chair
- screaming
- excessive talking
- running continuously in the house and sliding on the floor
- throwing his toys on the floor and laughing
- whining in the grocery store
- pushing his sibling (unless there is a wall or a hard surface into which he can push his sibling's head)

I observed one preschool child kicking the dinner table underneath him. His mother absolutely could not stand his behavior. She yelled at him several times to stop and he just kept on doing it and doing it. Finally, she screamed at him to stop at the top of her voice and he stopped . . . for just a few moments, and then he began to kick the table again! You should have an intentional and prescribed set of responses that you are ready to access at all times. It is vital for you to behave in a predictable and a responsive way, rather than behaving in a reactive way. If you react to your child's behavior, then you will be as out of control as your child!

Since we know that your home routine affects your child's socially inappropriate behavior, let us return to how to begin the process of redesigning your child's environment.

HOW DO I BEGIN REDESIGNING MY PRESCHOOL CHILD WITH ADHD'S ENVIRONMENT?

The very first thing that you should do is make an inventory of the environment in which your child lives and plays to determine if this setting will allow your child to function to the best of his ability in these areas according to his interests and needs.

Here are some questions to ask yourself:

- Is his space easy to clean up?

It is imperative that you have boxes or crates available and labeled in some way so that your child will know exactly where to put his toys away. If he does not read as of yet, use simple pictures pasted or glued to each bin so that he knows which toys go into which bin. He will be happy to know where to put his balls or his Legos, as well as the rest of his toys.

- Is his space comfortable so that he is able to play easily?

It does not matter if you have a spacious house or a two-bedroom apartment. What matters is if you have a comfortable environment so that your preschool child with ADHD can play easily. Make sure that you have a cushioned child-size chair or a bean bag chair for your child to sit on to do something quiet, such as reading or looking at books. At the same time, clear away one small area for him to spread out to build or to play with some trains or blocks, etc. You will soon find out what are your child's interests and be able to find some space for him to play with his favorite toys. If you have a small apartment, you may want to have his toy area be an integral part of your living room so that you can interact with him while you are doing something else.

- Are his toys and books located in a place where he can reach them or does he have to get up on a chair to do so?

As is dependent upon the area where his books and toys are located, make sure that when he tries to get to his belongings that he does not fall or lose his balance. Always have a safe stool or a learning tower on hand, but make sure that all of his belongings are of easy access. You certainly want to encourage independence, so make sure that he can always get to his playthings by himself instead of calling you several times an hour to get down his books and toys.

- Are his books and toys age-appropriate? Are his books and toys too juvenile for his interests or too much of a challenge?

One of the causes of frustration for preschool children with ADHD is that despite their high level of intelligence, they become frustrated very easily. If their toys and books are too easy for them, they become bored and behave inappropriately. If their toys and books are too challenging for them, they become frustrated and begin to behave in a socially inappropriate manner. Always provide books, puzzles, and toys that are not too easy for your child, yet not too challenging to frustrate him either. It is not an easy task to figure out sometimes, but if you watch your child play, you will soon see exactly where his strengths and weaknesses lie.

- Are his toys and books reflective of his interests or just random toys and books?

When you receive toys and books from other parents, grandparents, and friends it is particularly important that the books and toys that you actually give to your child to use are reflective of his interests. Clearly, each child is characterized by his own curiosities and interests. One preschool boy with ADHD I know loves trains, while another preschool boy with ADHD loves Legos. One preschool girl with ADHD loves dolls, while another one just wants to build. If you give each child toys in which they have no interest, they will not be very happy. Therefore, if you have been given books and toys that are not applicable to your child's interests, give them to someone else. Preschool children with ADHD, specifically, like to play with toys and read books that reflect their interests. You are more likely to observe your child behaving appropriately when he is playing with toys within his interest area than when he is not. Additionally, try also to introduce novel toys and books within your child's interest area so that he does not become bored. These new items will undoubtedly increase your child's engagement.

- Is his room compartmentalized into areas that are easy for him to keep in order?

You need to have your child's room organized in a simple way and labeled, (definitely labeled!) so that he can locate his personal items such as his pajamas and other such clothes. You want to begin to teach him to dress himself at this young age so that he learns a sense of independence. However, if he is not aware of exactly where his clothes are located, he will become frustrated easily and not be interested in getting himself dressed. You can label everything in his room in a colorful and bright way. These labels should include each of the categories of his clothes as well as his hamper and his books. Preschool children really respond to bright colors, which stimulates them and helps them to perform an activity. Ironically, as I alluded to previously, children who are characterized by hyperactivity need to be stimulated, so they will respond positively to the given instruction. We will discuss that conundrum on the next page.

Sometimes when I suggest to parents that their environment has to be organized, and their activities planned with ultimate consistency, they tell me that they are not that way themselves. They say that they are very "laid back." My point is always the same. This consistency and organization is not about *your* needs, but instead, it is about your child's requirements, as is consistent with the symptoms of his ADHD. The very first thing that you have to do is to look at how your child's environment is organized. Additionally, is your child's playroom or bedroom decorated with bright colors, so that he is stimulated?

DOES STIMULATION DIMINISH HYPERACTIVITY?

Preschool children who are diagnosed as having ADHD or those who exhibit symptoms that resemble ADHD sometimes feel stimulated by the colors and the design of their play and living areas, which is what they may need as some of the variables that are required to behave in a more appropriate way.

As I was just writing about how preschool children with ADHD need stimulation, I began to look back upon the very first year that I taught (which was in 1972, just so you have some time frame!). I taught thirteen boys with hyperactive ADHD. From the first day of school, my principal required all of the teachers to adhere to certain rules.

First, our principal mandated that the teachers were only permitted to wear neutral colors so that the children would not be distracted unnecessarily by the colors that we wore. Of course, we did not know at the time, however, that children with ADHD look for stimulation. What do I mean by that? One example might be that if the child needed stimulation, he might make a drum out of his desk and bang on it. Or, he might keep kicking his feet under his desk. Now we know that children with ADHD need to be stimulated to help them to diminish their hyperactivity! Therefore, if we do not provide stimulation for these children, they will create their own stimulation anyway!

Second, each and every morning, my principal would give me small cups of lukewarm coffee with sugar and require that I give one cup to each child in the morning and one cup to each child after lunch. I really did not understand why she wanted me to do so, but I certainly had to do as I had been told to do.

I then observed my students' behavior after they drank the coffee and quickly realized that the coffee had had a paradoxical effect! Coffee has caffeine in it, but when given to a child (or an adult) with hyperactive ADHD, their behavior calms down! I was stunned! These children were able to focus and to concentrate so much better than they had before they drank the coffee! The coffee had the opposite effect than I had thought! Wow! Certainly, as educators we would *never* do such a thing today as to give our students coffee, but I was required to do as my superior mandated that I do.

BACK TO REDESIGNING YOUR PRESCHOOL CHILD WITH ADHD'S HOME ENVIRONMENT

Let us return to the reasons that the above organizational and design changes are necessary. Preschool children with ADHD behave in a more acceptable manner if they are in an environment that is very predictable as well as one that makes it easy for them to become and to remain organized.

They also exhibit appropriate behavior more easily if they know that the discipline they receive as being consistent. Since preschool children with ADHD are so distracted and hyperactive, they respond better if they can predict whatever it is that they need to do to fit into their parent's plan of order and consistency.

Is there a safe place for your preschool child with ADHD to play energetically to dispel some of his hyperactivity? It is unlikely that you or anyone will be able to diminish much of the hyperactive behavior that your child exhibits for any prolonged time period. Hyperactivity, as I have stated before, is a paramount feature of preschool ADHD and may extend into the child's adolescent life. However, you can provide opportunities for your child to safely dispel some of his energy so that he can be as calm as possible.

What can you do? Depending on how much room you have in your house, you can create an obstacle course that your preschool child with ADHD can go through multiple times. Most children enjoy these activities so much that they keep doing it many times. There are also polyester tunnels that fold away for use at another time. They are very light so therefore, are easy to manage, especially if you live in an apartment.

Some of the activities that I have tried to implement with preschool children with ADHD to help them to work safely within their level of hyperactivity I found on the website www.handsonaswegrow.com. (This is also a great activity to practice cooperation, which we will visit below!) I subsequently modified these activities as per the child with whom I was working.

One of the activities required that I use some painters tape, so that it did not stick permanently to any surface and did not leave any residue. I then created a road that the child could use for his cars. You can also call them tracks so that if he really loves trains, he could use them as well. This activity worked out effectively.

Depending on the age of the child, he could also lay down the road or track himself or with help from you. This activity takes quite a bit of concentration and time, especially if the child is laying down the track or the road himself. Therefore, it is a very good activity to calm down some of a child's hyperactivity and encourage him to hyperfocus on one activity.

Movement calms preschool children with ADHD down. If you would like to read about the positive impact of exercise on hyperactivity, Ratey (2008) has found that exercise diminishes hyperactivity in children with ADHD.

WHAT DID MY DISSERTATION RESEARCH FIND OUT ABOUT TEACHING SOCIAL SKILLS?

As contrary to a predictable approach, the parents in my doctoral research thought that by modifying the environment they would find it easier to teach social skills to their children with ADHD.

> The parents modified the context: that is, the homeschool. The modified locations, activities, and instruction of the homeschool were all parts of the intervention that the homeschool parents employed to teach their children social skills. They changed the location where the instruction occurred, the time that the instruction occurred, and the people and the pets whom they permitted to remain in the teaching environment. The homeschool parents adjusted the context in order to enable their children to learn more efficiently (Rapoport, 2007, p. 242).

Although some of the parents stated that they taught their children social skills by implementing a plan, they did not consistently employ a plan to teach their children social skills. Instead, they taught social skills when their children's socially inappropriate behavior was intrusive to their teaching (Rapoport, 2007, p. 241).

So, therefore, the parents' social skills training in my doctoral research occurred just in reaction to their child's behavior. If the child with ADHD was with his sibling and he pushed him, the parent would say, "Stop that pushing. Don't do that." The child would stop for a few minutes only to push his sibling again and again. The parents' social skills interventions were designed reactively instead of responsively. These methods were not intentional and were not planned.

Did these parents' strategy work? My dissertation advisor called this strategy the "seat of the pants approach." It only worked for a very short amount of time, after which the child's socially inappropriate behavior would occur again. So, you can see that the only type of social skills interventions—and certainly the best approach to teaching social skills to preschool children with ADHD—that are effective over the long term are the ones that are *intentional* and *planned*, implemented *responsively*, as well as are enabled in *more than one setting*.

Before any infraction occurs, the parent should have a plan in her head as to how she will respond so that when her preschool child with ADHD exhibits socially inappropriate behavior, she will manage the child's behavior in an orchestrated, intentional, and predictable way. In that way, each and every time the child exhibits a similar behavior, the parent will respond in the same way. The child will then predict his parent's response and learn how to behave in a more socially appropriate way. As I have said above, think ahead of time as to how you would teach a specific social skill. Then, when you need to teach that social skill, you are teaching it in an intentional way. Additionally, teach the social skill in at least two settings so that the learning of that social skill will transfer across a couple of settings and endure over time.

Additionally, make sure that your preschool child with ADHD clearly understands precisely the behavior that he is exhibiting. Is his behavior socially appropriate or is his behavior socially inappropriate? As I have expressed here previously, much of the success of teaching social skills to preschool children with ADHD is ensuring that they understand what is being taught to them and why it is being taught.

You may need visuals to get the point of your lesson across. Preschool children with ADHD may therefore require visual cues to stimulate their learning of social skills. Visuals will stimulate these children so that they will be able to remember how to exhibit a specific social skill in an appropriate as well in an inappropriate way. These visuals may be pictures of the required activity, pictures of implementing the activity, stickers or whatever appeals to the children's interests. These visuals must be laminated onto stock cards and placed up at their eye level in their room or in their playroom.

Another advantage that the parent has when she thinks ahead of time about how she will respond when she sees her child exhibit an inappropriate behavior is that she will decide not to yell or speak in a negative, harsh manner. Behaving in that way is absolutely one of the most damaging things that a parent can do to a preschool child with ADHD! As I have stated previously, all that a harsh and negative response does is to increase a child's socially inappropriate behavior. My goodness . . . let us stay away from doing so!

Besides using visuals, how can you encourage your preschool child with ADHD to focus better so that he can learn a skill more easily? Can a preschool child with ADHD learn while being actively involved in another activity such as manipulating an object? One of the parents in my research explained the way that her son manipulated an object as well as how he learned through his own activity level:

Bess: He's just really bright and has difficulty shifting his focus from one thing that is interesting to anything else. He always has something in his hand, always plays with something in his mouth too, but yet it's not distracting. It helps him to concentrate.

Investigator: Why do you think that is?

Bess: I don't know, I don't know. It's similar to the chanting during our math workshop. He'll come with some nonsense chant that he'll do, just a couple of seconds, whatever. But he'll do the same, not every time, but if it's a long worksheet that he has to go through and he might have some trouble concentrating. So, you'll hear this chant all the way through. He'll just say whatever, make whatever noises and then give the answer, then repeat that for every one. At first it really bothered me, [laughs] 'cause I just thought, why are you doing this? And it's just slowing you down when you get to something really easy. But I finally realized that it's adaptive. It's helping him and he came up with this all by himself [laughs] and I shouldn't mess with it.

"Misinterpreting social cues in a school setting may be among many reasons that children with ADHD do not pay attention to another child's actions or words" (Rapoport, 2009, p. 65).

So therefore, feel free to let your preschool child with ADHD manipulate a stress ball or my favorite, Wikki Stix (www.wikkistix.com), as an adaptive way of learning a skill.

Let us continue on as to how you can teach social skills to your preschool child with ADHD. . . .

WHAT SOCIAL SKILLS DO PRESCHOOL CHILDREN WITH ADHD NEED TO LEARN? (WHAT DO YOU NEED TO DO BEFORE YOU TEACH SOCIAL SKILLS?)

Social Skill 1: Teach Your Preschool Child with ADHD How to Maintain Eye Contact

The first thing that you need to ensure is that your preschool child with ADHD is maintaining eye contact. If his eyes are wandering up and down and across the room, it will be much more difficult if not impossible to teach him positive social skills, as well as appropriate behavior. Because preschool children with ADHD are predominantly hyperactive, it seems to be a daunting proposition to teach them eye contact, but it can be done.

Many children with ADHD have difficulty maintaining eye contact, which is essential in terms of listening to another individual and responding to him. Remember that a child does not have to stare at another individual 100% of the time. He can look at the person and then look away. The key here is whether or not the child is paying attention to what the other person is saying in addition to whether or not he responds to that person (www.adhdanswers.blogspot.com).

The first thing to remember if you are concerned that your child does not maintain eye contact when you are with him, or when he is with other adults, is whether or not he maintains eye contact with his peers. I actually had an interesting conversation with a child to whom I teach social skills the other day. I asked him if he realized that he does not look at an adult when that adult speaks to him. He surprisingly told me that he does not know that he is not looking at that adult!

Then, I asked him whether or not he looked at his peers when they spoke to him. Surprisingly, he said that he *did* know that he looked at his peers when he interacted with them. I then asked why he thought that he looked at his peers but did not look at adults, such as his parents. He said, "Well, when other children talk to me, I know that everything that they say is important, so I always look at them." I was stunned, never having heard that logic from a preschool child with ADHD before or from any other child for that matter!

One vital reminder that I can offer you is that teaching eye contact is not a one-time exercise with these children. It is a continuous process to which you will have to keep returning to reinforce. Be careful, however, when you reward your child's effort in maintaining eye contact. Do not reward your child in an excessive way because if you do so the rewards will decrease in meaning as well as will work less effectively down the line.

As you speak to your child who does not make eye contact, make sure to look right into his eyes. Touch or hold his chin lightly in your hand and instruct him to look at you. You will undoubtedly have to repeat this command many, many times before you see your child comply with this task. Offer praise when your child looks into your eyes when you speak to him. You can say, "Good looking at me," or "I like the way you are looking at me when I speak to you." It is also a good idea to praise another child in the family who is maintaining eye contact as a model for the child with ADHD to follow. Be creative with the rewards you choose. Always remember to fade these rewards out after a certain period of time. In that way, your preschool child with ADHD child will have an opportunity to continue that behavior on his own with no reward following the required behavior, which in this case is maintaining eye contact.

How should you reward your child? It actually really depends on your child's temperament and his needs. Does he respond well to a high five or does he respond better to a sticker? Does he respond well to your verbal praise or the promise of a treat at the end of your session with him? As I have said before, the yield is most certainly based upon your child's interests. You will know better than anyone else as to your child's interests as well as to his personality and needs. Therefore, base your reinforcements on the above categories of interests, personality and/or needs.

Social Skill 2: Teaching Social Skills through Conversations with Your Child

Teaching social skills through conversations with your preschool child with ADHD may not be so easy due to the symptoms that your child exhibits. Let us return for a moment to the criteria in the *Diagnostic and Statistical Manual of Mental Disorders (DSM-5)* for diagnosing children with ADHD. Just to remind us, here are a few:

- is often easily distracted by extraneous stimuli
- often does not seem to listen when spoken to directly
- often fidgets with or taps hands or feet or squirms in seat
- often runs about or climbs in situations where it is inappropriate
- is often "on the go," as if "driven by a motor"
- often talks excessively
- often blurts out an answer before a question has been completed
- often interrupts or intrudes on others (American Psychiatric Association, 2013, pp. 59–61)

Conversations between you and your preschool child with ADHD occur throughout each and every day. I am not talking here about just speaking to another person. I am discussing using words to communicate ideas from one person to another. If listening acutely is an issue for your preschool child with ADHD, then it will be very difficult for him to converse with another person in a reciprocal way. Preschool children with ADHD are not typically adept at listening acutely, which is essential in any conversation between two people.

In addition to listening well to another person, what other social skill would be optimal for a preschool child with ADHD to learn through conversations? Children have to learn to attend to what other people are saying if they are going to be able to listen to them, in addition to being able to talk to them in a prolonged conversation. What method can parents use to ensure that preschool children with ADHD are attending and listening?

It is vital, as I said earlier, to make sure that the child with ADHD knows how to maintain eye contact. Just because a child is looking at someone does not mean that he is attending to or listening to that person, however. After the child maintains eye contact, he must pay attention to every word that another person is saying, as well as listen to every word.

How can parents help children with ADHD to attend and to listen better? A good method to try is to play a memory game. The efficacy of this game will depend on the particular child's developmental level, of course.

- Say a sentence to the child; for example, "Tigers have stripes on their bodies." Have him repeat the sentence back to you.
- Now, take some words out of the sentence (verbally). Say aloud, for example, "Tigers have on bodies." Ask the child to tell you what words are missing. In this example, the words that are missing in that sentence are "stripes" and "their."

Here are some other sentences from which you can verbally remove words:

- Firemen put out fires with big hoses of water.
- Polar bears live in the Arctic.
- I live in a brick house.
- Apples come in different colors. Some are red, some are green, and some are yellow.
- Trains run on tracks.
- Lollipops are sweet and sticky.
- Airplanes fly in the sky.

Have the child repeat a sentence. Then, remove some of the words verbally. Ask the child which words are missing in each sentence. If the child is able to write out the answers, have him do so. Otherwise, just have him tell you the answer. By achieving closure in terms of the sentences, children may be more likely to remember them. Hopefully, this technique will help your child to attend and to listen better. Feel free to revise my sentences to those that include topics that interest your child.

Now, let us use the visual modality to try to improve the auditory modality, which affects attending and listening. For younger children or for those who do not know their letters as of yet, you can draw pictures that represent the sentences above (or find pictures on the Internet, but check the legality of doing so please), on pieces of paper and paste them onto small pieces of cardboard.

Place the pictures in an incorrect order. Then, tell your preschool child with ADHD to move the pictures around until they are in the correct order to represent a meaningful sentence, excluding the missing words. Then ask the child which words are missing in the sentence.

For example, say the sentence to your child "Firemen put out fires with big hoses of water." Now say the sentence again but with words missing: "put out fires with big." Give your child pictures of firemen and hoses. Now have your child arrange the sentence with the pictures of the words firemen and hoses. Repeat the sentence to your child. Then ask your child what words are missing from the sentence. The words that are missing here are firemen and hoses of water.

This exercise is somewhat like a puzzle in terms of finding the relevant pieces to complete it. If the preschool child with ADHD likes to work with spatial objects (even though this is an auditory exercise), he may enjoy this particular exercise. Children with ADHD are often better listeners when they pay attention to visual cues.

When a preschool child with ADHD watches a television show or a movie that he likes, he can tell you what has happened, as well as the names of the characters. It is possible, therefore, that children with ADHD exhibit selective attention and selective listening. They may pay attention just to topics that interest them. Subsequently, they may only listen to conversations that they think may interest them or in fact, really do interest them.

Parents must work with preschool children with ADHD to attend to and to listen to topics in which the children are not interested as well as in topics in which they are interested. A negotiation or two may have to be made to incentivize these children to listen to something with which they are not interested in, such as a certain book. This lesson may serve as practice for them listening to an actual conversation about a topic in which they are not interested. Sometimes these children may be so distractible that they may not realize that most conversations may be interesting.

Here is an example of a conversation that a parent can coach so as to facilitate.

Five-year-old Charlie is interested in baseball, so he listens intently to any conversation about baseball. However, his friends are discussing topics not related to baseball.

Charlie's friend says, "I really like fast cars."

Charlie says, "How do you know? Have you ever ridden in a fast car?"

Charlie's friend says, "No, but I watch a television show about fast cars. Sometimes, I close my eyes and pretend that I am driving a fast car, like a race car."

Charlie says, "Then, you must really feel like you know what it is like!"

His friend says, "I do!"

The parent can explain to the child that talking about fast cars may be similar to talking about baseball players who are very fast at running the bases, such as those players who steal many bases. Hopefully, the next time someone has a conversation about a topic with which he is not interested, he may more readily remain in the conversation.

Conversations between you and your preschool child with ADHD about what are positive social skills are important so that he can learn to attend, and therefore, learn to listen better. Let us assume that the parent has taught her preschool child with ADHD to attend to and to listen more effectively. After the parent feels that the child has learned to do so, she can then begin to teach social skills with intent to him. She can teach these social skills intentionally by embedding the social skills training into everyday circumstances. If these children attend and listen better, they can be taught other social skills intentionally through conversations. Perhaps it is possible that if we help these children to listen more effectively, their interactions can hopefully be used to learn social skills.

Before we continue on to discussing how to behave in a polite manner, I want to tell you about a book that I came across that teaches that very lesson. It is titled *Modeling Social Skills with Max* by Amanda Riccetti. The premise of the book is a good one. A three-year-old boy whose name is Max is rejected by a friend when he asks to play with him. He then befriends a younger child and helps him to learn about manners and social skills. So, the message is an important one to help others, to be polite, and to be kind and helpful. The only negative about the book is that Max speaks and thinks in words and sentences that do not reflect a three-year-old child's thinking. Instead, these sentences represent those that an older child might say.

Teaching social skills through literature is an efficacious way to teach your preschool child with ADHD how to better listen and to pay attention. You can read the story above to your preschool child with ADHD, and/or read it into a voice recorder on your phone. Then, listen to the story with the child. Ask the child questions such as

- Which character do you like the most?
- Why do you like that character the most?
- What is the first thing that happened to that character in the story?
- What is the next thing that happened to that character?

The answers to the above questions will reflect whether or not the child listened. What should you do next? If he could not answer the questions, listen to the story again with your child. Now stop the voice recorder the first time something happens to that character and ask your child, "What just happened to that character?"

However you read the previous book to your preschool child with ADHD, these social skills lessons are important ones to learn. In fact, the social skill of being polite that is discussed in the book is a good segue to Social Skill 3: Behaving in a Polite Manner!

Social Skill 3: Behaving in a Polite Manner

One of the first social skills that a preschool child with ADHD needs to learn is reflective of a caring and warm child. These social skills are related to behaving in a polite manner. Some examples of these social skills are saying hello, saying good-bye, saying thank you, and saying please to people who enter into the child's environment. These individuals may include parents, grandparents, siblings, and friends. Even though a preschool child with ADHD may be inattentive at times, his parents must still teach him how to be polite, thereby teaching him to adhere to simple rules of etiquette. If they do not do so, impolite behavior may extend into his school life as well.

I know that preschool children with ADHD have difficulty imitating their parent's behavior because they simply do not pay attention to it for more than an instant. That being said, parents must still model appropriate behavior for their children. I was working with a child once when his dad came home from a week-long work trip. Not only did the child not say hello to his dad, but additionally, his mom did not say hello to her husband either! How in the world can we expect our children to behave in a polite way if we do not behave in that way ourselves? I was simply stunned.

Being polite is one social skill that needs to be talked about in a conversation. You may not realize it, but preschool children with ADHD *need to hear reasons* why they should behave in a specific way. It is not enough to just tell them that they have to be polite. They need to hear a reason why they must be polite. It may seem obvious to you, but it is clearly not apparent to these children.

You can explain the following to your preschool child with ADHD: "We are polite to people in our lives because we are kind and caring people. We want to be nice to people and like it when they are agreeable to us as well." For example, it seems natural for most of us to say good-bye to people who have visited us. For preschool children with ADHD, saying good-bye is not an automatic response, however. Their behavior is enigmatic. The preschool child with ADHD may want other people to say good-bye to him, yet he does not want to say good-bye to other individuals. I am still trying to figure that one out!

What you do not want to do is to argue about whether or not your preschool child with ADHD said good-bye to people whom he knows. That social skill should be required and automatic, in my opinion. There should be no room for discussion about doing so. For some children, however, every action that happens requires a negotiation from them.

Social Skill 4: Arguing with Disciplinary Decisions, the Negotiator

Do you have a negotiator? Here is an example: You say to your preschool child with ADHD, "Johnny, come out of the pool now. We have to eat dinner." He says, "No. I'm just going to swim to the steps and then get out of the pool." There is only one problem with this behavior. It is a ploy because he does not want to get out of the pool! How do you manage this behavior?

First of all, the intonation of your voice makes a big difference. Whatever you do, do not express any anger or negativity. Do not get me wrong, I *know* how exasperating this oppositional behavior can be because it is incredibly frustrating for your child to disagree with you. As I have said before, anger and negativity on the parent's part only breeds anger and negativity on the child's part. This type of behavior has a boomerang effect: everything comes back to you.

Take a deep breath and try as hard as you can to retain a sense of humor (I know that it is incredibly hard to do so!) Go into the water instead of becoming angry and say, "I will race you to the steps and then race you into the house for dinner." If necessary (and I know that some of you will dislike this suggestion!), you could try a bribe. You could alternatively say, "If we go inside the house for dinner now, we will have time to put our stickers in our new sticker book." You could try to suggest anything within your child's interest areas, of course.

The one thing that I need to stress again is do not argue and do not battle under any circumstances! Remember that negative attention encourages inappropriate behavior. Your preschool child with ADHD needs to interact appropriately when he is joining ongoing activities and play.

Social Skill 5: Joining Ongoing Activities and Play

It is sometimes difficult for typical children to join in when others are playing. However, preschool children with ADHD experience a more difficult time trying to join in play when it has been ongoing. Preschool children with ADHD typically do not know how to behave or what to do when they want to join in with children who are already playing.

How daunting might it be when a child sees several children with whom he wants to play and who are engaged in an intricate play, such as block building or playing with dolls in the setting of a doll house? The answer is that it can be very intimidating!

A typical preschool child may be quick to observe that these children are involved in an orchestrated and complex play. A preschool child with ADHD . . . not so much. However, if he does realize that the other children are involved in planned play, what can he do? If a preschool child with ADHD asks if he can play and is refused, he will feel bad. If he asks and is included, he might wonder, "Why did these children not ask me to play when they first began to play?" Additionally, many parts of the play session have already been set up. Will he interfere in a way that will be annoying to the others if he suggests a certain way to play? You certainly do not want your child to try join in with other children's play if he is going to be slighted and ignored. What type of behavior might a preschool child with ADHD exhibit that might annoy the other children?

I am sure that if you have a preschool child with ADHD, you have witnessed him running head-on into other children playing. Why does this happen? These children have great difficulty reading and interpreting other children's social cues such as body language and facial expressions, among others. ("Social cues are the signals people send through body language and expressions" [https://www.understood.org/en/friends-feelings/common-challenges/picking-up-on-social-cues/4-types-of-social-cues]; take a look at chapter 4.) Preschool children in general may become very annoyed all too quickly when they are interrupted in their play, which may lead to your child feeling spurned and excluded. My concern, of course, is your child's self-esteem, especially at such a young age. If you have more than one child, you might want to videotape them playing and more importantly observe how your preschool child with ADHD enters the play situation. If he barges into their playtime or stands over them as they play, viewing the videotape will serve as a good tool to teach your child how to enter the play situation next time. Another tool to help children with ADHD enter into a play situation appropriately is to recognize body language.

Body language is nonverbal behavior or a social cue that a person exhibits, such as the way people walk, the way they carry themselves (lean closely over to others, stay back from others, etc.); the gestures they make (pointing, putting their hand on someone's knee or shoulder, etc.); their facial expressions (frowning, shaking their head in frustration, holding their head down, looking away during the conversation, etc.),; or their eye contact; among others. Preschool children with ADHD must be accountable for their body language as well as their verbiage. We will go over the intricacies of recognizing another person's body language and what it means in the upcoming paragraphs. Therefore, it is imperative to teach preschool children with ADHD to observe other children's body language as a way of determining if it is an acceptable time for them to join in with other children's activities.

Being aware of social cues is an important tool to help preschool children with ADHD enter a play situation appropriately. In terms of social cues, these preschool children with ADHD do not have an understanding that when they want to play may not be the best time for them to play with other children. These children do not know that they should wait for an opportunity to play. You will see the discussion of social cues in the upcoming paragraphs. Specifically, concentrate on showing your child the facial expressions and the body language of the other children, so that next time he is more aware of these responses, which might prevent your child from being rejected. If you are unsure as to whether or not your child understands and recognizes facial expressions, please continue on to the information below to learn how to assess facial expressions.

Assessment of Facial Expressions

The first thing you have to do is find out if your child can recognize different facial expressions. How can you do that sort of assessment? Find or make some sort of wheel that your child can spin, either small or large, somewhat like a wheel at a carnival. Your child spins the wheel and when it stops, there are pictures of facial expressions on each part of the wheel that your child can recognize. You could probably buy such a wheel in a small size at a store like Staples. In fact, Amazon has this wheel that is a table top model. The WinSpin 24" Tabletop Spinning Prize Wheel 14 Slots with Color Dry Erase Trade Show Fortune Spin Game. The good thing about this model is that you can draw pictures of facial expressions with a dry erase marker on each and every part of the wheel.

Alternately, if you do not feel that you are such a great artist and/or you do not want to draw pictures of facial expressions, you can cut out pictures of the various facial expressions from magazines. Glue or paste or better still, Velcro the various facial expressions to each color or on the wheel or each part of the wheel. You will want to have the following facial expressions represented: happy, excited, sad, frightened, angry, surprised, etc., perhaps even an expression of someone who is busy. Since these children often enter into social situations with other children and immediately start talking, it is vital for them to learn when someone looks too busy to talk. This situation will also pertain to teachers. Additionally, these children will learn that when you are busy that they also have to wait.

Have the child spin the wheel. When it stops on a certain facial expression, have them identify the facial expression. You may want to repeat various facial expressions in two different places on the wheel, just as confirmation and validity that the child recognizes a particular facial expression. Another way of assessing as to whether or not your child recognizes facial expressions is to have him look at your face and/or his own face in the mirror making a certain facial expression. Then, ask him what is each facial expression that each of you are making.

Intervention: Mirror, Mirror on the Wall

> Mirrors are great tools for showing children who might not realize what a certain facial expression means to learn to understand their meaning. Either a teacher or another child can make a facial expression in the mirror. Ask the child with ADHD to name the facial expression (i.e., happy, nervous, afraid, etc.). Then, ask the child with ADHD to make the same expression in the mirror that the other child did. If the child with ADHD did not pay attention to the other child's facial expression, have the child make the facial expression again (Rapoport, 2009, p. 82–83).

Intervention: Candid Camera

It may be easier to teach facial expressions to preschool children with ADHD if they see pictures of themselves making the various expressions. They typically laugh and seem to remember these facial expressions because they view them as being personally relevant. Children with ADHD learn and remember when they are engaged in the learning process. When parents make learning experiences meaningful and relevant to children, they are more likely to remember what they have learned.

Digital photography offers another option to help you to teach facial expressions as well. After you take pictures, look at them with the child with ADHD and agree as to whether or not he has made a particular expression. If not, you can delete it until the child makes the facial expression that was discussed.

After you are sure that your preschool child with ADHD knows each and every facial expression, take pictures of him making each facial expression. Buy an index card book that is held together by a spiral margin and paste the pictures of one facial expression on each page. Sit with him and once again ask him to identify each and every facial expression that he made. If he knows each facial expression, then this particular lesson is finished. If he does not identify any of the facial expressions, teach him the facial expressions again using his own pictures. Voila! (Rapoport, 2009, p. 83).

If this technique does not work or if it does not fit within your child's interests, you can then teach facial expressions to your preschool child with ADHD through reading books to him that show facial expressions.

Learning Facial Expressions the Old-Fashioned Way

If your child does not fully comprehend what a specific facial expression means, read him *Today I Feel Silly & Other Moods That Make My Day* by Jamie Lee Curtis (1998). He can manipulate the facial expressions on the circular cardboard face at the end of the book himself. This is a great book that draws the child into it by the colorful illustrations as well as the dialogue. What comes next? So now that we assume that the child can recognize another child's facial expressions, he should therefore be better at judging as to whether or not the children with whom he wants to play are amenable to permitting him to join them in play.

Once again via the old-fashioned way of learning, read *Join In and Play* by Cheri J. Meiners (2004) to your preschool child with ADHD. If he has siblings, you can take advantage of that situation to teach him to join others when they are already playing. One of the parents with whom I was embedded during my dissertation research said the following about the learning of social skills through the conflict that a child may have with his siblings:

> I don't feel that I have to specifically teach them from books about social skills because they spend so much time together and I think that if you can learn to live peacefully with your brother or sister when you're not able to spend a whole day away from your siblings that's pretty good. And so, we work on social skills as conflict arises between the two of them.

You may have experienced a situation yourself where you enter a social situation by yourself, such as a party. As you look around, you notice that everyone is talking to someone and you are just standing there wondering to whom you should talk or what group you should enter so that you can be part of the conversation. The difference here is that most likely, you will weigh and measure what to do and then quietly join in with other people. What does your preschool child with ADHD need to learn to do?

Your child has to learn to look at the other child's facial expression to determine as to whether or not his peer is open to playing with him. You should teach your child social cues to look for when he wants to join in with other children who are already playing. A good thing to do is to wait until your child's sibling has a friend over (provided it is okay with your other son and the ages mesh) and then teach your preschool child with ADHD how and if he should join in with their play as a lesson.

What should you do next? Explain what body language means. If your preschool child with ADHD does not understand what you specifically mean by body language, show him some pictures of children's bodies facing the same and different directions. Ask him to choose which picture shows the children's bodies that are facing the same direction. Explain to him that if the children's bodies are facing the same direction, that is an indication that most likely these children are involved in an intricate way and they do not want to be interrupted in their play.

When his sibling has friends over to his house for a play date, as these children are playing, ask your preschool child with ADHD the following questions so that he will learn when and when not to try to join other children who are playing.

- Are the children's bodies facing in the same direction?
- Are the children's heads and faces close together?
- Are the children talking to each other?
- Are the children playing in a corner of the room away from others?
- Do the children look at your child when he moves toward them?

Go through each and every question with your child to see if he has an understanding of whether or not other children who are playing would be open to having him play with them. For example, if he observes that the children's bodies are not facing in the same direction, discuss what that social cue means to him. Does it mean that they are each playing by themselves and that he can approach them? Does it mean that each of the other children is choosing to play alone, so therefore, it is not a good time to intervene?

If the other children's heads are close together, is that a signal that they just want to play together without any interruptions? If the children are having a conversation with each other, is that a definite sign that they absolutely do not want another child to talk to them?

If the children are playing in a corner of the room with their bodies facing the same direction, as mentioned previously, it is a good indication that they just want to play by themselves. Does your child understand and accept that notion? If the other children look at your child as he moves toward them, is that a signal that they do not want to play with him or could it just mean that they are merely looking at him?

These are very important questions to discuss with your preschool child with ADHD who has to learn when and when not to try to join in with other children when they are playing. At some point, your child may just have to accept that the other children may want to play by themselves. It may or may not have anything to do with him. It may merely be that they are friends and they just want to play with each other.

Intervention: Some Steps for Your Preschool Child with ADHD to Follow

This is what your child who is trying to join the group who are playing might do:

- Look at the other children's body language.
- Determine if one of the other children says hi to your child.
- Determine if your child is being ignored.
- Does your child feel that he was ignored?
- If one of the children says hi to him, he can still ask if he can play.
- Even though none of the children say anything to him, he can still ask if he can play.
- He can find a toy or an accessory that might add an interesting change or a modification to the play situation, and may encourage the other children to permit your child to play with them.
- For example, if the children are building, your child can find a bridge and a sign and ask the other children if they would like to use the bridge and the sign as part of their construction project.
- If the other children begin to reject your child, he should just walk away and try to join in with other children's play.
- You could tell your preschool child with ADHD that the fact that these children only want to play with each other has nothing to do

with him. Instead, you can easily explain that they had already started to play with each other before he asked to join in their play and, additionally, that they had had a plan already organized.

Another strategy that you could try is to role play a situation with your child when he is trying to join in with children who are already playing. You could ask his siblings to pretend that they are other children with whom your preschool child with ADHD wants to play. Here is a typical role play.

His siblings are playing with trains on a track and have set up an entire city with buildings and bridges and train stations. The whole project looks finished. As your preschool child with ADHD approaches the situation, ask his siblings to say hello as he enters the play area. Then tell your preschool child with ADHD that this behavior on the part of his siblings is welcoming. Instead of asking if he may play, which may engender a yes or no response from his siblings, he can say, "I have a McDonald's building and a Burger King building. How can we add them to your city?" Then, if they answer his question, he can sit down and assume that they are open to playing with him.

It is always a mistake for a child to ask a question that yields a yes or no answer because after he receives an answer, no discussion will follow. If your child offers to add a building, and then asks how they can add it, hopefully, the other children will incorporate him into their play.

What do you do if that does not happen? Well, unfortunately, the reality of life is that sometimes we get snubbed or disregarded. Therefore, suggest to your child that he find other children with whom to play.

You should also try to teach your preschool child with ADHD how to judge as to whether or not another child needs help in any way.

Social Skill 6: Volunteering to Help Other Children

Why is volunteering to help other children important? Everyone needs help from time to time. I believe that young children inherently like to help one another. As a parent, I would not think that your child does not want to help another child. However, preschool children with ADHD may not naturally do so because they are so hyperfocused on their own play. What should you do first?

Make absolutely certain that your child understands what it means to help others. Ask him if he has ever needed help. Trying to get him to think about and remember circumstances when he needed help is not easy, give him specific examples such as

- putting his blocks away
- putting his toys away
- finding something that he has lost
- putting his socks and shoes on
- opening up the top of a water bottle

To further ensure that your preschool child with ADHD really comprehends what helping another child means, buy copies of both *The Berenstain Bears Lend a Helping Hand* by Stan and Jan Berenstain (1998) and *Helping Mom* by Mercer Mayer (2002) and read both books to your child.

Another option for you, the parent, is to write a social story using words and pictures as well that you can then read to your child. In that way, he will learn that it is important to help another child. The pictures are critical, however, because they will stimulate your child's mind so that he will remember this lesson. If you think that your child is at a developmental level where he can either give you ideas or help you to write, then please go ahead and follow that path. The social story should include an instance when one child asks for help from another child. How might helping another child impact your preschool child with ADHD's self-esteem?

Your child's self-esteem may improve when he realizes that he actually helped another child. Additionally, that lesson might generalize to your child being more successful in terms of making friends. The following are a few simple steps to which you can adapt and match pictures, so that you have a guide to teaching your child to help another child.

- Maintain eye contact with the child.
- Smile and use a kind voice.
- Say, "It looks like you might need some help putting away the blocks."
- Ask, "Would you like me to help you?"
- Help the child (adapted from Hensley et al., 2005, p. 162).

Social Skill 7: Inviting Others to Join Activities

In all of my years of experience in field research and treating children with ADHD, the sad but true wish that most of these children have expressed to me is that all they want is to have a friend. One vehicle toward making friends is for your child to ask another child if he would like to play with him. This request could occur in school, at a playground, or at your home with the child's siblings. Asking another child to join and play with him is risky for a preschool child with ADHD because it could lead to your child being rebuffed or rejected.

Depending on the age of your child and his level of awareness of another child's facial expressions and body language, this task could be fraught with either frustration or simply not comprehending what to do. Still, it is imperative to try to teach him these skills because over time he will pick up on the various social cues and body language, although that it may take some time.

Preschool children vary in their ability to pick up on social cues, so please be patient. Some of this lesson might be repetitive from the previous lesson. However, learning how to pick up on social cues is so important that if I repeat myself, you will hopefully understand my reason for doing so.

In order to learn how to invite another child to join him in an activity, first, the child with ADHD has to know how to read the social cues that the other child gives him that may be interpreted in a positive or a negative way. Second, the child with ADHD has to learn how to understand another child's body language, as we first discussed on the previous pages.

Body language frequently will give a child an idea as to whether or not the other child might be interested in playing with him. Many times, body language and facial expressions are the only hints that individuals express. Preschool children with ADHD need to see and to understand the relationship between body language, facial expressions, and behavior. Until they do, they cannot begin to interact in a more positive way.

When you are teaching your child how to exhibit any social skill, especially this one, it is vital that you break up the instructions into simple steps. What happens if you do not? Your child will get lost in the words and instructions, so in a very short time he will become unfocused, and not hear much of what you have told him. It will quickly become frustrating for you when he does not know and/or cannot repeat what you have told him, but quite honestly, you are not the most important person here!

Intervention: Recognizing Facial Expressions

Before you begin this intervention, once again revisit the topic of recognizing people's facial expressions with your child. Why? They are young, so it is imperative that they learn to identify facial expressions and understand that these expressions are social cues that they must recognize before they interact with children.

Find or design large pictures of facial expressions that represent many people's feelings. In fact, it often helps preschool children with ADHD to learn about and to recognize facial expressions if they make and/or draw these pictures themselves. Use brightly colored paper and/or vibrantly colored markers or paints to make the various facial expressions stand out. Additionally, you could have your child design the happy facial expressions in red and the sad or unhappy facial expressions in a dark color.

In fact, you can draw or paint one facial expression and your child can draw or paint the same facial expression. You will then have two sets of the same facial expression so that you and your child will be able to play a matching game. Being able to match the expressions with others of the same type is a good assessment tool. It is easy to draw the blank faces and print them out as many times as you like, so that you can use them again and again.

Here is an even yummier idea! Bake cookies together using refrigerated cookie dough, for ease and expediency. Then take some different colored icing for each facial expression and draw the various facial expressions. Make the cookies small, so that when your child recognizes the specific facial expression, you can both eat them as a reward!

Now, you certainly know and understand the more difficult issue of your child asking other children to play. If you have an older child, you can tell him to play the part of the child who is expressing each of the various facial expressions. This is a good lesson in cooperation for your preschool child with ADHD and his siblings as well.

Social Skill 8: Cooperation

As early as 1932, Parten explained cooperative play as:

> Cooperative or organized supplementary play—The child plays in a
> group that is organized for the purpose of making some material prod-
> uct, or of striving to attain some competitive goal, or of dramatizing
> situations of adult and group life, or of playing formal games. There is
> a marked sense of belonging or of not belonging to the group. The
> control of the group situation is in the hands of one or two of the
> members who direct the activity of the others. The goal as well as the
> method of attaining it necessitates a division of labor, taking of differ-
> ent roles by the various group members and the organization of activ-
> ity so that the efforts of one child are supplemented by those of another
> (p. 251).

Knowing how to cooperate sounds easy, right? No! Teaching preschool
children with ADHD to cooperate with other children is a challenge,
because they may not understand why they have to cooperate. Frequently,
these children are very self-absorbed so they primarily think about their
play as it pertains to them. However, learning to cooperate is a sine qua
non to interacting successfully. Therefore, as parents, you must teach
your preschool child with ADHD to cooperate. You must always look
toward the end goal, which is for him to become a social being and to be
able to make friends.

I want to repeat for emphasis that the one thread that ran true throughout every element of my doctoral dissertation field research was that
every single child said that he just wanted to have one friend, because he
typically did not. The problem was that these children's behavior was
generally obstructive, so other children did not want to be friends with
them.

As one mother told me about her son during my field research:

> Okay, so friends have been difficult, because he does have that impul-
> sivity, eventually, the hyperactivity. Kids can go with the flow with the
> hyperactivity. The distractibility, they're distractible too. Impulsivity
> is tough. People, kids get scared of him, because he'll do; he'll beat,
> he'll hit them, he'll poke them. He'll quickly become upset, and run
> away, and so he's very unpredictable in other kids' eyes, and they
> don't like that. So, friends are hard.

If your child learns to be cooperative, most of his energy will be generated toward that end, so perhaps some of his more obstructive behavior will drop out. How will you convince your child that cooperation is a valuable skill to learn? This is where conversation is essential. Even if your child does not want to cooperate with other children, he will definitely be more amenable to that task if you explain to him the value of cooperating with other children. Give him several examples, but be sure to permit him to express his opinion as well. It is not assumed that preschool children with ADHD will see beyond their own needs, as I have said before. Therefore, it is up to you, as a parent, to explain why learning to cooperate is so imperative to him making friends, as well as enjoying playing with other children to an optimal level. In fact, any lesson in which you teach your child to cooperate with you will in all likelihood transfer over to your child cooperating with another child.

An Additional Point!

Please remember that cooperation is important when your preschool child with ADHD is interacting with you as well. It is imperative that your preschool child with ADHD is cooperative as he interacts with you in various situations throughout the day. The following are examples of instances in which your child needs to learn to cooperate with you.

- getting dressed in the morning
- getting into his car seat when it is time to go to school
- sitting in his chair at dinner instead of walking around
- not jumping on your furniture
- being quiet when you are on the phone or talking to someone in person

These instances of cooperating are not only related to listening to you, but also to accommodating your requests as well. Let us look at some possible ways to encourage cooperation with you by your preschool child with ADHD, as well as when he interacts with other children. But before we do so, you need to design standards of behavior. Please read on . . .

Intervention: Designing Rules

The first thing that you need to do is to create a list of rules and post it at the child's eye level, so that every child in your house will abide by the rules for consistency. Even though in most cases your preschool child with ADHD is not able to read as of yet, he will still be able to understand the rules of your house *if you explain them to him.*

Make the list of rules readily available to your child and accompany each rule with a *clear picture* of a child abiding by that rule. You can draw a picture, find one in a magazine, or find one online. If you teach and explain the rules of your house through a picture, enforcing these rules will be easier. Make sure that your child understands each and every rule. Go through each rule and then explain each one to him. Then, tell him to describe what he should do. Your list of rules should only include three to five rules. Write down what you want your preschool child with ADHD to do, instead of what you do not want him to do.

Some of the rules may be as follows:

- Greet people in a welcoming, nice, and polite way.
- Take turns talking.
- Think about others before you act.
- Be kind to others.
- Respect other's belongings.

Back to cooperating. . . . Remember that when you are trying to teach preschool children to cooperate that they are still rather concentrated around themselves and their own needs. I am repeating this fact so that you will recognize that learning to cooperate is a difficult task for preschool children with ADHD. However you teach your child to cooperate, please be aware that your input into his playing with other children is imperative to him learning that skill. You are an invaluable asset when he is playing with other children because you can tweak his social interactions as he is playing.

Young boys are typically very often interested in cars and trucks. (These interests somehow have not changed!) I know that I mentioned this activity above, but it is just such a perfect way to teach cooperation. Take some painters tape, (which does not stick to any surface permanently), and make a road for the cars on a floor of your house with the child working with his sibling, another child, or you.

This intervention is a perfect example of each child having his own ideas and being rigid about translating these ideas into the completion of a project. Observe these children and tweak each moment of rigidity to see if you can convince your child to accept the other child's ideas. Once again, you will need to explain to your child that each person's ideas are valuable and that these ideas will add to the most creative and broadest completion of their project.

If you have a girl, you probably have a doll house. (Certainly, boys play with dolls as well, however!) I used to love dolls as a child. Learning to cooperate while playing with dolls is very important here as well. I certainly cooperated with my cousin as a child until she systematically cut off all of my dolls' hair! I am still asking myself, "Why?" In fact, I have never actually asked her that question!

At any rate, if you do have a doll house, there are separate floors. See if the children choose different floors in which to have their doll play. If they do, then monitor their play. If they both want to have their doll play on the same floor and if an argument ensues, explain to the girls the benefits of having both dolls playing together on the same floor.

The benefit of doing so is clearly that when both girls play with their dolls at the same time on the same floor, they can play together. Additionally, when two people are playing together it is twice the fun. Furthermore, if you explain to your preschool child with ADHD about the advantages of cooperative play, your child will really understand what you are saying and therefore learn to cooperate when he otherwise might not have done so.

The most successful interventions in terms of teaching cooperation to your preschool child with ADHD are the ones with shared goals. Puzzles; building sets like Duplo Legos with a specific, predetermined setup; and the Tall-Stacker Mighty Monkey Playset by Lauri are all toys that have shared goals. In other words, these toys are conducive to more than one person playing with them as well as requiring cooperation to complete the setup.

In terms of learning to cooperate, is every child's level of maturity the same? Please remember that children with ADHD are not typically as mature as other children of their same age. In a study funded by the NIH, Shaw et al. (2007) found in groundbreaking research, "that in youth with attention-deficit/hyperactivity disorder brain (ADHD), the brain matures in a normal pattern but is delayed three years in some regions, on average, compared to youths without the disorder" (p. 19649).

Therefore, even though some preschool children with ADHD will see and comprehend the importance of working together, other preschool children with ADHD may be far less mature and most likely will not have that same understanding of the importance and the value of cooperating with another child or a sibling. Therefore, they need to be taught the importance of cooperation as well as how to cooperate.

How else could you teach cooperation to preschool children with ADHD? The absolute best way to teach your child to cooperate is to begin an actual project together that will yield real results. In that way, he will see the benefit of cooperation in real time.

Intervention: A Cooperative Project

For example, if you live in an area where you have space, you can start a garden of any kind, either vegetable or flowers. I would actually recommend planting a flower garden, because vegetables may take up to 80 or 85 days before your plants will yield those vegetables. Remember, however, that you should break the work involved in your garden into many simple steps.

You certainly do not want your preschool child with ADHD to become overwhelmed and lose interest. Very importantly, do not use yourself as a barometer as to when you feel that you have done enough work in the garden. Take a look at your child and see if he gives out clues that he has done enough for one day. Does he look tired? Is he walking around and not focusing?

I would also not recommend growing seeds with preschool children with ADHD because they really need more instant gratification than planting seeds will yield. You can break the planting of the garden into several components so that your child will see the benefits of planting it together. I would like to give you a little bit of advice here: Buy a few extra plants so that if your child does not take the plants out of their containers correctly and they are ruined, you have extra ones to plant.

Here are some steps to planting a garden cooperatively.

- Decide on a color scheme.
- Choose carefully and decide as to which plants will grow depending on the number of hours of sun that shines on the garden. Make a trip out to the patch of land several times a day where you are growing your plants. Why should you do so? In that way, both you and your child will learn information about how much sunlight that area of land receives per day as well as how much sun and how

much shade your plant will receive. (Your child will depend on your horticultural expertise here, or you can always Google your question about the number of hours of sunlight that a certain plant requires!)

- Additionally, choose the size of the plot of land where your plant will grow depending on how much space you are allotting for your garden. You certainly do not want to grow sunflowers in a very small area because they need room to spread out vertically and horizontally! For example, New Guinea Impatiens need some sun and some shade, while the old-fashioned regular Impatiens need full shade. Vincas require full sun but can withstand drying out in hot weather.

- Go to the garden center and choose small plants together depending on your color choice and your size requirements. If you draw up a design format on paper (using symbols that your young child can understand), your child will quickly understand your restrictions. Ask the person who works at the garden center as to the type of soil that you will need, as well as any fertilizer and when to apply it. *Here is an important caveat! Buy plain soil with no included fertilizer so that your child will not be working with any soil with fertilizer in it, which could cause your child to experience an allergic reaction. Only buy fish fertilizer and/or fish/seaweed fertilizer for your plants. They are the absolute best fertilizers and are *nontoxic* for your child to use.

- Have your child cooperatively help you every step of the way, especially in terms of taking the plants out of the car and putting them in a safe place until you are ready to plant them.

- When you plant, explain to your child how to release the plants from their temporary pots. Then, show him how to release the plants from each temporary container, and help him to insert the plant into the ground. Tell him how far apart the pots will be planted. Show him how to put extra soil around each plant.

- Tell your child how to water, meaning to water until he sees the water drip down out of the bottom of the plants. If it is possible, avoid getting water on the flowers. (When water gets on the flowers, they will be stained a bit.)

- Finally, give your child praise as to how well he cooperated with you to plant the flowers.

- Each day, take your child to view the plants and talk about the changes that you both see. In fact, you might even want to graph the changes in a picture format so that your preschool child with ADHD can see the changes over time.

If you live in the city and do not have room for so many plants, you can still execute this intervention. If you have room for a medium size to a large pot, go through the same steps as above, except for designing the garden, of course.

Social Skill 9: Compromise

Cooperating and compromising share similarities yet are very different. What does it mean to compromise? It typically means that each person is willing to give up something in an effort to settle their differences. Additionally, each child must feel as if he has gotten an advantage or has won. When a child sees that another child compromises with him, he is more likely to play with him and even to become friends. The goal of compromising, therefore, as it relates to preschool children with ADHD, is to make and to keep friends. The reason why learning to compromise is so vital for preschool children with ADHD is that often they find it very difficult to even make one friend. Children with ADHD are frequently unwilling to compromise with other children, however. They are very egocentric and typically want things to go their way.

Preschool children with ADHD may seem to interact in more situations that require compromising than typical children. This may not always be true. However, I am making that inference after many years of helping children with ADHD to interact more positively with their peers. Perhaps they become involved in the same number of acrimonious interactions as typical children. However, they seemingly have a more difficult time compromising. We often see preschool children with ADHD being asked to compromise with their siblings at home. The home can serve as a safe, natural practice ground for these children.

During my field research, I met Ellen who talked to me about how her child was stubborn at times and did not want to compromise.

> It's very difficult to figure out how to put it in words. You can teach, but teaching doesn't make a person learn. He can only learn what he

chooses to learn from what is being taught. He has to have the teachable spirit. He has to be receptive. I can teach, teach, and teach, and if he doesn't want to learn it, he's not going to learn it. So it doesn't mean I'm a bad teacher. It just means he's choosing not to learn because of a stubborn rule system, so it's trying to get through that stubborn willfulness without breaking his spirit of learning.

When two children successfully compromise, they have to agree to give in to the other's actions or intent. However, it is problematic at times to convince the young child with ADHD to do this. Many children with ADHD want to maintain control and are not interested in complying with any agreement. How can you convince your preschool child with ADHD to try to compromise when the situation arises?

First, you have to make sure that your preschool child with ADHD understands what the word "compromise" means and how positive a tool it can be when dealing with other children. Second, you have to make sure that your preschool child with ADHD is willing to learn how to compromise. Getting your child onboard is half the battle.

Cooper (2005) talks about four steps to coming up with a solution that involves compromising.

- Choose to resolve the conflict.
- Define the problem. What exactly is the conflict and what do you want to happen? What does the other person want?
- Think of some win-win solutions and suggest them to the other person. Ask for the other person's ideas, too.
- Choose a win-win solution with the other person, and act on it (p. 47).

Even though it may sometimes be a challenge to convince the preschool child with ADHD to compromise, this does not mean that the preschool child with ADHD cannot be taught to compromise. However, to compromise or not to compromise is a choice. Offer your preschool child with ADHD an option as to whether or not he will compromise with other children. It is up to him whether he decides to do so. If your child thinks that another child is behaving in an unreasonable manner, explain to him that by compromising, a good solution to the problem may be found.

*Intervention: Effecting a Compromise Between Two Preschool Children
(One with ADHD)*

Here is an example of effecting a compromise between two children. The parent of two preschool boys (one with ADHD), takes their children to a monster truck show where they buy one flag for the family. When the children arrive home, they begin to argue over who can hold the flag. One of the boys runs around with it and says, "You can't have it." The other boy says, "But I want it!" They run around in circles chasing one another until the preschool child with ADHD is crying.

That argument might have been solved in this way: The parent tells her children that first, the older boy will hold the flag for the time it takes the Time Timer flag to wind down. Then, the preschool child with ADHD will hold the flag for the time it takes the Time Timer flag to wind down a second time. If either child will not agree to compromise, then you can tell them that for *now*, neither of them will get to hold the flag. You can then tell both children that when and if they decide to compromise, each of them may have a turn holding the flag again.

This intervention might fit into the category of taking turns as well as compromising. However, both children are making a choice as to whether to give his brother a turn, which is a compromise. Do you remember that I said that in a compromise that one person has to give something up? Well in this case, both brothers have to give up the right to hold the flag for the entire time. The only way that either of them can hold the flag is to compromise.

Intervention: Building Together

Here is another example of compromising: One child wants to play with the large, wooden blocks and build a construction site in the only place in your house that is large enough to allow him to do so. The other child wants to build tracks and play with trains in the exact same area. What should you do to help them to compromise? You could suggest that preschool children with ADHD could use the large building blocks to design a town and include the trains as part of the town. Easy? Absolutely!

However, preschool children with ADHD need to be coached along to develop and to include that kind of compromising solution. If they do not want to agree to compromise, then you can tell them that they both have to choose another toy with which to play. They may be able to choose as to whether or not to compromise, but you are always the person in charge.

Social Skill 10: Asking Permission to Use Other's Property

Preschool children with ADHD often do not follow guidelines when it comes to touching or using another person's property. Most of us would understand and respect the fact that individuals own items and want to be the only ones to look at or touch them. Preschool children with ADHD, however, do not typically internalize the same standards.

What is the main important issue that people have with preschool children with ADHD when they touch other people's possessions without permission? Simply put, no one wants their personal possessions touched and inevitably become very annoyed at these children for doing so.

For example, if you attend a family get together, you typically place your pocketbook down in a specific place along with your cell phone. Let us say, for example that you are eating and when you finish your meal you go over to obtain something from your pocketbook.

As you walk toward the area where you left your handbag, you notice that your comb, your private supplies, and your cell phone are strewn about and are accompanied by a child who is continuing to go through your pocketbook! What is your response?

I would imagine, because I have experienced an identical situation, that you react instead of respond. You undoubtedly wonder who is responsible for this child's actions! There are several reasons why you are annoyed, not the least of which is a concern on your part that some of your things might be lost. Hopefully, however, you do not lash out at this preschool child with ADHD who is the cause of this infraction. This is such a typical example of a preschool child with ADHD touching other people's possessions without permission. As I have said previously, this type of incident has happened to me. I did not reprimand the child. Instead, I just put my possessions back into my pocketbook and held it for the rest of the night.

As a parent, how do you teach your preschool child with ADHD to stop going near and certainly not touching other people's possessions? You may begin by talking about personal privacy. You may use as an example, how attached your preschool child with ADHD is to his own belongings, such as his stuffed animals. You might ask him how he would like it if people merely went into his room and took his stuffed animals out. It is always best to discuss any rules with preschool children based upon what is important to them. Preschool children are typically attached to their stuffed animals, so this would be a good place to start.

As I have said before, preschool children with ADHD need to understand the rules of behavior. They need to comprehend that they simply cannot do whatever they want to do despite an adult's disapproval. There are social mores and rules that most people follow and the sooner that they learn and understand them, the easier and better life will be for them. Why? If they behave according to the standard rules of sociability, fewer people will be annoyed with them (although they certainly may not realize this fact as of yet!).

Intervention: Role Play

A good thing to try to teach preschool children with ADHD is to not touch other people's possessions. You may facilitate a role play situation where one person takes away or touches another person's possessions without their permission. Due to the fact that preschool children with ADHD are inattentive, you could videotape the role play. These children love to watch themselves on video. Then, talk to your child about what happened in the role play and see if you can encourage him to express his feelings. Ask him open-ended questions only. For example, "When you saw Sam go into your room and take your stuffed animals, what were you thinking? How did it make you feel?"

Encouraging your preschool child with ADHD to be aware of his feelings and to express them to you may be an arduous task, but one that is well worth it. Here is a role-play idea that you can execute (videotape the role-play so that you can view it along with your child).

Here are the following simple steps to the role-play:

1. Have the first child place his toys down and then walk out of the room.
2. Instruct the preschool child with ADHD to touch or to move the other child's toys.
3. Have the other child come back to see his toys strewn about and moved.
4. Watch the role-play with your child.

If you cannot convince your child to express his feelings, ask him specific, open-ended questions beginning with the child's behavior, such as

- What did the other child's facial expression look like to you? Did the other child appear to be happy after he realized that you touched his toys? Was he smiling?
- What kind of noises or sounds has the other child expressed, such as grunts to show that he is annoyed?
- What else did the other child do to show annoyance, such as rolling his eyes? What does it mean when he does that?

Now, ask him open-ended questions about his own emotions, such as:

- How do you feel about the fact that you touched the other child's toys without asking him?
- What expression was on your face when you touched his toys? Look at the video to remind him of the expression that the other child had on his face when your child took or moved his toys. Show him a mirror so that he can recognize his own facial expression. Alternatively, show him a digital picture that you took of his facial expression when he touched the other child's toys.
- What do you think the other child thought of you touching his toys without him telling you that it was okay?
- If you noticed that the other child had an annoyed face (for instance, he rolled his eyes), what were you thinking? What words did you hear yourself say as you walked away from him?

Social Skill 11: Sharing and Taking Turns

Learning to share is one of the most important skills for a preschool child with ADHD to learn. It is related to taking turns, which I will explain to you later. Sharing may not be an easy skill to hone because as I have stressed before, these children become very involved with their own needs and desires. It is all about *them*—unfortunately for the parents who are trying to teach them new skills! Still, sharing is essential to learn when preschool children are playing and interacting with other children. Imagine a scenario where two children are playing together and one of them holds his toys off to the side and refuses to share. Playing with another child is certainly not the time to play by himself and to be stubborn about sharing!

Just to remind you: the goal of social interaction for preschool children with ADHD is to make friends, since frequently their behavior may be abrasive and annoying to other children.

Intervention: Playing Together Is Much More Fun!

The first thing that I typically do when I work with these preschool children with ADHD is to explain to them (remember that I told you how important it is that they understand every phrase and nuance of what you are trying to teach them?) why sharing is so important in terms of the results that sharing hopefully will yield.

If you can convince your preschool child with ADHD to share one time, the response of the other child should be positively reinforcing to him. Your child should be very happy to enjoy a reciprocal social interaction. Ah, but how do you convince a stubborn (often these children may be stubborn) child to share? First, I point out the benefits of being able to play with other toys in addition to those that belong to him. For example, say that the preschool child with ADHD has some trucks with which he is playing. The other child has wooden blocks and men that will most likely fit into your child's trucks. During a play date, I point out that playing with trucks is enjoyable but it would be much more fun if he could build some bridges over which the trucks could drive.

However, how would he get to build these bridges? Well, he would have to let the other child play with his trucks while he built a bridge from the other boy's blocks! They could therefore share both the blocks and the trucks. By playing together, your child should quickly see that it would be so much more fun!

I mentioned previously the similarity and/or the relationship of taking turns and sharing. Okay . . . just to clarify . . . sharing implies that your child and another child are playing with something at the same time, whereas taking turns suggests that first one child plays with a toy, for example, and then the other child plays with the same toy.

Convincing a preschool child with ADHD to share, as I have said, is not so easy. On the contrary, if you succeed in getting your preschool child to share, teaching a preschool child to take turns can be easier to accomplish. How? It is *all* about the use of a timer. If you observe a situation when two children want to ride the same car, you can say, "First, you have a turn," and then you would allow the first child to ride the car for several minutes. "Okay," you say to the second child, "it is your turn now." But does this method work for you? Not so much. . . . Why not? It does not work because the decision of who should have a turn next is random. Additionally, preschool children with ADHD need structure. When they do not know when it is their turn, it may become difficult for them to understand how long they have to wait.

What works effortlessly to determine who gets each turn is to set up a Time Timer, which is essentially a timer that has a flag that winds down the time so that the child can clearly see it. This type of device is vital at four and five years old because children cannot tell time as of yet at these ages. Here, however, they clearly observe a demarcation of time that has gone by even though they cannot tell time. The Time Timer works simply and effectively.

The adult pulls the flag over. (To eliminate an argument over who pulls the flag over, I would say to your child that it is a grownup's job to pull the flag over!) When the time expires, the flag is gone. I prefer the Time Timer that is the tabletop version instead of a digital version, because on the tabletop version, the child can clearly see when the time is up for either child's turn.

As I indicated, the Time Timer may also be purchased at the App Store for your phone if you prefer that format. However, I believe that the stand alone one is a better option for preschool children. If you use the tabletop version of the Time Timer, the child clearly understands when his turn is over with hopefully, no arguing and no bickering! No argument can ensue at that point over whose turn is coming up next . . . we hope! But what happens if your preschool child with ADHD has an auditory strength instead of a visual one? Try using audible task cards! Read on!

Intervention: Audible Task Cards

Preschool children with ADHD typically cannot read as of yet. Therefore, task cards with written instructions on them, even if these words are accompanied by pictures, are not always workable for four- and five-year-old children with ADHD. Audible task cards incorporate instructions that are spoken. These "cards" are created by you. They are not cards that you can purchase. You can read the instructions below into your voice recorder on your phone.

Children today, even ones as young as preschool age, are very adept at using cell phones. Therefore, just show your child the location of the voice recorder on your cell phone and explain to him how to start and stop the voice recorder on your phone. Then, he can follow along with your audible instructions as he is playing, which will hopefully encourage sharing. Your child may try out the instructions first with siblings as a role play, of course.

The following are the specific social skills that a parent is trying to teach. Additionally, included are the instructions that the parent should read into the voice recorder *after* she makes sure that her preschool child with ADHD understands each and every word that she has said. Therefore, the child will know exactly what to do.

You or your preschool child with ADHD should start the voice recorder and listen to an instruction. Then, your child should do what the instructions say to do. After he does so, he can then continue onto the next instruction and follow it. He should then continue on from there.

Intervention: Sharing a Toy With Which Another Child Is Playing

Read the following into the voice recorder on your cell phone. After you do, have your child listen to the recording.

- "Look around and see if anyone is near you who might want to share the toy with which you are playing
- Decide on the toy or the material with which you want to play.
- Notice which child has that toy.
- Ask that child if he is finished playing with that toy and whether or not you may have a turn playing with it.
- If that child is not done or will not share the toy with you, choose another toy with which to play" (Rapoport, 2009, p. 115).

Intervention: Sharing a Toy With Which You Are Playing

Read the following into the voice recorder on your cell phone. After you do, have your child listen to the recording.

- "Look around and see if anyone is near you who might want to share the toy with which you are playing.
- Offer to share the toy or wait for them to ask to play with the toy.
- When they ask if they can play with your toy, you can say:

- 'I will share the toy with you when I am finished with it' or 'I will let you play with my toy if I can play with your toy'" (Rapoport, 2009, p. 115).

We will discuss the options for helping your child to wait to share several times in this book. It is difficult, but it *can* be accomplished! Please remember that preschool children with ADHD need to be stimulated so that they will pay attention. By using a voice recorder, the preschool child will be stimulated so that he hopefully will be able to follow your instructions as to how to wait to share a toy.

Intervention: Waiting to Share a Toy

Since preschool children with ADHD may have difficulty remembering, a memory game might help them to recall what to do while they are waiting to share a toy with another child. For example, for the social skill of Sharing a Toy with which Another Child is Playing, which we discussed previously in this chapter, how do you teach your preschool child with ADHD to wait to share a toy?

You can enrich your lesson by drawing your own simple pictures, using digital pictures or finding some images in magazines to stimulate your child so that he attends more effectively. Then, order the pictures of the steps below for waiting to share a toy.

- "A child watching another child playing with a toy that he wants.
- A child deciding with which toy he wants to play.
- A child noticing which child has a toy.
- A child asking if another child is finished with a toy and whether or not he may have a turn playing with it.
- A child who is not done playing with a toy or will not share it so the other child will have to choose another toy.
- A child asking another child if they can play with his toy, and the child with the toy says, 'I will share the toy with you when I am finished with it'" (Rapoport, 2009, p. 115).

Go over the correct order of the pictures as they pertain to the steps above so your preschool child with ADHD will learn how to wait when he wants to share another child's toy. Then, mix up the order of two pictures at a time and see if he can correctly reorganize the pictures for the memory game. Then, mix up the order of two more pictures and see if your preschool child with ADHD can reorganize these pictures correctly again. Finally, mix up all of the pictures and see if he is able to place all of the pictures in the correct order. You can either use actual objects or pictures of objects.

- You can use an actual watch or a picture of a watch to represent waiting to share.
- You can use a picture of a child thinking and trying to decide when he can ask if he can share.
- You can use a stop sign or a picture of a stop sign to represent waiting to actually ask if he can share.
- You can use a cartoon bubble with a question mark inside of it to represent the actual words that he can use when he asks if he can share.

If your child exhibits excessive verbiage, especially during the time that he is waiting to share another child's toy, that is another behavior that you will want to diminish. Keep reading, please. . . .

Social Skill 12: Incessant or Excessive Talking

Frequently, all preschool children with a diagnosis of ADHD, as well as typical preschool children, ask lots and lots of questions. However, preschool children with ADHD ask even more! As you are driving, the following questions, among others, are ones that they might ask one after another.

- "What does it mean to hurry?"
- "Why does the light change colors?"
- "Mommy, what are you talking about with Daddy?"
- "What is that wire up in the sky?"
- "Why does it rain?"
- "What does 'pleasant dreams' mean?"
- "Is it Saturday or is it Sunday? What day is it?"
- "Why don't turtles talk, Mommy?"

It is easy for parents of preschool children with ADHD to become exasperated with their child's constant verbiage. However, should you stifle your child's curiosity? How many questions are too many? There are many layers to these issues that are associated with these questions. One layer is the interrupting that your child exhibits as well as a constant barrage of questions.

First things first . . . preschool children with ADHD typically interrupt constantly and continuously. It is one of the paramount symptoms of ADHD. However, when we are talking to these children and they are trying to produce an answer to our question, we must wait anywhere from eight to ten seconds (approximately) for them to answer. Please be patient as you wait because these children have so many thoughts running around in their head that they need time to form the answer to your question. Try to anticipate your preschool child with ADHD's interruptions so that you can figure out ahead of time how you will handle them. Try to show him in some way, perhaps by a pat on the shoulder or a "thumbs up" response that you *will* listen to him.

That being said, these children must learn to judge whether or not other people are immersed in a conversation. If you are conversing with another person, merely saying, "excuse me" and still interrupting is of no real help. They *must* learn to wait while other people are conversing. However, preschool children with ADHD have a very difficult time waiting! They basically have a fuzzy concept of time because they are so young, so therefore, they would not even know how long to wait! What is the answer?

Intervention: Waiting to Talk

Here once again are the benefits of using a Time Timer. However, when you are conversing with other people, I would suggest using a Time Timer that is an app on your phone so that you or your child can hold the phone. Take a look at your choices at www.timetimer.com in advance of this situation occurring, however, so that you can purchase the specific timer that is best for your child.

You may also need to give your preschool child with ADHD some incentive. It might suffice to give him the type of book that includes pictures with invisible ink. After the ink dries, the original pictures appear again time after time. Go to www.melissanddoug.com and look for Water

Wow books. You can say, "By the time you color two pages, then it will be time to ask your question."

One of the most important issues is that in consideration of the fact that preschool children with ADHD are so distractible, how would they notice if two people were immersed in a conversation? Once again, I would suggest setting up a scenario with family members so that your child can learn when another person's body language indicates that they are talking, and when they have finished talking as well.

Create something of a script with your preschool child with ADHD's older siblings, cousins, and/or his other parent that is accompanied by pictures. In that way, you will be able teach your child, and hopefully he will learn when another person's body language shows that people are engaged in a conversation. Before you will have your child observe the faux conversation, give him a sheet of paper with a checklist on it with pictures of the following to check off during the conversation.

- Two people talking to each other where they are leaning toward each other to converse.
- Two people using hand motions to indicate that they are talking.
- Two people showing happy facial expressions to indicate that they are engaged in conversation.

The above indicators are really all that a preschool child can internalize at one time. Next, give him some brightly colored markers and have him circle the picture in which he sees the people in the faux scenario exhibiting the previous body language or facial expressions. These indicators, as you should explain to him, show that two people are having a conversation so therefore, he must wait to speak.

As I stated before, waiting is very difficult even for typical children. One accessory that will help preschool children with ADHD to wait to speak are Wikki Stix. They are soft, pliable, colored, sticky long strands that can be twisted and manipulated in as many ways as you desire. You can buy them either at www.wikkistix.com or on www.amazon.com. Your child can play with these Wikki Stix while waiting to speak.

The newest trend in terms of manipulative toys are fidget spinners. These are toys that spin easily when they are held between two fingers. Preschool children with ADHD seem to become transfixed by gadgets that spin. They can be purchased at www.fidgetspinstore.com or once again at www.amazon.com. Remember that preschool children with ADHD need to be stimulated to become calmer. Therefore, generally speaking, anything that you can offer them in that direction might be very useful in terms of helping a preschool child with ADHD to wait for just about anything!

You can also take out some Playdoh and a kit that includes molds for these preschool children with ADHD to use while they are waiting. Playdoh is really perfect developmentally for this age group. Preschool children with ADHD ask many questions, therefore, you might want to keep a pad and washable crayons and/or markers readily available so that they can try to draw a picture of what they are asking. They can also use stress balls. Remember that even though your preschool child with ADHD's drawing may be vague and simplistic, the most important issue here is that he knows what he is drawing. This strategy may help him to remember his question as well as to encourage him to wait to ask his question.

In consideration of the fact that many preschool children excessively talk, they also interrupt when parents and teachers give them instructions.

Social Skill 13: Listening to All Instructions Without Interrupting

Does your preschool child with ADHD have difficulty listening without interrupting? One four-year-old typical child said to me, "Do you know what Gramma loves? When people listen!" That principle may not be so present in the social interactions of preschool children with ADHD. Have you noticed that many two-year-old toddlers stammer because they have so many thoughts swimming around in their head at the same time? In a similar way, four-year-old and five-year-old children with ADHD are characterized by having many thoughts that occur in their heads as well. What is the result of these preschool children with ADHD having so many thoughts in their heads at the same time? They just cannot wait to express all of the thoughts and ideas that are spinning around in their head, so they just blurt out words and interrupt others who are speaking.

Just so you know . . . the social skill deficit of verbal impulsivity or excessive verbiage might take a significant amount of time to inhibit and to therefore diminish. Teaching a preschool child with ADHD to listen and not to interrupt is a long process, but I hope that if you follow my interventions, your child's behavior will improve over time. It is imperative that you try to anticipate interruptions and how to handle them *intentionally*. In fact, after you explain to your preschool child with ADHD why it is important not to interrupt, and have also worked on inhibiting his excess verbiage, he will still require a great amount of prompting for him to remember what you have taught him.

One typical four-year-old said to his grandmother, "Gramma, I remember everything that you tell me." Unfortunately, the same is not true for preschool children with ADHD. We *must* help these children to remember as well, in this case, to remember to listen without interrupting. They will only be able to do so, however, if they are encouraged by their parents. Parents should say to their child, "Yes, you can! Yes, you can!" This message is similar to the one expressed in the book *The Little Engine that Could*, written by Piper and Hauman. By reading that book to a preschool child with ADHD, you can show your child how to feel good about his effort to remember to listen without interrupting, if he only tries!

Continue reading to learn about an intervention to diminish your child's interrupting.

A General Intervention: Teaching Your Child Not to Interrupt

The main challenge with getting the preschool child with ADHD not to interrupt is to teach him to wait to say what he is thinking. One simple way is to show him how to take several deep breaths. This method may sound kind of silly, but it works with some children. By taking deep breaths to the count of ten, preschool children with ADHD may be able to wait to speak more patiently. By the time that they are finished taking their deep breaths, the adult has finished speaking and they can take a turn to say what is on their mind.

I often hear preschool children with ADHD negotiating to speak before their parent speaks: "Let me speak first. No, I need to say something. I need to talk." One other idea for the preschool child with ADHD to do when he feels like he just desperately needs to speak is to grab a crayon or a marker (which should always be available), and have him draw a picture of what he wants to say. By the time he has drawn his picture of what he wanted to say, it will be his turn to speak. Parents must cooperate with both of these interventions, however, so that the preschool child with ADHD will get a chance to speak after he has waited.

Please check out a more detailed intervention below.

A Detailed Intervention: Getting Your Child to Listen to Instructions Without Interrupting

After you have repeatedly told your preschool child with ADHD to listen to your instructions and he has not been able to do so, try the following.

- Change the volume of your voice to a very low level, a little above a whisper.
- When your child pays attention to your instructions, then speak to him in a voice with a typical volume.
- Each time the child does not listen or interrupts, change the volume of your voice.
- After the lowering of the volume of your voice no longer affects the child listening to your instructions, change the volume of your voice to a moderate level.
- Repeat the above steps again until the child consistently listens to your instructions correctly and follows through on them.

Hopefully, this vocal intervention will help your child to have an easier time when it comes to him listening to his parents discussing upcoming transitions.

Social Skill 14: Transitions

Transitions are one of the most challenging areas of difficulty for both preschool children with ADHD and their parents. There is a higher likelihood that these children can learn to behave appropriately when they are surrounded by structure and consistency. However, life is characterized by lots of changes. Therefore, due to all of these changes, living a daily existence as a parent of a preschool child with ADHD may be very difficult.

One of the moms from my field research for my dissertation told me about her son Aaron's negative experience with transitions:

> For Aaron, there was the emotional part, which manifested itself very early on, and he had great difficulty in transitions. And I didn't realize at first what that meant, what was going on in his head. From the time that he was big enough that I couldn't physically strap him into his car seat, that I needed his cooperation, there was trouble. He was never a

child to just "go with the flow." He's not the kind of kid to just do what everybody else is doing just because that's what everybody else is doing.

What can you do to ease transitions for your preschool child with ADHD? You can recognize that the more they know, the more they will understand. For example, say that your child has been taking piano lessons and a recital is coming up. (My daughter took violin lessons and had recitals at four years old . . . they went well enough, but I thought that it was too young for a child to perform in public.) Certainly, children who take music lessons, even preschool children, know that recitals are part of the requirement of learning how to play music and typically comply with that requirement.

However, imagine if the location of the recital had been changed and you took your child to the new location when he expected the recital to be at the previous location? I would not be at all surprised if your child was upset, perhaps even refusing to play or, worse than that, had a temper tantrum. What could you have done differently? The answer here was easy: You should have told your child that there had been a change in the location of the recital. In fact, in order to try to make sure that your child would not have an adjustment issue as related to the new location, you should also have brought him to see the new location a few days before the recital.

Preschool children with ADHD expect routine and predictable circumstances. The more that you get your child to successively comply with these requirements, the better he will behave. It is imperative for parents of preschool children with ADHD to be intentional.

Intervention: Be Intentional

Preparation and intentional actions on your part are a key to helping preschool children with ADHD to manage transitions. You may not expect changes in your child's behavior to occur, but if you start to see tantrums or behavior that is atypical for your child, be aware that these behaviors could be related to his response to some change in his life (check out chapter 7 for a discussion of life changes).

You should be intentional in your approach and try to anticipate any changes in your child's behavior. For example, if you are changing preschools, make sure that you bring him to the new preschool several times.

Take him to see each and every room that he will be using, including the bathroom. If you usually have your child's grandparents babysit for your child and you are having someone else babysit for him, make sure that you have that person come over a few times when you are in your house, (even if you have to pay them to come over, it is well worth it).

I would also be honest with your child about any change that will be occurring. You can be positive about the change that will occur, but just make sure that you tell him the truth. These explanations are also critical for new experiences as well. When he goes to the dentist, tell him exactly what the dentist will do, so that there are no surprises in store for him. You want as many of these transitional and/or novel experiences to be successful. It is up to you to make these experiences as positive as possible, as you prepare your child for each change. Sometimes, however, no matter what you do to prepare him, it may not work. However, at least you will know that you have tried.

The old-fashioned method of reading books about changes in your child's life will still be helpful. One inevitable change in your child's life will be potty training. For example, when you are trying to potty train your child, you can read him a book such as *Big Boy Underpants* by Fran Manushkin. If your child likes fire trucks and fire fighters you could read him *Even Firefighters Go to the Potty: A Potty Training Lift-the-Flap Story* by Wendy Wax (this book is hilarious!).

One other idea that you could try in this new incredible world of technology is to use any technology that you can find to familiarize your child with something new. There are YouTube videos on everything! As related to my recital example, you could show him digital pictures of the building online of the recital venue so that he knows precisely what it looks like, both inside and outside.

Social Skill 15: Staying in His Seat for Meals

Save yourself some stress by not expecting your preschool child with ADHD to sit still during a meal. In fact, one of the most aggravating behaviors that occurs with preschool children with ADHD is their reluctance to stay in their seats at meals. Why does this behavior occur? Well, some reasons might be that they are not hungry or that they see something else that interests them. Additionally, they may be copying their sibling.

The reason that they are not staying in their seat at meals does matter, however.

The point is that it is very hard to have an enjoyable family meal with a preschool child with ADHD jumping in and out of his seat. All you find yourself doing is reprimanding your child, which ends up stirring up more negativity between the two of you. Your end goal is for your child to stay in his seat at meals. Before you begin to implement any intervention, design an ABC chart similar to the one that I have included here in appendix B. Your data from the chart will show you what happened before your child behaved in a certain way, what was the behavior that he exhibited, and what happened to maintain the behavior such as a reinforcement, a reprimand, or praise. Also included, is the date that the behavior started and ended. This data is invaluable in trying to get your child to stay in his seat at meals. Hopefully, you will gain an answer as to how to get him to stay in his seat at meals successively and over time.

Additionally, try using a bit of self-talk. Say to yourself, for example, "I am not going to get annoyed. I will not show him that he is driving me crazy! I will remain calm and figure out a way to maintain my composure and keep my sense of humor."

Of course, as I have said before, the real trick to not allowing yourself to become annoyed and aggravated, and showing your child that you are disgusted and upset is to think ahead of time about what you will say. Fewer mistakes are made when you decide ahead of time exactly what to say to your child. Try to turn each and every negative situation into a positive one.

I clearly realize that whether you have been working all day or staying at home with your child, you have a right to sit down to a calm and relaxing dinner. That being said, find something that your child is doing that is positive and praise that behavior. It could even be, "I like the way you are spearing your pasta with your fork. You are being so neat when you handle your pasta in that way." Praise goes a long way when it is used with preschool children with ADHD.

Additionally, try to get your child to move before he sits down for a meal. Put on music, so that he will naturally move and/or dance. The more movement that he does before meals, the longer that he will be able to sit in his seat at meals.

Intervention: Positive Reinforcement

I have found a really great book that is literally titled, *It's Time to Sit Still in your Own Chair* by Lawrence E. Shapiro. The author suggests an intervention that just might work with preschool children with ADHD, so I would suggest that you obtain that book and see what the author suggests to do. In fact, this book along with other similar books written by the same author is available on Amazon.

Okay, so what should you do now to try to help your preschool child with ADHD to sit in his chair for a meal? Instead of looking for a long-term yield of having him stay in his seat for thirty minutes at a time, set up a regimen where the goal of how long he sits at the table is shorter, for example, two minutes. This time, use a kitchen timer instead of the Time Timer. Even though your preschool child with ADHD can undoubtedly not tell time, he will be able to at least see the two-minute mark on the timer.

If you really want to be creative, buy an Amazon Echo and set a timer on it. Your preschool child with ADHD will think it is fun, which will make your entire experience a more positive event. You can set the Amazon Echo's timer for any increment of time. You can set the timer by using your voice. You can also ask how much time is left on the timer and cancel the timer. For example, you can say, "Alexa, set the timer for three minutes." In fact, if you are wondering how much time is left, you can ask Alexa. When the time is up, an alarm will sound.

Some type of reinforcement is in order here, so think of something small that is in your preschool child with ADHD's interest area. If you decide to use stickers, for example, do not just give him a sticker that he puts on his body or on the table. Buy him a blank sticker book so that your preschool child with ADHD can see the stickers accumulate that he received when he behaved in a socially appropriate way. Remember, in addition to these short-term goals, you always want to keep in mind the longest-term goal of all, which is, as I have said previously, positive self-esteem.

What would you do if your preschool child with ADHD does not really care about stickers? Find out what he really cares about, whether it is playing on an iPad for five minutes, watching a few minutes extra of his favorite show, drawing with a new marker, eating a snack after dinner such as fruit snacks, drawing outside with sidewalk chalk, blowing bubbles, or counting all of the change that you have collected in a cup in your room! In fact, you can give him one fruit snack (to be eaten after dinner), for each minute he remains in his seat at a meal! The only thing that matters here in terms of the value of the reinforcement is whether or not he has a real interest in that reinforcer or reward. Oh, and you may have to change the reward frequently so that it does not lose its value.

You may also have to frequently change the schedule of the reinforcement. For example, you may begin this intervention by giving your preschool child with ADHD a sticker each time he stays in his seat for two minutes. Then, you can give him a sticker for every other time he stays in his seat for three minutes. When you switch to four minutes and then five minutes, follow the same plan.

I am repeating this information for emphasis: you may have to change the reward as well as the reinforcement schedule. You will carry out this intervention in an easier way if you design a chart similar to the ABC chart that I have included here in appendix B, that includes the start and the end time of the task; the antecedent, or what happens before the preschool child with ADHD exhibits the behavior; the behavior; and the consequence, or what happens that maintains the behavior. Then you can complete each element of the intervention and see if he is improving in the amount of time that he is sitting in his chair at meals. You can use the chart for two meals per day. In that way, you will be able to look at your data and try to determine if your preschool child with ADHD sits longer at one meal than another. Additionally, you will have data-driven proof, so that you can try to ascertain as to why he sits longer at one meal than another. Also, collect information such as the following: Are his siblings at one meal and not another? Do you and your spouse actually eat at one meal and not another? Does your preschool child with ADHD eat with his siblings? Does your preschool child with ADHD eat by himself? Are you on the phone when he is eating during one meal and not another? Are you rushing out with your preschool child with ADHD in the morning meal to get him to school and are more relaxed at dinner?

If your preschool child with ADHD attends school, ask his teacher if he stays in his seat at the meals that he eats there. How long does he stay in his seat while eating at school? Ask his teacher to write down the length of time that your preschool child with ADHD sits in his seat at school when he eats. In that way, you can compare the time period that he sits at his seat at a meal at school to the time period that he sits in his seat for a meal at home. If you can answer these questions, then you can try to figure out which variables might possibly influence how long your pre-school child with ADHD sits at a table at meals. What other situations that are similar to staying in his seat at meals are challenging for your child in terms of remaining in one place?

Social Skill 16: Staying in One Place

Staying in one place is a similar behavior for your preschool child with ADHD as is staying seated at a meal. Here is one example: Your child is attending a classmate's birthday party and there is a line to enter the bounce house because it is too dangerous to have more than a few pre-school children jumping around at the same time. You can see your preschool child with ADHD waiting in line and beginning to walk and wander around. This is indeed a difficult situation because he is out in public in front of his friends and his friends' parents, so your avenues of whether or not he adheres to your rules may be tenuous.

Intervention: Using a Manipulative

What can you do to ensure that your preschool child with ADHD patient-ly awaits his turn while not touching other children? Remember when I said that it is always a good idea to think of solutions to challenging situations before they occur?

- First, use your judgment as to how much close supervision is simi-lar to the other parent's supervision.
- Second, if your child does need close supervision, your only choice is to do whatever is best for your child. If he requires closer super-vision than you observing him from across the gymnasium in the party to avoid negative interactions with other children, then you have to do what is in the best interests of your child.
- Third, always carry Wikki Stix with you so that as he is waiting for his turn, he can manipulate them in a constructive manner.

Manipulating Wikki Stix is a much better activity than irritating another child. Make sure that you are aware of when your preschool child with ADHD's turn comes up well before he enters the play situation. You certainly want to make sure that you take the Wikki Stix away from him before he enters the play situation to avoid arguments with him over whether or not he can bring the Wikki Stix into the bounce house, which may not be a safe idea, among other reasons. As you give him the Wikki Stix, if he says to you, "I don't know what to make," always offer him creative ideas within your repertoire. Trust me . . . while waiting in line for a bounce house is *not* the moment to wait to hear your preschool child with ADHD's creative ideas! What happens if the other children want to manipulate the Wikki Stix as well? This is a great opportunity to share so make sure that your preschool child with ADHD tries to do so!

ONE CAVEAT! SIBLING INTERACTIONS: HELP!

One of the more challenging situations to manage is the interaction between the preschool child with ADHD and his siblings. At times, it appears as if these children have been brought up in two different households in terms of their ability to listen to instructions and to adhere to them, how to behave toward others, and to use correct social skills in a myriad of other behaviors. Why is there such a difference between these children's behavior? The disparity in their behavior is due to the symptoms of ADHD in one of these children. As I have discussed before, the preschool child with ADHD may not have developed the necessary social skills as has his sibling, which actually has nothing to do with the fact that both children are being brought up in the same household!

Due to the distractibility that characterizes the preschool child with ADHD, he may not pick up on the same social cues as has his sibling. Typical children internalize the behavior that their parents model. Preschool children with ADHD are too inattentive or have too many interfering behaviors to internalize these same social skills.

What happens when these two children with disparate skills interact? *Clash!* The typical child goes his merry way (except for a few exceptions) listening to instructions and adhering to the family rules. The preschool child with ADHD goes his merry way not paying attention to instructions and not adhering to the rules of the household. These siblings are bound to clash. Frequently, there is a communications gap because the typical sibling does not understand why his brother is acting so differently from him. The preschool child with ADHD is often in his own world and does not realize that he is behaving in an annoying way to his sibling. In fact, I would not encourage your preschool child with ADHD to get involved in a competitive game with his sibling. The reason for my statement here is that some preschool children with ADHD are vulnerable, so therefore, if they lose at a game, even if there is a reward for effort, he may feel as if he has failed.

What can you do to achieve some sort of balance between your preschool child with ADHD and his sibling in terms of positive social interaction? (As an aside, I would not encourage your preschool child with ADHD to get involved in a competitive game with his sibling. Many preschool children with ADHD are vulnerable, and if your child loses at the game, even if there is a reward for effort, he may feel that he has failed.)

Intervention: Getting Along With Each Other

- Make sure that you have a set of rules written down that you design collaboratively with all of your children.
- Include visual cues—for example, pictures—so that any of your children who do not read yet will be able to understand the rules.
- Go over the rules many times.
- If at all possible, act out the required behaviors that are included in the rules. For example, have each child ask his sibling if he can play with the toy that his sibling has in his hands. If the sibling refuses to permit the other child to play with that toy, instead of becoming upset, the other child should choose a different toy. You may have to act out this behavior more than a few times.
- Make sure that you have a place for a separate, quiet time for each child. One example might be a tepee where he can listen to music or an audible book. He can even draw in his quiet place.
- Instead of becoming involved in negative comments or yelling at your children when they do not get along, always refer them back to the rules.

Give all of your children some cue words that will encourage them to get along. Have them practice saying them. Here are some phrases, depending on the circumstance.

- Keep the peace!
- Keep going!

- Keep the faith!
- Way to go!
- Good listening!
- I like the way you sat there waiting for your dinner!
- I like the way you shared!
- I like the way you took turns!
- Great helping each other!
- You guys did such a wonderful job cooperating with each other!

DEVICES AND ACCESSORIES TO CALM YOUR PRESCHOOL CHILD WITH ADHD DOWN

Do you need devices to help to calm your child down? If your child is wiggly, you can try a Kore Design Wobble Chair. It is supposed to exercise muscles and relax children so that they are less hyperactive. Here are some more accessories that you can find on https://www.funandfunction.com/ or sometimes on https://www.amazon.com/.

- My Magical Cushion—This is a fidget seat that is supposed to reduce the wiggles.
- Mushy Smushy Beanbag Chair—This chair is marketed to produce calming benefits.
- Fishy Gel Cushion—This chair is supposed to permit the child to wiggle while he is doing something else.
- Mini Mushy Smushy—This chair is supposed to control the wiggles.
- Tactile Sensory Ball—This ball is supposed to make sitting more stimulating.

Some other chairs and cushions that may help soothe your child's energetic nature are the following.

- Hokki Stools—These stools are available on www.amazon.com and are marketed for children who are ages five to eight, so make sure that your child is at least five years old. While sitting still, this stool moves so that your preschool child with ADHD can use his energy as he sits and has a conversation or is involved in a quiet activity, such as coloring or drawing.

- Disc 'O' Sit Jr. Cushions—These cushions are available on www.amazon.com. They help a preschool child with ADHD to achieve a balanced position when he is sitting.
- Howda Chairs—These are also available on www.amazon.com. These chairs are roll up, portable chairs. They can move back and forth and have adjustable straps in case you want your preschool child with ADHD to feel snug or loose.
- The many types of seating for active children found on the website www.moving-minds.com.

ALTERNATIVE TYPES OF TREATMENT

Two alternative types of therapy are worth considering in terms of improving the social skills of preschool children with ADHD. The first treatment is Canine-Assisted Therapy. The research is still limited on Canine-Assisted Therapy for children with ADHD, however. It makes practical sense, though, that animals offer both comfort and unconditional love to young children. If a preschool child with ADHD's dog or cat sleeps next to him in his bed or on the floor, he may feel a new sense of calmness upon going to sleep. Additionally, preschool children with ADHD can be taught to learn to be responsible by being intimately involved with the daily care of their pets.

The second type of treatment is called Equine-Assisted Therapy, which also has had a limited amount of research completed on children with ADHD. However, this type of therapy, in addition to possibly helping strengthen muscle tone, involves riding, feeding, and caring for a horse, which are all good lessons in responsibility. A strong, bonding relationship may build between the young child with ADHD and the horse he is riding, which may engender a calming influence on the child.

Both Canine-Assisted Therapy and Equine-Assisted Therapy may offer stimulation to a preschool child with ADHD, which may affect their focus in a positive way. They may become hyperfocused on their responsibilities and hopefully, will have an easier time attending to other activities as well.

Technology also stimulates preschool children with ADHD, whether we are discussing apps, television shows, video games, or computer games. Move ahead to chapter 6 to learn about apps that your preschool child with ADHD might try if they match up with his interests and strengths. Your challenge as parents is whether or not you feel that permitting your child to experience screen time is a beneficial idea. We will discuss that issue in chapter 6, so read on!

6

TECHNOLOGY FOR PRESCHOOL CHILDREN WITH ADHD

This chapter was edited by Jake Rapoport, MS Education, Education Technology Specialist

SHOULD YOU PERMIT YOUR PRESCHOOL CHILD WITH ADHD TO ENGAGE IN SCREEN TIME?

You have probably observed that your preschool child with ADHD needs stimulation and is always looking for something to do, which in many cases involves a screen. Therefore, it may be your cell phone, an iPad, a tablet, a computer, or a television. Do parents (including me!) employ these screens as a respite from the behavior that our children exhibit that is negative or socially inappropriate? Absolutely! Who could blame you? No one! What is the influence of screens on preschool children with ADHD?

Screens offer preschool children with ADHD the opportunity to hyperfocus, or to lock in with intense concentration. These children need stimulation, and rewards and screens satisfy these needs. Preschool children with ADHD may become what I call "zoned out," whether they are watching a television show or playing a game on an iPad. You may be confused by the term "hyperfocus" and ask yourself, "What is she talking about? My child has difficulty focusing so how can she be talking about an intense focus?"

Hyperfocus is the ability to zero in intensely on an interesting project or activity for hours at a time . . . the tendency for children and adults with attention deficit hyperactivity disorder (ADHD or ADD) to focus very intently on things that interest them. At times, the focus is so strong that they become oblivious to the world around them (Flippin, 2005, np).

Have you called your preschool child with ADHD to a meal, or asked him a question when he just stares ahead and does not answer you? Children and adults with ADHD have difficulty shifting attention from one thing to another. If they're doing something they enjoy or find psychologically rewarding, they'll tend to persist in this behavior after others would normally move on to other things. The brains of people with ADHD are drawn to activities that give instant feedback (Barkley, 2005, np). Preschool children with ADHD appear to exhibit less hyperactivity and/or inattentiveness during a period of hyperfocus, which typically occurs when they watch a television show, play a computer game, or a game on their iPads.

Is hyperfocus a good thing? It is advantageous to intensely focus on completing a puzzle or building an intricate Lego structure. Many young children play iPad games or watch television. However, there may be damaging effects of these screen-involved activities depending on the length of time that they are engaging in them. There is much research that indicates that there may be some negative side effects as related to your children using screen time.

As your child grows, keep in mind that too much screen time or screen time that is of poor quality has been linked to

- obesity
- irregular sleep schedules and shorter duration of sleep
- behavioral problems
- loss of social skills
- violence
- less time for play (www.mayoclinic.org, 2017, np)

A better goal for the parents of preschool children with ADHD for their child is to build their child's creativity and independent play, which they are not going to do while he is concentrated on a screen.

If your child is sitting on the couch staring at the television watching a show, or playing a game on an iPad, is he using his mind for creative play? My opinion is probably not, though there is room for some imagination when a child is accessing apps. I am not advising you to never permit your child to have screen time. Instead, I am saying that it would be smart on your part to limit the time that your child spends on screens, as well as make sure that he independently plays.

Just to explain a bit more about the negative effects of your preschool child with ADHD spending time on screens: When your child is involved with screen time, he is inactive. Radesky and Christakis (2016) found that "heavy media use during the preschool and early school-aged years is associated with increases in body mass index (BMI)" (p. 834). Therefore, if your preschool child with ADHD is involved with screen time, make sure that he gets some regular exercise as well to counterbalance his inactivity.

Should you permit your child to use a screen during a meal? Just to return to your desire to keep your child seated at meals once again, please do *not* permit him to use any device with a screen that might zone him out during meal time. Meals should be a social time of finding out about your child's day and simply conversing about everything. If your child is using an iPad or a mobile device during a meal, he will only be paying attention to exactly what he is doing in a hyperfocused way. In other words, your child may not be accessible to you during these meals if he is viewing anything with a screen.

That being said, why would you introduce your preschool child with ADHD to apps? Why would you not just have your child play with typical toys? As I have said before, preschool children with ADHD, especially those who are hyperactive, need stimulating materials and activities to grab their attention. Therefore, apps for preschool children with ADHD are worth trying if you think that these children will be successful at them. They should be colorful and interesting to your child, however, accompanied by pleasing sounds and positive reinforcement.

There are two caveats, however. The first caveat is to be aware at all times of what app your child is accessing and what activities are included in the app. I know that parents have so much to do each day, especially those who work. However, please supervise your preschool child with ADHD on whichever device you choose for him to use. If you are not available to supervise your child, please have another adult oversee him.

Additionally, you need to make sure that the activities on the app are just challenging enough to be interesting yet not too challenging to be frustrating to your child.

The second caveat is to be aware of advertising that may be embedded in some Android apps.

> One of my big concerns about why apps might not be educational was because of the presence of distracting features such as banner ads that sit along the top of the screen and which contain stimuli that are irrelevant to the learning objective," Dr. Radesky said. "And we were expecting to see those (https://www.nytimes.com/2018/10/30/style/kids-study-apps-advertising.html).

However, Bowles (2018) stated that "Jenny Radesky, a pediatrician who wrote the American Academy of Pediatrics guidelines for children and media . . . reported in a study in the *Journal of Developmental & Behavioral Pediatrics*" (https://www.nytimes.com/2018/10/30/style/kids-study-apps-advertising.html) that 95% of commonly downloaded apps marketed to be played by children ages 5 and under contain at least one type of advertising.

> In apps marketed for children 5 and under in the Google Play store, there were pop-up ads with disturbing imagery. There were ads that no child could reasonably be expected to close out of, and which, when triggered, would send a player into more ads. Dancing treasure chests would give young players points for watching video ads, potentially endlessly. The vast majority of ads were not marked at all. Characters in children's games gently pressured the kids to make purchases, a practice known as host-selling, banned in children's TV programs in 1974 by the Federal Trade Commission. At other times an onscreen character would cry if the child did not buy something (https://www.nytimes.com/2018/10/30/style/kids-study-apps-advertising.html).

Finally, set up some sort of timer and manage the time that your child spends watching television or playing a game on an iPad or a computer. Do not permit your child to watch more than one hour a day or play an app or a game on an iPad more than one hour a day. Interestingly, Steve Jobs, who was the CEO of Apple, apparently restricted his children's access to screen time! This exchange is so interesting between a reporter in 2014 and Steve Jobs, the CEO of Apple regarding his children's use of technology:

> When a reporter asked Steve Jobs about his children's use of iPads, "So, your kids must love the iPad?" I asked Mr. Jobs, trying to change the subject. The company's first tablet was just hitting the shelves. "They haven't used it," he told me . . . "we limit how much technology our kids use at home" (Bilton, 2014, np).

If the former CEO of Apple restricted his children's time on screens, what should that tell you? However, let us talk about the reality of your life with a preschool child with ADHD. Your child may be hyperactive and/ or inattentive, which makes it difficult for you to perform typical household responsibilities, such as making dinner or doing laundry. He may require your attention most of the time to make sure that the interactions among your family members remain calm. I know that logic may fall apart when the responsibilities of everyday life come into focus. I also clearly understand that you may need some time for yourself to make dinner or settle some plans. However, young children with or without ADHD need guidance, judgment, and time management when it comes to them accessing apps. The use of apps is not a babysitter, but instead, a different way of stimulating your child, so that he is more concentrated and less hyperactive for a short period of time. Additionally, your choice of which apps to use will be dependent upon your child's developmental level.

Just remember how young your preschool child with ADHD may actually be in terms of being at an immature developmental level as a result of his ADHD. Check out later in this chapter as to what I reported from Shaw et al.'s (2007) research about the immature developmental levels of children with ADHD. In addition, make sure to read the policy statement below written by The American Academy of Pediatrics in terms of the recommended restrictions of the use of digital media for young children.

GUIDELINES

The AAP designed a policy statement titled "Media and Young Minds" that "reviews the existing literature on television, videos, and mobile/

interactive technologies; their potential for educational benefit; and related health concerns for young children (0 to 5 years of age)" (American Academy of Pediatrics, 2016b, 1–5). The guidelines address the recommended time limitations on the use of digital media for young children from two to five years of age:

> For children 2 to 5 years of age, limit screen use to 1 hour per day of high-quality programming, co-view with your children, help children understand what they are seeing, and help them apply what they learn to the world around them (p. 3).

They emphasize that these children have enough time to be involved in activities that are important to their health and development (p. 5). The report also accentuates the recommendation that parents should engage with their child as they involve themselves with technology.

Here are some more examples of what is suggested to parents in these guidelines as related to the use of technology with young children.

- Avoid fast-paced programs (young children do not understand them as well), apps with lots of distracting content, and any violent content.
- Turn off television and other devices when not in use.
- Avoid using media as the only way to calm your child. Although there are intermittent times (i.e., medical procedures, airplane flights) when media is useful as a soothing strategy, there is concern that using media as strategy to calm a child down could lead to problems with limit setting or the inability of children to develop emotion regulation.
- Monitor children's media content and what apps are used or downloaded. Test apps before the child uses them, play together, and ask the child what he or she thinks about the app. (In the app section of this chapter, I reviewed the apps in detail that I suggested are effective and safe).
- Keep bedrooms, mealtimes, and parent-child playtimes screen-free for children and parents. Parents can set a "do not disturb" option on their phones during these times.
- No screens 1 hour before bedtime, and remove devices from bedrooms before bed (p. 4).

The AAP also recommends completing a Family Media Plan, that is available at www.healthychildren.org/MediaUsePlan. They claim that by completing this plan, families will become more aware of when each person in their family uses media and for what purpose they are using it. They also state that the media plan, which includes a media time calculator "will help you to think about media & create goals & rules that are in line with your family's values" (https://www.healthychildren.org/English/media/Pages/default.aspx, np).

You can enter each of your children's names who are between 18 months and 18 years old on the calculator. You can also choose categories where you list the time spent in each one. Some of the categories listed are family time, free time, meals, personal care, physical activity, and school, among others. Additionally, you can create categories of your own choosing. Inclusive within the calculator is the recommended number of hours of sleep and exercise. Once you complete the calculator, you should be able to see how much time is left in your children's day for media use. Voila! So . . . next, let us discuss technology and its possible influence on preschool children with ADHD's understanding of social skills.

THE USE OF APPS TO TEACH SOCIAL SKILLS: THE VERDICT?

Some television shows contribute to children's understanding of social skills. "Regarding social skills, evidence shows that quality TV programmes such as *Sesame Street* and *Mister Rogers' Neighborhood* improve children's understanding of concepts such as friendship, feelings and how to treat people" (Kucirkova and Falloon, 2017, p. 19). These concepts are instrumental for preschool children with ADHD to learn in terms of playing with their peers.

Some researchers believe that apps diminish the indigenous value of play. Kucirkova and Falloon (2017) state that games "such as Cookie Monster Challenge and Daniel Tiger's Grr-ific Feelings app . . . do remove the naturalistic and social components of nondigital play that have long been the basis of learning social-emotional skills" (p. 19) (see my review of these apps later on in this chapter). In other words, the argument here is that apps do not offer the child the same skills that old-fashioned play has contributed to the learning of social and emotional skills. You are the parents, so you have to decide as to how you feel about permitting your preschool child with ADHD to access these apps.

Radesky and Zuckerman (2017) recommend the following rules of thumb for teachers who want to decide which apps a child should use (as a parent, of course, you can adapt these for your own use).

- The app needs to be aligned with the specific activity, skill or experience you aim to foster.
- The app needs to enrich the activity you have in mind.
- Open-ended apps offer more opportunities for children's own creativity and exploration than template-based ones.
- Apps which support shared engagement with others can foster social skills.
- Discuss your choices with other parents, teachers, and the children themselves. Consider the added value of the app's use for the offline version of the same activity (pp. 260–61).

Just to reiterate, this list can be adapted and used for parents as well.

HOW DO I START USING APPS? WHAT SHOULD I DO FIRST, SECOND, AND THIRD?

First, the most important thing to do is to determine which topic you want the app to incorporate. For example, do you want an app that is specific to social skills, (though these are difficult to find for preschool children, but are available as you will see later in this chapter), emotional skills, or academics? How would you determine the category of the app? This part is not easy for parents to determine. (Believe me, I know because I am a parent and a grandparent as well!) Additionally, when I work with young children with ADHD, I need to determine the most important category at the onset.

Second, as we enter into this new world of technology, all of us need to make sure that it is the right time for your child to enter that world. Additionally, you should insist on the parameters of when, where, how, and why you are permitting your child to use those apps. You certainly do not want to encourage your child to be dependent upon technology, especially in consideration of the possibility that preschool children with ADHD may latch on to technology. We know that parents need a break, but please still be mindful of the pitfalls of using technology for young children!

Third, researchers have questioned as to whether or not there is a delay in the maturity of the brains of children with ADHD or if their brains develop differently than typical children. "Since its earliest description, there has been debate as to whether the disorder is a consequence partly of delay in brain maturation or as a complete deviation from the template of typical development" (Shaw et al., 2007, p. 19649). As reflected in the previously mentioned longitudinal research, children with ADHD are less mature than typical children. Shaw et al. found, in groundbreaking research, that

> in youth with attention deficit hyperactivity disorder (ADHD), the brain matures in a normal pattern but is delayed three years in some regions, on average, compared to youth without the disorder, an imaging study by researchers at the National Institutes of Health's (NIH) National Institute of Mental Health (NIMH) has revealed. . . . The delay in ADHD was most prominent in regions at the front of the brain's outer mantle (cortex), important for the ability to control thinking, attention and planning. Otherwise, both groups showed a similar back-to-front wave of brain maturation with different areas peaking in thickness at different times (https://www.nih.gov/news-events/news-releases/brain-matures-few-years-late-adhd-follows-normal-pattern, np).

Why is this information important for parents to know? The ages that are listed as appropriate for your child on the apps may not be accurate for their developmental level. Just to emphasize this statement: There are so many apps out there, so just make sure that the app that you teach your child to use is reflective of his appropriate developmental level!

So, do you want your preschool child with ADHD to use the apps to teach him about social skills or academics? Additionally, do you want him to use apps that cause a hyperfocus, so that his hyperactivity may be temporarily diminished? Answer these questions and let us move on!

A FEW MORE SUGGESTIONS BEFORE YOU BEGIN WORKING WITH APPS

You need to explain precisely to your preschool child with ADHD how to work a specific app because frequently the instructions are just not that explicit, or in fact, may be nonexistent! You also want to ascertain which level of the app is the most effective for your own child. Additionally, and very importantly as well is do not deny yourself the pleasure of seeing your child actively solving a problem, which you might not typically observe. Let us look at some apps to determine which ones are the best for preschool children with ADHD.

As far as I know, there are few if any apps that are specifically designed for preschool children with ADHD. Therefore, you will have to adapt the apps that are available for your child's age and developmental level according to his interests and needs. I cannot evaluate hundreds upon hundreds of apps so I will describe and analyze a selected number of apps here instead.

As a preview, the categories into which I delved were pre-academic skills, such as memory, letter recognition, spatial awareness, and color recognition; and emotional skills such as shyness, feelings, self-reliance, and problem-solving (which incorporates planning and social skills such as manners and being polite).

PRE-ACADEMIC APPS

Memory Match and Learn (Apple)

This app is clearly one that is a memory matching app that includes matching games. These games involve the teaching of the alphabet, as well as shapes, colors, numbers, nature, vegetables, and fruit. It is a very child-friendly app. It downloads perfectly easily for a preschool child's use. If you do not want commercials and you would like some more intricate game choices, then you can download the complete app and purchase it for $7.99. Otherwise, you may be very happy with the free version for your preschool child with ADHD. Be careful, though, because I honestly did not see the price until I purchased it.

How does the app work? When a match is made, it is paired with a soothing voice that is very pleasant. When the child makes a mistake, he will hear a soft buzz. The name of the object is offered at the bottom of the screen, which may encourage the child to begin to learn to read or at least to be able to recognize some of the words that are written down. The music is not distracting.

I really liked this app due to the colorful objects, the soft music that was played, the encouraging sound that the child hears when he is correct, and the nonabrasive sound that he hears when he makes the wrong match.

Abby Monkey Basic Skills Pre–K (Apple/Android)

This app is clearly a basic skills app (as in the title!). The cost is $0.99. The child will need an adult to operate this app. It begins by the character announcing who she is: Abby the Train Driver. She is trying to pick up train passengers and asks for the child's help. There are instructions for each page at that point, which includes completing patterns, matching, touching the toy that starts with a letter, and making pairs. One issue that I had was that it asked the child to tap the toy that started with the letter *B*. I would rather have had the instructions state that the child should tap the toy that starts with the sound of the letter *B* instead of the name of the letter. Perhaps the child does not know the names of the letters with which objects start but might know the sound of the letters.

Then, instructions are given to drag the wagons to make a train, which is a creative opportunity for the child. The positive praise for correct responses is pleasant. The responses for incorrect answers are innocuous such as "ee" that is paired with an embarrassed face. After you make a correct pattern, the app plays a cute melody. At that point you are finished, unless you want to upgrade to a version for which you have to pay. At some point, after your child has completed all of the games, you may want to upgrade, because there is nothing else that is offered to do, except to go back and play the games again that your child has already played.

The only real negative here is that the app plays monotonous music in the background. You will have to judge if that music annoys your child or not. It certainly annoyed me, but I am not four or five years old! Additionally, the games that are chosen are seemingly random. Finally, at the end of the games the child is offered stickers. However, there is no evidence that these rewards are contingent upon getting a certain number of answers correct. I would say that this app is entertaining enough for specific children but does not offer enough in the free version to continue to engage preschool children with ADHD for a longer time period.

Dino Learning Games: Dinosaurs Puzzles for Kids (Apple/Android)

This is a very cute app for preschool children. However, when you open the free app, which clearly requires adult intervention, your child can only complete three out of the eight puzzles because the others are locked. The puzzles are really well-illustrated and easy enough to do. However, when I accessed the Parents button and tried to pay $1.99 and unlock the games so that I could do the other puzzles, it just did not work after I tried it several times. I restarted my iPad and then *finally* it took my purchase. Parents must read the directions to hold down the button for three seconds.

There are no real instructions, which is unfortunate. However, in consideration of the fact that most children are adept technologically today, they would know that they have to drag pieces from the side to the puzzle. One nice feature is that if you drag the incorrect piece, all that happens is that the piece floats right back to the side. There are not any negative comments if the child is incorrect. This lack of negativity is great for preschool children with ADHD because they meet negativity each and every day. When you complete a puzzle correctly, colorful balloons come up and the voice says a positive phrase.

The additional puzzles are challenging, (maybe it is just me!) so that they require adult intervention, unless your child is very good at spatial awareness. That being said, the challenge is great to try to get your child to concentrate. However, as I said, these puzzles may require some adult help. It is a very good app, once you pay the $1.99 to access all of the puzzles. It seems that most, if not all of these apps have background music that may be annoying, however. Hopefully your child is either unaware of the music or ignores it because it is repetitive.

Preschool Math App—First Numbers and Counting Games for Toddlers and Pre–K Kids (Apple)

I simply would not bother with this app. That is as direct as I can be! There are only a few parts that you can do without paying $1.99 for each other part. You could be spending too much money on this app, because each part is $1.99, and each workbook is $1.99. The parts that are free are simply a picture of a ladybug and a voice that says the number, such as the number 1, unaccompanied by some animation, which is just plain boring.

Preschool Games for Kids (Android)

The first thing that you notice when you download this app is the repetitive music, which I personally found to be very monotonous. Perhaps preschool children with ADHD would like the music as a backdrop, but I did not. At any rate, you then see a choice of games for your child to play, which includes words, drawing, shapes, a sandbox, coloring, comparing numbers, fishing, and the clock.

There appear to be no instructions. It is possible that children will know that when letters drop down, the letters at the bottom are supposed to be dragged up to the letters on the top of the page. I did notice that when you drag the letters at the bottom of the page up to the letters at the top of the page, a pleasant voice says the word that you spelled, and then the object that the letters represent, such as a dog, appears. One huge mistake in the design of the app is that you can spell the word backward or forward and the voice will spell out the word anyway. I do not think that that is a good idea in consideration of the fact that children at these young ages are learning to read so therefore, they need to see a model of the correct way to spell and to read.

The drawing element is fine. The app shows the child examples of circles and squares and tells them to draw as many as they would like. From the last section forward, there seems to be simple instructions at the beginning of each section, which is good. The shapes section tells the child to tap on the screen to see whichever shapes he wants to see. That is fine. In the sandbox section, the child matches the shapes that are in the sandbox.

By the way, your child can always return to the choices of sections to access by tapping the house at the bottom left corner of the screen. In the section where your child colors the alphabet, he first chooses a colored pencil and then drags his finger up and down the letter. Different from other apps that include letter work, there are no arrows that guide the child as to the correct way to draw the letter. It is impossible to go out of the lines, however, because the app will not permit you to do so.

In this next section, the instructions ask you to choose which number is bigger. If you choose the incorrect number, nothing happens. When you choose the correct number, a pleasant voice tells you various positive phrases such as "Awesome!" and "Wonderful!"

In the fishing section, your child is supposed to fish for numbers. If he does nothing, the number flies back and comes back. It is unclear as to what your child is supposed to do here. The numbers come flying by and if you drag them up into the open area, a voice says the number. I would think that the idea would be to hook the number onto the character's fishing pole, but it does not seem to work that way.

Finally, the clock section asks your child to state the time. If you make a mistake, a pleasant voice says to try again or nice try. When you get the correct time, it just repeats the correct time and does not praise the child. One huge problem in this section is that only part of the times that are listed can be seen. They are cut off of the page for some reason, which might be confusing to your preschool child with ADHD.

This app is good for the youngest children in the preschool group. Parental supervision is necessary. It is entertaining to a degree and is easy enough for these children to do without being boring to them, except for the repetitive music!

Kids Preschool Learning Games (Android)

This is a free app. After you register, there are six sections to which your child may have access. These sections are alphabets, numbers, colors, fruits, animals, and shapes. Within the alphabet section, for example, are other sections. In the alphabet section, there are letters, alphabet practice, and words. The first two sections are virtually the same except that one is lowercase and the other is uppercase. The instructions say to tap the letters. The practice section is clever. However, because there are no instructions except to complete the pattern, it is trial and error as to how to complete the pattern.

As it happened, I found out that if you tapped the correct letter at the bottom, it showed at the top and cracked the egg as it sat up on the letter, which was very cute. The word section simply associated and spoke the object that was associated with the letter, such as *A* for apple. The numbers section is quite good. The first part says to tap the numbers and then a pleasant voice says the numbers. The next part counts the number you tap and has an associated picture, which the voice identifies.

The practice section requires an adult to read the instructions. Your child is supposed to tap the number in sequence. When he taps an incorrect number, a mildly annoying sound occurs. When he taps the correct number, the voice says the number and then, the balloon holding the number bursts, which is stimulating for preschool children with ADHD and is really pretty cool!

The last game section in numbers has simple instructions, so that it is possible that an early reader might be able to read them. You are supposed to touch a number and when you touch the correct number, the voice says a word of praise. When you touch the incorrect number, that annoying sound occurs. Additionally, at the bottom of the screen there is a train with absolutely no purpose, which was puzzling to me.

The colors section says that we should learn colors, but it does not offer any instructions. You have to assume that you need to tap a color to hear the voice say its name. There are flashcards that say the color. However, I accidently touched the accompanying picture which says the name of the object as well as the color. If I had not done so, I would not have known that the name of the object or the name of the color would have been stated. The quiz asks the child to touch a certain color, and once again that train is there with no purpose!

The practice section instructs you to find the matching pairs. In the coloring book section, which young children will certainly enjoy, your child can touch a color and then draw on a blank palette. However, once again, he would have to figure out these instructions, so he would know exactly what to do.

This app is pretty good, except for the instances when they do not give specific instructions. There are elements of this app that are more suitable for younger preschool children, but there are also sections that are suitable for preschool children who are on the older side of preschool. Parental supervision is necessary here, however, due to the lack of instructions offered.

Attention Trainer for ADHD: ADHD Pig (Apple/Android)

I know! This is a simply an awful name for an app! I am not sure if that title was the app builder's sense of humor or not. Since most of your children do not read as of yet, I would call it another name, such as Pink Pig or whatever. This app also requires some adult supervision because the game instructions are written on the screen. After you touch the place that says Game, you then choose the game that you want to play: spots, letters, colors, or size. Whichever game your child chooses, the instructions for the game are written in small letters at the top of the screen, which requires an adult to read. When the pig floats by that satisfies the parameters of the game, such as the pink pig, your child taps it. When your child chooses the correct pig, he gets a number score at the bottom of the screen. When he taps an incorrect pig, there is a buzzing sound. This is a good enough app for encouraging your child to focus. I am guessing, however, that your child will get tired of it fairly quickly.

APPS ABOUT FEELINGS AND SOCIAL SKILLS

Even Monsters Are Shy (Apple)

Even Monsters Are Shy kept a smile on my face throughout my entire experience with it. An adult has to operate this app, however, because your child has to choose one of two options that are written on the screen that are Read to Me or I Can Read. Clearly, if your child cannot read as of yet, he will not be able to choose an option without help.

This is a story app that talks about a boy whose best friend is a monster who is shy. Many preschool children with ADHD are either shy or anxious when it comes to talking to other people, especially people who they do not know, so this app is a good fit for these children. I will not ruin the message of the story for you, but trust me, it is a wonderful message that pertains to how to overcome shyness.

Just a little note about shyness. . . . It can be quite typical for many preschool children with or without a diagnosis of ADHD to be shy. One of the three-year-old boys whom I know is very shy initially when he is in groups of more than a few people, even when these people are his family whom he knows very well. In fact, before a recent family gathering, he was told by his dad that the family would be visiting after his nap. When he got up from his nap, he said immediately to his dad, "Hold me Daddy, hold me." He had never said that before!

I asked several preschool teachers who stated that shyness is often seen among preschool children in their classrooms. It is always so interesting to see if that shyness continues throughout childhood and into adolescence for preschool children with ADHD and without ADHD. It is a good idea to work on impacting a preschool child with ADHD's shyness, even though it may continue into childhood and adolescence.

How does Even Monsters Are Shy deal with helping a child to overcome shyness? It is interesting in fact that the monster overcomes his shyness by being with other children besides his best friend who is not a monster. This app includes diverse characters which is imperative for preschool children who live in such a diverse world today. Including diversity is a real plus for this app. However, by not including instructions, it becomes more difficult to fully take advantage of all of the options that are available within the app.

After researching so many apps, I found myself experimenting with the objects and the characters on each page to see if by tapping them they made any sounds or spoke any words, which they certainly did! It would have made it more user-friendly for me if they had offered instructions to do so, but when I explored and found these features, it was really exciting! It was really cool!

I would happily recommend this app to parents of preschool children with ADHD, whom I am sure would have the character read the story to their child over and over again. This story has a very important message, including the steps to overcoming being shy. It is a clever and a colorful app. What more could a parent of a preschool child with ADHD who is shy want? This is an awesome app!

What will I Find at the Company Page?

Of course, after simply loving the Even Monsters Are Shy app, I went to the company page, the Busy Bee Studio page on the App Store. What did I find? I found a bundle of two apps for $1.99, which seemed like a good deal. They also offer bundles of four apps at a slightly higher cost. The app Tracks and Trains is certainly a clever app but seems (to me, any-way), far too difficult for a preschool child with ADHD who may not have the patience to figure it all out. There *is* a detailed list of instructions for the parents on the home page, but it was quite complex, even for me to follow.

The other bundled app, The Zoo Train, as I have found with several of the apps that I have researched, does not include instructions. That being said, it is fairly straightforward as to what to do. However, it is also possible if not probable that young children are more adept at using these apps without any instructions than adults! It took me several minutes, for example, to figure out if I should drag a letter to its same letter that had to be placed on the train or if I should tap it.

One other criticism is that the words that the app designer was trying to teach the children either to recognize, to read or to spell were random. In fact, I did not know how the app designers decided on the word "banjo" at all, because I did not think that many preschool children with ADHD would have that word in their everyday vocabulary. (Maybe I am incorrect?) This app, however, has a positive feature of having the con-ductor respond pleasantly when the child drags the correct letters to the train, which has the same word spelled out. In these circumstances, the conductor blows his whistle.

Additionally, a voice says "Awesome," or some other positive re-sponse, but says it randomly as well. Perhaps the unpredictability of positive responses encourages the child to complete the task. The voice then repeats the name of the object and spells it out. Soon afterward, the image of the object appears on the screen so that the child can associate the spelled word with the object that it represents.

Another word train comes along immediately. After the child spells a couple of words correctly, a suitcase comes rolling along where (without instructions again) the child can choose a sticker. Finally, if your child chooses the incorrect letter to spell the word on the word train, that letter simply floats up to the top without any negative response by the charac-ter. The randomness of the word choice really bothered me, however, in terms of helping the child to recognize words. However, other than that criticism, it really is a pretty good app, accompanied by bright colors, pleasant sounds, and challenges that are not too difficult yet not too easy for preschool children with ADHD to manage.

Breathe, Think, Do with Sesame (Apple/Android)

I highly recommend this app, which I truly love! It teaches problem-solving of everyday problems such as the child being frustrated putting his shoes on, not wanting to separate from his mommy when he goes to school, becoming upset when the building he made fell down, being impatient when he has to wait his turn to go down a slide, and being afraid of the dark when he goes to sleep. Before I forget to tell you, you can listen to this app either in Spanish or English, which is a real plus.

The app opens and shows a friendly monster, whose name is Mando, telling your child to choose an activity. When he taps on an activity, the narrator explains the monster's problem. Then he tells the child to tap on the monster's belly to help him to put his hands on it. As the monster does so, the narrator states that he is taking three deep breaths, which helps him to calm down.

As the monster calms down, the narrator tells the child to think of a plan to solve his problem. In order for the child to do so, he is told to pop bubbles with thoughts of planning in them, so that the monster can think of a plan. After the child pops the bubbles, which he just does by tapping on each bubble, he is shown a plan of action that the monster may take. When he is finished popping the bubbles, the monster has decided upon three plans of action to solve his problem, which the narrator goes over again at the end of each problem-solving example.

Therefore, the child has three possible plans from which to choose, which the narrator states again and has the child make a decision as to which plan to choose. The bubbles come up, accompanied by very pleasant, light music somewhat like a triangle or a xylophone. At this point, the child is shown the importance of developing a plan again and how to make one, including beginning with taking three deep breaths. He tells your child to breathe, think (of a plan), and do (carry out) the plan. The instructions continue with the monster experiencing another problem. The same instructions follow for each of the monster's problems. The instructions are the same, so therefore are predictable, which is perfect for a preschool child with ADHD who does best with routines. This is executive function exemplified!

Another great part of this app is the parent's section, which is easily accessible by dragging the rectangle to the lower-right-hand corner of the iPad. Parents are offered tips and strategies for everything from strategies for persistence and coping with separation to other tips about issues that are not included in the apps, such as adjusting to a move and managing sibling rivalry. This is just awesome!

There is also a Let's Breathe option that is explained in more detail within the app. Finally, and really the best part, is a section where you can encourage the monster to think of plans using your child's own voice! Just amazing! What a great innovation!

Here is a fabulous bonus! If you go to www.sesameworkshop.org, you can access (for free!) videos of characters learning to be patient, not giving up, and saying bye-bye for now. For example, when you listen to the videos, a character talks in a rhythmic way, offering your child examples of what to do when he is waiting so that he can remain patient. There is simply no negative that characterizes this app for preschool children with ADHD—with supervision, of course!

Daniel Tiger's Grr-ific Feelings (Apple/Android)

This great app is from the Public Broadcasting System (PBS) and the Fred Rogers Company. I absolutely love it! The $2.99 that this app costs is well worth it and more. The app begins by having Daniel Tiger introduce himself as your neighbor. He says, "Let's play some games that are about feelings." One of the games is the Trolley Game, which includes a train that your child moves around the track according to an arrow that he spins. The trolley game discusses feelings such as calming down, feeling proud when the character cleans up his toys, feeling sad, happy, mad, scared, being afraid of the dark, and feeling happy. Daniel Tiger says that the child should tap any of the games pictured to play. Your child is told to go to a specific shape stop.

The app also includes Daniel Tiger singing a song about each of the feelings. One negative is that the instructions are not that precise, but I am sure that a young child will be able to know when to drag one object to another. If he is correct in his choices, a pleasant sound occurs, and if he is incorrect in his choices, a sound occurs that is nonabrasive.

The next game is Daniel Tiger's Sing Along. Daniel tells the child to choose one song out of eighteen songs. The songs are illustrated in a very colorful way and are somewhat diverse within specific songs. Each song explains how one feels such as being afraid, alike and different, brave, calm, determined, disappointed, frustrated, helpful, jealous, mad, proud, reassured, sad, sorry, thankful, and worried, among many other feelings.

In the parent's section, which is easy to access, is a choice of mini-games which allows the parents to go over the songs again if there are specific feelings that they want to reinforce in terms of how to manage them. Additionally, within the parent's section are instructions and explanations in Spanish.

The next game is the Drawing Easel. Daniel states that sometimes when he feels happy, sad, or mad he likes to draw. He then asks the child if he wants to draw a picture with him and instructs him to tap the easel. He says that sometimes he likes to draw about how he feels on the inside or about something that has happened. Your child has a choice of many art tools such as markers, paints stickers, etc. As your child chooses different scenes, he can also choose which specific drawing vehicles to use, such as markers or stickers. There is a pleasant voice announcing the particular choice that he has made.

There are no specific instructions, so to be honest, I found it a little difficult to figure out exactly how to use the various drawing devices. After a while, I figured out that I had to tap the markers and then choose a particular marker color. After choosing a color, I could then drag the color onto the picture. The app designers even have a section where you can access your pictures on your iPad and then paste them on the picture.

The only caveat, however, is that you have to grant permission to access your pictures, which is easy and is simply agreeing to what it says in the box asking you to do so. As I have said, before, however, I am SURE that even young children are more adept at figuring out what to do in terms of working these apps in 2019 than many adults could do! (including me!)

The last game is the Feelings Photo Booth. This game requires access to your phone's camera and pictures, and adds the pictures to the camera roll but does not place it side by side to Daniel's face which I was copying, which is unfortunate. Therefore, I really did not understand the point of this game. This game, if I am correct, is no different than just using the camera on the iPad, so it was a bit of a disappointment. This game also permits you to take pictures with a regular camera as well as taking a selfie. However, there were no more instructions. Therefore, it was not clear when the game ended.

This app, in general, does an excellent job of helping preschool children with ADHD to recognize and to name their feelings, which they specifically may have a difficult time doing. The concept and the justification for the app is that if the child understands his feelings, then perhaps he will be able to control them. The illustrations are bright and cheery, and the songs are catchy, rhythmic, and entertaining. Children love to draw, and the game that helps them to sketch their feelings may be very useful to them.

The Trolley Game additionally permits the child to have his own control over learning how to manage each of his feelings as well. When the part of each game is completed, the app plays a pleasant song going over the specific feeling again. I just loved this app and would highly recommend it to parents who are trying to help their preschool child with ADHD to recognize and to understand his feelings.

All by Myself by Mercer Mayer (Apple/Android)

This is a really excellent app that incorporates a story that can be read to your preschool child with ADHD. It includes the dimension of him turning the pages, putting the story on auto play where the story is read to him and the pages are turned for him, or alternately, you can read the story to him. If your child is an early reader, then he can read it to himself. This app is a story that discusses all things that are related to independence. For example: finding his socks and putting them on, buttoning his pants himself, tying his own shoes, and pouring some juice for his sister, among others.

The colors are bright and appealing. The diction in the reading is crisp and clear. This is an all-positive app that encourages self-esteem as related to all of the skills that your child can do by himself. Parental assistance might be necessary to get started, but after the child is shown which format to choose, he will be able to manage the app by himself, which is the self-reliance that the app teaches!

Daniel Tiger's Day and Night (Apple/Android)

This is another superb and well-designed app. Some of these apps are free, but this one is $2.99 and is well worth it. This app offers a choice between how to get ready for school and how to get ready for bed. When the app begins, a pleasant voice asks you what you would like to play next. If your child does not respond, Daniel tells him to tap on the sun or the moon to play Good Morning or Good Night. The app asks questions such as, "Will you wake him?" However, if your child does not respond, a voice says to give Daniel "a little nudge to wake him."

A song then reminds your child what to do in the morning. He asks what he should do first. If your child does not respond, a voice tells him to tap on one of the icons. An absolutely adorable part of the app is that it permits your child to help Daniel, such as zipping up his jacket by using his finger to pull the zipper up.

A similar format occurs with getting Daniel ready to go to bed at night. Some adult assistance is necessary here, until your child becomes accustomed to the instructions. One negative is that when Daniel asks if you want to play make-believe, the app does not work until you tap the button on the bottom right. In fact, it takes some trial and error to manipulate the colors of the actions that Daniel has exhibited.

Additionally, your child can choose what to do in the self-help activities such as setting the table. (What a great idea it is to offer independence skills for your child to emulate!) One final criticism, however, is that the background music may be a little monotonous because it is very repetitive, but this is certainly not a major issue.

All in all, Daniel Tiger's Day and Night app is excellent as well as entertaining in terms of teaching specific tasks and colors and offering some enjoyable activities and fun things for your child to do. Most importantly, however, is that the app accentuates the important message of self-reliance, which is so important for preschool children with ADHD to learn.

Manners (Apple/Android)

This app costs $2.99 and includes a social story about the importance of being polite. It was created by Touch Autism. However, this app is perfect for preschool children with ADHD because of the strong visual supports from which these children can benefit. Upon opening the app, you have four choices, which are: Start the Story, Manners, Read to Me, and Read Myself.

The app also includes a section where you can tap and listen to each type of polite statement such as, saying Thank you and Please, among others that are accompanied by visual reminders as well. Once you begin to have the story read to you, colorful illustrations are offered that includes the correct behavior as well as the incorrect behavior. Some of the pictures of the behavior that is not appropriate are actually very funny.

This app includes a convenient and practical story that teaches an important lesson to preschool children with ADHD that many may not use in their everyday conversations and interactions. Parental assistance is definitely necessary here in terms of which rectangle to tap to either hear the included manners, the story that is read to your child, or the story that he can read.

Feelings—Emotional Growth (Android); Feelings—Baby Bus (Apple)

This app, which is free, helps young children to recognize when they are feeling a certain way, which preschool children with ADHD need to learn. Additionally, and importantly, it teaches them how to work through these feelings and how to solve the issues that are causing them to feel in a specific way. Typically, preschool children with ADHD may not understand the problem-solving that is involved in understanding feelings such as sadness, anger, and frustration, among other feelings.

Parental assistance is definitely necessary here because there are no explicit instructions included. When your child sees the word "feelings," which he undoubtedly will not be able to read at four or five years old, he needs to touch an arrow that brings up four characters who talk about their problems.

Each character experiences the same feeling, but their experiences are different. There are no instructions here, unfortunately. Your child would have to know to tap the character and then drag what he needs to do to solve his problem. Additionally, some of the other screens are very cute as well, but also come with no instructions to tell your child to either tap or drag or execute both of these actions to solve his problem. All of these scenes, therefore, are trial and error in terms of what your child should do.

One related criticism is that I expected several feelings to be explored, but unless I am incorrect (I just might be, because it is so unclear!) all of the characters only discussed the fact that that they were sad. That being said, in terms of what I said about the fact that there are no instructions, children on the younger end of preschool will be able to learn about how to manage their feelings through this app. It is a good app, yet certainly not a great app. Preschool children with ADHD will need total supervision here by an adult when they use this app, due to the fact that there are no instructions included.

MY OWN SUMMATION OF THE USE OF APPS FOR PRESCHOOL CHILDREN WITH ADHD

My review of apps should merely be used as a guide. There are thousands upon thousands of apps, many of which purport to be appropriate for your preschool child with ADHD to use. I chose a cross-section of apps that reflects the types of apps that you might want to use with your preschool child with ADHD. This survey should in no way be viewed as a comprehensive examination of the marketplace.

I have tried to give you a good sample of both pre-academic apps and apps that concentrate on social and emotional areas. However, I do feel obliged to tell you about my overall app experience. The apps that I have included here consistently work and are easy enough to access and to use.

There were many apps that were well recommended. However, after I spent ample time trying to figure them out, they either did not work, worked after much duress, or turned on and off. Additionally, there were some apps that I just could not figure out—and I am an adult! I am pretty adept at technology, but dealing with apps can be a very frustrating experience. While I obviously have some recommendations as to which apps to avoid and which ones to seek out, hopefully, my analysis of these apps will inform you of the potential strengths and weaknesses that you may come across in other apps that you find in order to decide which are appropriate for your preschool child with ADHD.

You are all set, however, because I only recommended those apps that easily worked for me and were good at facilitating the lessons that your preschool child with ADHD needs to learn. I covered both the Apple and the Android platforms. Please read the final analysis of each app because some of them were absolutely excellent and would really help your preschool child with ADHD to learn the skills that he needs to learn, as well as keeping him hyperfocused (which is a good thing sometimes!) when he becomes hyperactive.

7

THE CHANGES IN LIFE THAT MAY AFFECT YOUR PRESCHOOL CHILD WITH ADHD

There are so many changes that may happen in life to a family or to people in general that may affect a preschool child with ADHD. There-fore, in response to these events, your child may exhibit behavior that you have not previously observed or display his same inappropriate behavior at a more frequent pace. Your preschool child with ADHD may exhibit new behaviors if an outside event occurs that upsets him or gets him excited. Some examples of these events may be the following:

- a new baby in the house
- the death of a grandparent
- moving to a new neighborhood or to a new city
- a friend moving away
- a child bothering or bullying him at school (yes even in preschool! Check out chapter 8)
- a natural event like a hurricane or a snowstorm

You undoubtedly become upset or emotional at the various changes that occur, as does your child. Therefore, you are the best person to explain to him why you are distressed or excited, and can explain to him how you will manage your own feelings, as well. If he sees that you have a method to try to diminish your vulnerable feelings, he might very well try to manage his feelings in the same way.

HOW TO TEACH YOUR PRESCHOOL CHILD WITH ADHD TO BEHAVE WHEN YOU ARE UPSET

Your preschool child with ADHD may have low self-esteem as well as being vulnerable. Therefore, when he hears a conversation in which he observes you upset, how will he respond to what he hears? His response is very much dependent upon how you respond instead of how you react. Sometimes, however, one cannot help but to cry or to be upset. These are natural emotions that do not signal to your child that you are behaving in an unmanageable way. On the contrary, you are showing your child that it is perfectly acceptable to show emotion, which is imperative for your preschool child with ADHD to observe because these children may have difficulty getting in touch with their own emotions.

We all cannot be in a happy and relaxed mood each and every day. You may have experienced this situation. Perhaps you came home from a day at work and you were very upset because your boss criticized and embarrassed you in front of the other employees. You are clearly worried about your job performance and, therefore, your job security. Upon arriving home, you collapse into your recliner, close your eyes, and are visibly upset.

Your child sees your body language, and as many preschool children with ADHD typically do, he does not pick up on your social cues. You do not tell him anything as to what happened to you and why you are sitting with your eyes closed in the chair. He comes right up to you and begins to talk excessively, as do many preschool children with ADHD. You become quickly annoyed and say to him, "Calm down. What is your problem? I just got home. Can't you go and do something?" Of course, you immediately feel terrible about what you said.

What should you say to your child when you are upset, as in this example, so that you can help him to be sensitive to your emotional state? I do not think that it is necessary—and in fact, it may add more worry than necessary—to tell a child all of the details as to what happened to you at work. However, what you can say is that you did not have a good day at work and that you are very exhausted. In that way, he does not think that you are upset with him, and with a little guidance from you, he will learn to wait until you are ready to talk to him.

Here is an example of what you can say to him: "Jimmy, I did not have a great day at work today and I am very tired. I will rest for a little while and then we can talk, okay?" In that way, the child knows that you will talk to him later, but for now, you need some time to relax. In addition to responding in an intentional way to a transient event, it is imperative to respond in an intentional way when a major event occurs.

QUESTIONS TO ASK YOURSELF TO HELP YOU TO RESPOND TO A LIFE CHANGE INSTEAD OF REACTING TO A LIFE CHANGE

You must always respond intentionally to any possible changes that occur. In that way, you are able to reply to a change in a calm and thoughtful way, instead of immediately reacting, which may result in undesirable and negative behavior by you. The following section is a list of questions that you should ask yourself as a parent before a major change occurs in your family's life.

- How will you respond to the major change that has just occurred?
- How will you describe your emotions?
- How will this change affect your level of anxiety?
- How will you be able to maintain your composure while interacting with your child?
- What effect do you feel your response to the change in your life will have on your child?
- How will your preschool child with ADHD's behavior change or will it remain consistent?
- What will be the reactions of family members and friends to your child's behavior, as related to the change in your life that has occurred?
- What sentiments and/or emotions will your child mention to you that he is experiencing, due the change that has occurred?

As I have said before, and am stating again now for added emphasis, your responses to a change in your life will serve as a barometer for your preschool child with ADHD's responses to the changes in his own life. The above questions are sine qua non, so that you are prepared for any change that occurs in your life. In that way, you will be able to help your child to respond in a reasonable way.

QUESTIONS TO ASK YOUR PRESCHOOL CHILD WITH ADHD ABOUT A CHANGE THAT HAS JUST OCCURRED

The most important thing that you can do when a drastic change occurs in your family's life is to try to immediately have a conversation with your preschool child with ADHD about that change. I am going to list some possible questions here. However, here is a caveat: If your child does not want to talk, do not try to force him to talk about the change that has occurred. Instead, see if he will draw some pictures to represent how he feels, or tell you what to draw that will represent how he is feeling. If he will not draw, just wait it out in the hope he will be ready to talk very soon. If he is a very talkative child and he simply stops talking, I would consult a physician or a psychiatrist to see what are the next steps that you should take.

Here are some questions to ask your preschool child with ADHD.

- Does he realize that a change has occurred?
- What does he think about the change that has occurred?
- What are his feelings related to the change that has occurred?
- Has he spoken to anyone about the change that has occurred? If he did so, about what did they talk?
- What changes has he noticed in his own behavior?
- What changes has he noticed in his sibling's behavior?
- What changes has he noticed in his parent's behavior?

As you are reading my list of questions, please realize that the answers to these questions will be dependent upon the level of maturity and/or developmental level of each and every preschool child with ADHD. One child may be able to answer only one question while another child might be able to answer all of these questions. Just have patience while you are waiting for the answers to these questions because preschool children with ADHD will need approximately eight to ten seconds to form their thoughts and respond to each question. It is possible that by employing resources such as reading books about similar life changes to your preschool child with ADHD, he might be able to answer these questions more easily.

SOME RESOURCES THAT WILL HELP YOU TO TALK TO YOUR PRESCHOOL CHILD WITH ADHD ABOUT A CHANGE THAT HAS OCCURRED

A wonderful and poignant book to read to your preschool child with ADHD about someone close to them who has died is *Always Remember* by Cece Meng. This beautifully illustrated book talks about the contribution of the turtle who died and how his legacy will live on forever. Children will feel that they have not really lost their turtle because his memory will be everlasting. This is an excellent book because the message is one of consolation and solace to those children who read it.

My Best Friend Moved Away (*Nancy's Neighborhood*) by Nancy L. Carlson is a great book about a child whose best friend has moved away. The narrator tells the reader about everything that the two friends have shared, from soccer to chicken pox. Bright and beautiful illustrations highlight each of these events. This book offers reassurance and comfort to children after their sadness at having a best friend move away, by showing the reader that she soon made new friends.

A good book about having a new baby in the house is *We Just Had a Baby* by Stephen Krensky. This is a humorous book that is written from the sibling's point of view. The older child's perceptions are both poignant and comical. A simply fabulous book that I just bought and read to a four year old about bullying is *The Pout-Pout Fish and the Bully-Bully Shark* by Deborah Diesen and Dan Hannah. In this book, the Pout-Pout Fish, who always has a great message, teaches a Bully-Bully Shark not to be mean, but instead, to be kind as well as how to become a friend. The Pout-Pout Fish doubts how he, just one little fish, can possibly make a difference, but he certainly does make an impact!

In order to find a good book on moving, we returned to 1981! *The Berenstain Bears' Moving Day* is as good as it gets in terms of reading about moving away from their treehouse to another part of town and therefore leaving their good friends. As a bonus, this book comes with lots and lots of stickers.

Here is an example of an environmental change that may occur and what a parent should do.

HOW TO MANAGE YOUR PRESCHOOL CHILD WITH ADHD'S BEHAVIOR WHEN A NATURAL DISASTER OCCURS

In many areas of the country, there have been hurricanes and heavy rains and winds. Due to the eight to ten inches of rain that you may have received, the clean-up may be overwhelming. As our children grow out of their toys and clothes, some of us are savers and those who are so, (like me!) have an overwhelming amount of work to do in terms of cleaning up. These cleanups do not just take an hour or even a day, but sometimes, weeks and months.

So here is the scenario: You begin to clean up that incredible mess and your preschool child with ADHD somehow gets in the way. What can you do to keep him busy so that you can do whatever you have to do in terms of cleaning up and clearing out the debris from the flood?

The solution is quite simple. Give him one and only one specific job at a time, whether it is taking Legos out of a wet box and washing and drying each piece; that is the idea. Just to continue, he can categorize the Legos into different colors and then count how many there are of each color. Hopefully, this task will give you at least an hour of uninterrupted time, so that you can clean up. Events such as natural disasters are typically predicted, so you will be able to plan how you will be able to manage their detrimental effects. Life changing events for which you cannot plan are more difficult to manage.

LIFE CHANGING EVENTS FOR WHICH YOU CANNOT PLAN

Life changing events for which you have time to plan are quite different from events that occur suddenly. Presumably, your family will have advance knowledge of a new baby, moving to a new neighborhood as well as a friend who is moving away. However, the death of a grandparent may be an event that happens suddenly and without warning. It may be complicated and confusing for a preschool child with ADHD who does not have a precise sense of time, a real understanding of age, and a deep comprehension of what it means to die. Your child may be very close to his grandparent, so this loss may be difficult to manage. All of a sudden, the child's grandparent is not present and will never be again.

Preschool children with ADHD may have difficulty comprehending the big picture of a grandparent dying. Your child may seemingly say, "She died because she was old," but then expect his grandparent to come over to see him the next day. Additionally, preschool children oftentimes have not grasped as of yet the relationship of you to your mom or you to your dad, as well as the relationship of your siblings to you. I often ask a four-year-old child whom I know well, "Who is daddy's mom and dad and who is daddy's brother and sister?" Even though he knows these people well, he somehow becomes confused by these relationships.

The concept of grief that is associated with dying is complex and difficult for adults, nonetheless for preschool children with ADHD. Grief is a particularly powerful emotion and one that may make your child anxious due to his incomplete understanding of it. Be patient because your child may latch on to or hyperfocus upon a single aspect of the dying process. In turn, he may ask the same question over and over again even though you are convinced that you explained the answer to him many times in several different ways.

Two other areas of difficulty for preschool children with ADHD may be affected by the death of a grandparent. These are impulsivity and transitions. Be prepared for your child to exhibit impulsive behavior. This behavior may or may not be related to the death, so be prepared to respond to that behavior in a non-threatening and calm manner. Your family's activity may be disrupted as well, which your child will certainly not understand and with which he may not be happy. He may say something like "Why can't I go to swimming or soccer?" or "I want to see my friend" or "Why can't I go to play with him?"

The first thing that you can do is answer every single question honestly, and there will be many, in the simplest terms possible. You know your child's developmental level as well as depth of understanding better than anyone, so have confidence in what you are telling your child. The second thing you can do is to try not to become annoyed if your child's behavior is exaggerated during this sad time because the persistence of that behavior may be related to the death in the family.

The website www.understood.org has outlined six suggestions in terms of helping parents to assist their children in coping with grief. These are the following:

- Observe their responses and take cues from them.
- Let them know what to expect.
- Speak with empathy and try not to judge.
- Create safe places for your children to talk.
- Notice and reward positive behavior.
- Maintain schedules and routines as well as you can (np).

Typical children need time to manage their feelings when it comes to death and mourning. Preschool children with ADHD need even more time and understanding than typical children do, however. You may notice your preschool child with ADHD exhibiting more repetitive behavior. That behavior may be the only response that these children can manage in response to something that has happened for which they are just not yet developmentally ready to understand.

They may appear to be more vulnerable than they were previously, so be on the alert for them to be a good target for bullies. Vulnerability may be perceived as weakness, upon which bullies thrive. Read on to the next chapter to find out about preschool children with ADHD being bullied as well as being bullies themselves.

8

BULLYING

Bullying frequently begins at a young age and then continues throughout a child's elementary, middle school, and high school years. Bullying has a detrimental effect on children. One ten-year-old child, who had been bullied since preschool, talked to me about how he felt:

> I try to [have a positive outlook] but sometimes it's just too hard. I don't know if you go through a certain amount of stuff in public school. It's just hard to look and to feel positive. The kids get in there and leave a permanent scar and you just can't get rid of it.

There are some children who are bullied more than others. Perhaps they come across as vulnerable or perhaps the bullies just try to abuse each child along the way and see which ones they can manipulate. It is all very sad and difficult to hear. However, it is imperative that we are all aware of children who are being bullied and do our best to help them to stop this abusive behavior.

In this chapter, I will discuss bullying in preschool children. First, I will offer you the research data so that we can determine if preschool children have actually been bullied. Second, I will offer you some techniques so that if your child has been bullied, you can try some ways to stop him from being bullied. Here we go!

WHAT DOES THE RESEARCH SAY?

Overall, bullying in schools has become a national epidemic. According to the National Education Association (NEA), bullying impacts approximately 13 million students every year. A 2010 survey of NEA members reported that "62 percent (of educators and professionals) indicated they'd witnessed bullying two or more times in the last month. Forty-one percent indicated they'd witnessed bullying once a week or more" (NEA.org, 2012, np). We do not know the exact number of preschool children with ADHD who have been bullied, but we do know that it happens all too frequently.

When you saw the title of this chapter, did you say to yourself, "That is ridiculous! Preschool children with or without ADHD are not bullied! They are too young"? Well, I am sorry to say that preschool children are not only bullied but may act as bullies as well. There is limited research, but there *is* research:

> The findings emanating from the limited number of studies available indicate that preschoolers can be the perpetrators and victims of both direct and indirect peer aggression and that children of this age are capable of displaying different forms of bullying such as verbal, physical, social exclusion, and rumor spreading (Vlachou et al., 2011, p. 333).

How has bullying been defined? Olweus and Limber (1999, p. 31) have delineated three criteria for describing bullying: It is (1) an aggressive behavior of intentional "harmdoing" (2) carried out repeatedly and over time (3) in an interpersonal relationship characterized by an imbalance of power.

The above definition of bullying is widely agreed upon. However, some researchers feel that the term "bullying" should not be used for these young children. Instead, they state that since

> This may be associated with the social skills instability characterizing this particular age . . . some argue that the term 'unjustified aggression' might be more proper for describing 'bullying' in early years . . . children are the victims of unjustified aggression by others when they are attacked physically, verbally, or psychologically without there being a justifying reason or motive for the act (Vlachou et al., 2011, p. 331).

Bullying is regarded as a specific type of aggression that is accomplished by a stronger culprit toward a weaker individual. Therefore, there is an imbalance of power. Be mindful, however, that "playful fights/disputes between two parties of equal strength should not be regarded as bullying" (Vlachou et al., 2011, p. 331).

One very important caveat here is that it is believed, according to research on preschool children, that most victims as we shall call these preschool children who have been bullied, tend not to be repeatedly bullied over a long period of time. Instead, they are bullied for short periods of time.

> During early childhood . . . most victims tend not to be repeatedly victimized over long periods of time during early childhood but experience victimization only for brief periods of time (Vlachou et al., 2011, p. 331).

The whole idea of your precious young child being bullied is an atrocious thought. However, I am sure that you are saying to yourself, "But my child is only four years old. He cannot have been bullied!" Vlachou et al. (2011) found that "aggressive behaviors that could be bullying and peer victimization have been identified in children as young as 4 years in several countries" (p. 332). So, there it is . . . children as young as four years old have been bullied and may be bullies!

Is it true that preschool children who have been bullied have few friends, which may cause them to be more vulnerable than those who have not been bullied? This statement is research supported.

"On the one hand, victimized preschool children's lack of friends might render them psychologically and socially vulnerable and thus more prone to becoming easy targets" (Perren and Alsaker, 2006, p. 45). Therefore, the bully victims have few friends, which causes them to be vulnerable. The bullies, however, are sought after by other children to be their friends. Therefore, children, especially boys, want to be friends with the bullies: "on the other hand, bullies seem to be more preferred playmates, particularly for other aggressive boys" (Perren and Alsaker, 2006, p. 45).

Here are some key findings from a kindergarten study that may apply to your preschool child with ADHD:

> Compared to non-involved children victims were more submissive, had fewer leadership skills, were more withdrawn, more isolated, less

cooperative, less sociable, and frequently had no playmates. As expected, bullies and bully victims were generally more aggressive than their peers. In addition, bully-victims were less cooperative, less sociable, and more frequently had no playmates than non-involved children. Bullies were less prosocial and had more leadership skills than non-involved children. Bullies belonged to larger social clusters and were frequently affiliated with other bullies or bully victims (Perren and Alsaker, 2006, p. 45).

Finally, are there differences in girls who have been bullied as compared to boys? Yes! Did girls who had been bullied interact well with their peers? "Among girls (but not among boys) bully victims were more isolated than non-involved children. Moreover, female bullies were more isolated than male bullies . . . they often had nobody to play with" (Perren and Alsaker, 2006, p. 53).

So, you can see that there are signs of being a bully or having been bullied that you can investigate in your own preschool children. Here are some questions that you can ask yourself:

1. Is my child vulnerable?
2. Is my child isolated?
3. Does my child have friends?
4. Does my child play and/or congregate with children who are aggressive?
5. Does my child have difficulty asserting himself?

Remember to be aware, if your child is submissive, that "victims had problems asserting themselves: they lacked leadership skills and were highly submissive. The latter may contribute to their victimization" (Perren and Alsaker, 2006, p. 52).

IF YOUR PRESCHOOL CHILD WITH ADHD HAS BEEN BULLIED, WHAT CAN YOU DO TO STOP HIM FROM BEING BULLIED?

The very first thing that you need to do is to decide how you will approach talking to your young child about such a complicated and sensitive subject, such as bullying. At this young age, you cannot exactly talk to a preschool child with ADHD who is being bullied about aggressiveness or isolation, and therefore not having any friends.

The first thing that you must do, as is similar to teaching your child social skills, is to maintain eye contact. Why? If your child does not maintain eye contact, he will not pay attention to what you are teaching him in terms of how to behave. Second, you must try to get him to concentrate and to understand what you are teaching him.

I *know* that I am stating that you need to control both of these behaviors in a preschool child with ADHD, which may be difficult, but you must try. If your child is not looking at you and not concentrating on what you are saying, then he will not learn how to help himself in terms of not being bullied or to stop bullying others.

If you have been teaching your child social skills as per the interventions in this book, then he should be already accustomed to maintaining eye contact. If not, then please go back to the section on maintaining eye contact in chapter 5 and read the relevant section.

HOW IS BULLYING DESCRIBED IN PRESCHOOL CHILDREN WITH ADHD?

Bullying may include kicking, hitting, tripping, pinching, kicking or punching. It may also be knocking someone's blocks down or ruining their art project. On the other hand, it could also be that the child refused to play with a peer, made fun of a child, or acted generally mean and appearing happy that he had done so. Are there signs that may alert you that your child has been bullied?

HOW DO YOU DISCOVER IF YOUR PRESCHOOL CHILD WITH ADHD HAS BEEN BULLIED?

Here are some signs that your preschool child has been bullied. You must be vigilant (we all miss seeing cues, however!) and try to determine if your preschool child's behavior has changed. For example,

- He loved going to preschool school and now he either hesitates, dawdles, or refuses to go.

- He has several bruises that he cannot or will not explain to you as to how he got them.
- All of a sudden, he complains of not feeling well or having stomach aches.
- He does not want to have another child over to play, either one child or any of the children in his class.
- He does not want to go over to any child's house for a play date.
- He tells you that another child is bothering him at school or on the bus.
- He becomes dependent on you or wants to stay with you most of the time.
- He talks about himself in negative terms, indicating low self-esteem (adapted from Carpenter, 2017, np).

HOW DO YOU CONVINCE YOUR PRESCHOOL CHILD WITH ADHD TO TALK ABOUT BEING BULLIED?

In my opinion, this is the most difficult part of the preventative process and then subsequently, the healing. We are talking about four and five-year-olds here, most of whom have not yet developed a sense of time. I have heard one of these children say, "Six years ago, no two years ago, no two weeks ago." It is cute in a way, but also sad to hear these children grapple with a sense of time, although this confusion about a sense of time is quite normal.

That being said please do not put too much emphasis on when the bullying happened but concentrate more so on exactly what happened. Even though you may have built a close system of communication with your child, talking about being bullied may be a difficult topic for him to understand, no less to discuss. An easier way to help your preschool child with ADHD to discuss what has happened to him is to read him one of the several books on bullying that applies to young children. The following (some are ebooks, and some are paperback books) are some well-recommended books on bullying that are appropriate for young children, all available on Amazon.com.

- Alexander, C. (2008). *Lucy and the bully*
- Best, C., and Potter, G. (2001). *Shrinking violet*

- Henkes, K. (2008). *Chrysanthemum*
- Otoshi, K. (2008). *One*
- Pearson, T. C. (2004). *Myrtle*
- Seskin, S., and Shamblin, A. (2002). *Don't laugh at me*
- Thomas, P., and Harker, L. (2000). *Stop picking on me*

My suggestion is to read a particular book once to your preschool child with ADHD. Ask him about what was the topic of the story. Then, read the book again to your child and slowly talk about the bullying that occurred in the book. First, see if you can get him to talk about any bullying that he has observed. Second, ask him if anything similar has happened to him as well as the trajectory of what happened. If your child begins to discuss the bullying that has happened to him, try very hard to just listen. It will be difficult for your child to talk about the negative experiences that he has had with other children, so you certainly do not want to interrupt his train of thought. At this point, you certainly want to learn techniques for trying to prevent your child from being bullied again.

TECHNIQUES FOR TRYING TO PREVENT YOUR PRESCHOOL CHILD WITH ADHD FROM BEING BULLIED

Children generally are bullied because they appear vulnerable to other children. The best thing that you can do to prevent your preschool child with ADHD from being bullied is to promote better self-esteem in him. You certainly want him to learn how to behave in a positive way. It is important that you realize that it will be challenging for you to act in a positive way, because you are so upset about the fact that your child has been bullied.

Your heart is broken when you hear about other children biting, hitting, or kicking your child. That being said, you must become an actor and behave in a positive way so that your child does not think that he should be blamed for being bullied. If you are encouraging, then hopefully he will feel more positive. Please remember that if your child picks up on any of the nuances of your negative feelings, he may very well internalize these feelings, which is not fair to him. This may be a long process, so just be determined that you will help your child for as long a time period as is necessary.

Okay, so back to what techniques you can try. Since you have already worked on helping your child to recognize certain facial expressions, go over what a person looks like again when he is angry. In that way, he may be able to recognize when a child is preparing himself to bully another child. Then, practice what a face that shows pride would resemble. Young children in 2019 have a good knowledge of digital images such as emojis.

You can show him the variety of emojis on alternate platforms such as Apple or Android. Then, print out the specific emojis. In fact, you can make stickers with the proud emoji on them, and then, print them out. Look for an emoji with a thumbs up or any look that would resemble confidence. Design your own reinforcement schedule so that you will give the emoji stickers to your child at an optimal time. Remember, do not give him too many stickers, and fade the stickers out after a while.

Then, talk to your child about feeling proud of himself and confident as he can see in the emoji's facial expression. Converse with him about his strengths, i.e., being a kind person, being funny, or being good at a sport, such as soccer. Set up a role play with a sibling, if possible. In the role play, tell your child to walk up to another child and appear proud and confident. Remember as to whether or not you have decided to give him a sticker here for behaving in that way. If he learns to produce a body language where he exudes confidence instead of vulnerability, there will hopefully be fewer bullying events.

Encourage him, in addition to feeling proud and confident, to stand up tall instead of looking down at the ground, which some children who are vulnerable with a lack of confidence appear to do. Explain to him that if he looks down at the ground when he walks, other children may think that he is not being friendly. Additionally, he may appear as having a lack of self-assurance, which may encourage bullies to engage with him in a negative way.

What other methods could you try to help your preschool child with ADHD to better interact with a bully? You could use puppets. Create a situation where one puppet is being mean to the other, either hitting him or pushing him. Teach your child how to manipulate the puppets himself so that he can practice using the puppets to be assertive. You definitely do not want the puppet to yell or to scream. Explain to your child the difference between being assertive and aggressive, though clearly not using these words.

I personally would not have your child practice saying, "I don't like when you do that" because quite honestly, a bully typically does not care at all about your child's feelings. Instead, if your child says a phrase such as "Don't push me again, or don't hit me again," and then walks away, that assertive behavior might work to discourage further episodes of bullying. Typically, once a bully finds out that he cannot impact your child, he will probably stop doing so.

If your preschool child with ADHD is playing with a doll or a truck and does not allow the bully to take it by saying in an assertive way, "Stop taking my truck from me. I was playing with it," generally the child who was bullying him will back down. Even though it is imperative to teach preschool children with ADHD to take turns and to share, you certainly do not want him to be bullied into compliance.

I know that these instructions may seem complicated for a preschool child with ADHD. However, if you explain them to him slowly and in simple terms several times, your child will develop a full understanding that appearing weak and unsure may lead to him being bullied.

Try to make any conversation about bullying very low key from this point forward. You certainly do not want your child to feel that he has to report progress to you each and every day after school. If your child does talk about being bullied and it appears that he is handling it and that there are fewer bullying events, praise him. Preschool children with ADHD children need to be praised by their parents for exhibiting positive behavior.

I am sure that if the number of times that he is being bullied decreases, then that situation would be a reward in itself. The realization that your preschool child with ADHD has been bullied is painful enough, nonetheless finding out that he is a bully as well!

IS YOUR PRESCHOOL CHILD WITH ADHD A BULLY?

The possible realization that your child is a bully may be stunning. You are bringing your child up to be a kind and caring person who is nice to other children. How could it happen that instead of being nice to other children, he is being mean and aggressive? It has been reported that children who have been diagnosed with ADHD are three times as likely to be bullies. Additionally, preschool children with ADHD generally exhibit behavior problems before entering school, which may match up with bullying behavior in fourth grade, as reported by their parents.

> Children diagnosed with situational or pervasive ADHD in fourth grade report being active bullies about three times as often and being bullied often 10 times as often as other children. The risk increase was similar in children who fulfilled the ADHD criteria in one or two settings (home and school) (Holmberg and Hjern, 2008, p. 136).

> The high predictability of parental reports of behaviour problems when entering first grade for being an active bully in fourth grade indicates that ADHD–related behavioural problems most often were present before entering school in these children, thus establishing a tentative causal link between the presence of these symptoms and developing bullying behaviour in school in these children (Holmberg and Hjern, 2008, 136–37).

Why does bullying occur? Well, when your child exhibits negative behavior, it may be simply that your child is trying some behaviors out. Some hitting or pushing does occur in preschool settings. However, if you see that your child is enjoying the reaction another child has to his aggressive behavior and even laughing, that behavior is considered unacceptable. Alternatively, he may not feel so good about himself in terms of self-esteem, so that making another child upset might augment his own beliefs about himself. You seemingly have noticed if your preschool child with ADHD is mean to other children, including his siblings. This negative behavior is hard to miss. Does he push or shove another child? Does he knock over structures that they have built? Does he hit or bite the other children?

What are some signs that might alert you to the fact that your preschool child with ADHD is a bully?

- Your child seemingly has a desire or a need to be more powerful than the other children.
- Your child becomes angry quickly and then becomes aggressive.
- Your child feels that he is always right in most situations.
- Your child seems not to care about another child's feelings. He behaves in a cavalier way when he hears that another child is upset.
- Your child is aggressive toward other children or adults (adapted from an article by Carpenter, 2017, np).

What can you do about your child bullying other children? If you witness his inappropriate behavior in a natural setting you must put a stop to it immediately. If you permit this abrasive behavior to continue and hope that it passes, you are giving license to your child to continue his bullying. You must immediately stop aggressive behaviors like holding a sibling down or holding another child down. He must learn that he cannot behave in that way and be told so immediately and consistently. In that way, he is learning about your standards of behavior as well as your household rules.

Each parent has varying ways of making a child realize that a certain behavior is unacceptable. These methods may include time out; not permitting your child to do something that he loves, such as riding his scooter; or merely having a conversation with him. Do whatever works for you, your child, and your family.

Speaking of rules, it is imperative that from a very young age you require that your child learns and adheres to the rules of your house. Even though he most likely cannot read as of yet, you can tell him one rule at a time and associate a picture with each rule so that he remembers each one. How do you know if your child has been following your house rules in settings outside of your home? Unfortunately, you are dependent upon other people telling you about his behavior. If his behavior is harmful or hurtful, I can guarantee that other adults will tell you that your child has behaved in an inappropriate way.

How do you discuss your child's bullying behavior with him? Very carefully! Whatever you do, do *not* reprimand your child for being a bully and do not yell at him! Instead, if you receive information from his teacher or from another child's parent, ask him what he thinks occurred. It is imperative that you do not accuse him but instead, ask him about his behavior.

You can start in a general way. For example, "Is everyone with whom you play nice to one another?" "When you are playing with other children, what do you do to be kind to each other?" "Does anyone hit another child when you are playing?" If your child does not admit to exhibiting any bullying behavior, ask him how he feels when someone is not nice and instead, is mean to him.

A good way to delve into a conversation about bullying is to read your child the book *Hands Are Not for Hitting* (which I love!) by Martine Agassi. The authors discuss the positive things that hands do. Alternately, they discuss the fact that using your hands for hitting is not friendly and may hurt the other person. Does your behavior toward your preschool child with ADHD impact how he behaves toward his peers?

HOW DO YOU BEHAVE TOWARD YOUR PRESCHOOL CHILD WITH ADHD?

Here we are discussing how to teach your child to behave in a kind and thoughtful way toward other children. However, what is the model that your child is observing every single day and night? Is his model his parents who are a calm and guiding force even though they require him to adhere to house rules that mirror positive social skills? On the contrary, is the model your child is imitating parents who are negative, harsh, belligerent, and belittling?

As I have said previously, children with ADHD may be characterized by low self-esteem and vulnerability. Additionally, if they are constantly yelled at and reprimanded, how will they feel about themselves? How will that internalized negative feeling affect their interaction with other children and their building up of positive social skills?

Let us go back a moment. We all know that preschool children with ADHD may be extremely difficult to manage. They may be inattentive and therefore may not listen. They may be hyperactive, as well as forgetful. As I have said before, it may be difficult for you to get much done when you are supervising these children. However, let us be realistic here . . . you are the adult and must retain the responsibility of behaving in a calm and nonabrasive way to your children. Many of us who have had to manage our children with ADHD have found it a challenge to manage our home environment.

Any negative and abrasive behavior may be imitated by your preschool child with ADHD. So be careful to monitor your own behavior so that you do not act in a way that your child might internalize and then exhibit similar behavior with other children. If your child is a bully, what principles do you need to teach him?

IDEAS AND PRINCIPLES THAT YOU NEED TO EXPLAIN AND TEACH TO YOUR PRESCHOOL CHILD WITH ADHD IF HE IS A BULLY

Behave in a Nice and Kind Way

It is imperative to bring up the conversation with your child of behaving in a nice and kind way to other children. Be very careful not to accuse your child of bullying. Instead, explain to him how other children feel after someone is not kind to them. Talk to him about how *he* feels when and if another child is mean to him. These feelings might be experienced in preschool in terms of not allowing someone to play with the group, ignoring another child, hitting, pushing, or knocking over a finished project. Try to explain to your preschool child with ADHD that another child's feelings are important, so therefore, it is not acceptable to hurt another child's feelings. How does maintaining a routine affect your preschool child with ADHD's behavior?

Design a Schedule and Set Up a Routine

As we have discussed before, it is vital to design a schedule for your child with him and to adhere to that routine. He will behave more positively if he knows what to expect in terms of his environmental procedures. It is vital that you praise him when you see that he is exhibiting positive behavior. Perhaps if he hears your approval when he behaves in a positive way, his bullying may diminish. Additionally, in order for him to build positive self-esteem, he needs to be rewarded for exhibiting positive behavior. How would you know if your preschool child with ADHD was behaving in a socially appropriate way?

Set Up a Time for Conversation

It is very important, especially if you have more than one child, to set up a time each day to listen to your child's stories of what occurred on that day. In that way, you will hopefully be able to connect with him in a meaningful way when he expresses his feelings, so that you will be able to develop an accurate perception of his behavior. If he begins to tell you that someone else was not nice to him, try to ascertain as to exactly what happened. There is usually an antecedent, or what came first, the behavior, and the consequences of that behavior, or what maintained that behavior. You need to find out if the other child was mean to him first or if he was mean to the other child. It is a difficult challenge to get your child to admit that he was mean, but it is imperative to try to solve that puzzle.

Encourage Your Preschool Child with ADHD to Discuss His Feelings

In addition to trying to convince your child to admit that he bullied other children is the task of helping your child to feel and to express his thoughts about bullying another child. You are working against two issues: first, preschool children are often not able to realize and/or express their feelings; and second, if your child is not in touch with his feelings, he may not be able to discuss as of yet whether or not he feels badly in relation to the fact that he was mean to another child.

The following are some questions to which you might try to obtain some answers when you are trying to teach your child about the feelings that are typically associated with being a bully.

- What feelings did your preschool child with ADHD express that showed that he was aware that he was mean to another child?
- What kind of an understanding did he have that what he did was called bullying?
- What did your preschool child with ADHD say about possibly feeling badly about what he did to another child?
- What did he say about caring or not caring about what he did to another child?
- What did your preschool child with ADHD express about having been bullied himself, so that he would have a better understanding of how it felt when another child has been bullied?
- What did he say about whether or not he admits that he has been bullied himself?
- It is characteristic of bullies that they laugh about the mean behavior that they exhibited toward another child. When you discussed the issue of your child being mean or being nice to another child,

what did your preschool child with ADHD express as to whether or not he laughed or smiled, and why he did so?

- What was the level of remorse that he expressed, if any?
- What did your preschool child with ADHD say about the fact that he behaved in a mean way toward another child?

After your preschool child with ADHD answers these questions in a meaningful way, what should he say to the child who he has bullied?

SHOULD YOUR PRESCHOOL CHILD WITH ADHD APOLOGIZE TO THE CHILD HE HAS BULLIED?

If your child does not understand what he did, then it will be very difficult for him to apologize. Instead, I would just continue to teach him positive social skills leading towards him developing more positive self-esteem. Additionally, keep an open dialogue with him about his interactions with other children. If you have a relationship with his teacher, then perhaps you will receive feedback from her as well.

If your preschool child with ADHD does realize that he has been mean to another child, then instead of apologizing to that child, perhaps explain to him the importance of behaving in a kind, nice, and caring way toward that child whenever he interacts with him. Children of the preschool age may or may not remember something that happened to them in the recent past. However, thinking about how he might behave in the future might be a very constructive approach for him.

If your child brings it up again, the other child may not remember it, or more likely, is not prepared to discuss it. If the other child brings up the topic to you or your child, then most definitely have your child apologize. I guess the best practice here is to play it by ear, see what evolves, and make a judgment as to the subjects that are brought up.

If your child has a play date with the child whom he presumably bullied, I would keep my eyes and ears open, and supervise the play date carefully to manage any continued attempt at bullying by your child. As I have said previously, if you observe your child exhibiting inappropriate behavior, whether on the playground, in the supermarket or in your house, be vigilant in terms of putting an immediate stop to it.

It is also imperative to be cognizant of positive behavior that your child exhibits so that when and if he exhibits positive behavior, you can reward it immediately. You can say, "Good job" give him a high five, or just tell him that he did a good job. Each child will respond differently to a specific type of praise. Find out what reward works best for your child and implement it immediately after observing your child exhibiting positive behavior.

CONCLUSION

What have you learned about preschool children with ADHD after reading this book?

Ideally, you have learned the definition of attention-deficit/hyperactivity disorder (ADHD) according to the *Diagnostic and Statistical Manual of Mental Disorders, 5th Edition (DSM-5)*. You have learned that preschool children with ADHD exhibit persistent hyperactive and inattentive behavior differently and in a more extreme sense than typical children do in two settings. Additionally, you have learned that the paramount symptom of preschool children with ADHD is hyperactivity. You have also learned about the *American Academy of Pediatrics Clinical Practice Guideline for the Diagnosis, Evaluation, and Treatment of Attention-Deficit/ Hyperactivity Disorder in Children and Adolescents* as it pertains to the diagnosis and treatment of preschool ADHD, which helps to inform parents about the recommended treatment for their child as they go to see a professional. These guidelines focus on behavioral interventions being the first line of treatment for preschool children with ADHD.

Parents are an instrumental source of information about their preschool child who exhibits the symptoms that may correspond to a possible diagnosis of ADHD. Therefore, the importance of parents being observers of their preschool child with ADHD's behavior has been highly recommended, so that they can judge their child's behavior as compared to a typical child of the same age. Parents were given many questions to answer about how their preschool child with ADHD behaves in several different settings, which is imperative information to give to a professional who is trying to determine if he fits into the criteria for a diagnosis of ADHD. In that way, parents of a preschool child with ADHD will be able to inform the professional if their preschool child's behavior is different in an extreme sense from other children of the same age.

Parents of preschool children with ADHD experience stress, anxiety, and guilt as associated with their preschool child's ADHD. Hopefully, hearing real-life quotations from other parents about their children who had diagnoses of ADHD who misinterpreted social cues, exhibited impulsivity, and socially inappropriate behavior, has helped these parents to feel as though they are not so alone in their plight. They have been taught how to deal with the unpredictable and inconsistent behavior of their preschool children with ADHD.

You have then learned how to exhibit positive and constructive parenting, so that you will impact your preschool child with ADHD in an affirmative way. Most importantly,you have learned to respond to his socially inappropriate behavior instead of reacting to it. This type of treatment is imperative because research has found that critical, harsh parenting is associated with an increase in socially inappropriate behavior in preschool children with ADHD.

You have learned the definition of social skills. You have also learned the reason that preschool children with ADHD do not learn social skills as easily as their siblings. Additionally, you have learned the importance of parents having knowledge of their preschool child with ADHD's social skills. It is vital to know this information because preschool children with ADHD have poorly developed social skills, such as difficulty following instructions, not listening well, and therefore interrupting others, among other negative behaviors. Since they do not have intact positive social skills, they become vulnerable and are therefore at risk for negative and difficult social experiences such as bullying.

You have learned about social skills deficits, which are at the core of the difficulties that preschool children with ADHD display. Additionally, we have discussed how these difficulties interfere with these children's interactions with their peers, as well as with their family. Interventions were delineated to teach these children to share, take turns, and manage transitions, which are some of the problem-solving areas with which these children grapple.

In terms of treatment, techniques such as social skills training, positive reinforcement, ignoring of certain inappropriate behaviors, controlling your own behavior, and maintaining an organized home routine have been taught to you, so that you will be able to manage your preschool child with ADHD's socially inappropriate behavior. These techniques incorporate the goal of building positive self-esteem in your preschool child with ADHD, which is often lacking even at this young age. You have also heard suggestions on how to build and maintain affirmative interactions with your preschool child with ADHD.

You have learned about detailed interventions and activities that the parents of preschool children with ADHD can follow to make morning and evening routines easier. Additionally, by collaborating with your child to make these rules, (I know that he is young, but in this way, he will feel ownership!) you will experience fewer arguments and negotiations with him.

These techniques will also help preschool children with ADHD to self-regulate their behavior, including their excessive verbiage. Additionally, parents have been offered numerous meticulously detailed methods and interventions inclusive of sixteen social skills. Before you teach these social skills to your preschool child with ADHD, however, you have learned that it is essential to teach him to maintain eye contact or he will not be able to pay attention to the social skills that you are trying to teach him. These social skills included are: Behaving in a Polite Manner, Joining Ongoing Activities and Play, Inviting Others to Join Activities, Cooperation, Compromise, among many others. Also listed and explained as well are a list of devices and accessories to calm down your preschool child with ADHD, as well as some alternative treatments.

Many times, parents of preschool children with ADHD look to technology to diminish their child's hyperactivity, even for a short period of time. Therefore, the role of technology for preschool children with ADHD has been dissected and analyzed. You have studied the advantages and disadvantages of these children using screens and technology. Guidelines have been included to explain the amount of time that researchers have found it safe for your child to use technology. I have included comprehensive reviews of a select group of apps for both the Apple and the Android platforms. I have also offered you a family media plan as designed by the American Academy of Pediatrics (AAP) that will help you to think about and be aware of the purpose of your child using media, as well as how long he accesses it.

The very important topic of dealing with changes in life has been discussed. These issues include a new baby in the house, moving to a new neighborhood or to a new city, the child's friend moving away, among others. Parents have had access here to specific, open-ended questions that will encourage conversation with their preschool child with ADHD about these changes that have occurred. These interactions will hopefully show him how you have responded to these events instead of having reacted. The topic of how to deal with life-changing events for which you cannot plan has also been discussed, such as the death of a grandparent, a hurricane, among others. Resources have been offered here to encourage dialog with parents and their preschool child with ADHD.

Bullying has become all too prevalent in preschool children with ADHD. These children have been bullied and may be bullies, as well. Parents are told about signs that will alert them as to whether or not their child has been bullied, as well as to whether or not he is a bully. Techniques have been delineated that will hopefully prevent your child from being bullied. Additionally, ways to encourage a conversation with your child about bullying has been delineated. Also included were some ideas and principles that you need to explain and teach to your child if he is a bully, such as learning to behave in a nice and kind way. Since it may be difficult to discuss bullying with your preschool child with ADHD, I have provided you with the names of several books on bullying that are appropriate to read to young children.

Finally, a bibliography and a resource list has been included that will help parents of preschool children with ADHD to learn about their child's ADHD as well as how manage their behavior. The topics that the books listed concentrated on having a new baby, sharing, learning about emotions, joining in play, being polite and kind, learning to listen, and using one's hands in a non-aggressive way, among others. Suggestions were made for you to set up a time for a conversation, as well as to encourage your preschool child with ADHD to discuss his feelings.

I hope that this book was helpful to you on your wonderful yet challenging journey with your preschool child with ADHD. The message that I really need to communicate to you is to try to be optimistic and positive at all costs while you are teaching social skills to your preschool child with ADHD. The more positive you act, the more positive your child will feel. The more that you respond, instead of react, the more socially appropriate behavior your child will exhibit. I know that the challenges that you face seem overwhelming. That said, please reach out to support groups at the Children and Adults with Attention-Deficit/Hyperactivity Disorder (CHADD) so that you do not feel so alone.

APPENDIX A: DOES ADHD HAVE A HISTORY?[1]

The derivation of ADHD has a storied past, as does the definition itself. Still (1902) observed behavioral symptoms in certain children when he first focused attention on the hyperactive child. The symptoms that he saw in those children were similar to those that teachers and parents see today in children with ADHD.

Still spoke about children's moral control of their behavior. He referred to what we know as hyperactive and impulsive behavior today, neither of which the child can control. He found that "a deficit in moral control could arise as a function of three distinct impairments: (1) a defect of cognitive relation to the environment; (2) a defect of moral consciousness; and (3) a defect in inhibitory volition" (p. 1011).

From 1917 to 1918, an epidemic of encephalitis caused individuals to experience symptoms that were the result of brain damage. This encephalitis outbreak was the impetus for people to investigate the causes of ADHD.

Werner and Strauss (1941) and Strauss and Lehtinen (1947) developed the concept of the "brain-injured child," which was pervasive throughout this era. They found that this brain damage could occur to the infant either before or after birth. "The behaviors of the brain-damaged children were described as hyperactive, distractible, impulsive, emotionally labile, and perseverative" (Meyen, Vergason, and Whelan, 1993a and b, p. 246). The term "brain-injured child" applied to children with behavioral characteristics similar to those of children with ADHD today as well.

Ironically, these children had no evidence of brain damage! How could those distractible, hyperactive, and impulsive children, the researchers asked, be taught effectively in traditional classrooms with variable routines and typical classroom noise? They suggested that these children be placed in smaller, more organized classrooms, with as few distractions as possible (Barkley, 1998, p. 7).

I remember that the principal of the first school in New York City where I taught children with ADHD required that all the classrooms have white walls with no pictures. We had to wear clothes that were monotone in color such as beige or gray so nothing would distract the children we taught.

Little did we know as first-year teachers that these children would distract themselves! They would jump up and down, twirl their hair, tap their fingers on the desks, and walk around in circles! The term "brain-injured" child was soon to be replaced, however.

During the 1950s, the term "brain-injured child" was replaced with "minimal brain damage." "Scholars suggested the term 'minimal brain damage,' a designation indicating that the brain damage was slight" (Meyen et al., 1993a and b, p. 247). After suggestions by the National Institutes of Health (NIH), the preferred term next became "minimal brain dysfunction" (MBD; Clements, 1966, p. 9). Just in case you are interested in the definition of MBD that was used at that time, here it is:

> Children of near-average, average or above average general intelligence with certain learning or behavioral difficulties ranging from mild to severe, which are associated with deviations of function of the central nervous system. These deviations may manifest themselves by various combinations of impairment in perception, conceptualization, language, memory, and control of attention, impulse, or motor function (Clements, 1966, p. 9).

As things go, the designation evolved and changed again in 1957 to "hyperkinetic impulse disorder" because researchers such as Laufer and Denhoff (1957) believed that these children had a deficit in the central nervous system—specifically, in the thalamic region. This definition-specific term would have fit my brother perfectly. He spent his time in elementary school jumping over other children's desks in a leapfrog fashion. My brother was never evaluated, but if he had been, I believe he would have had a diagnosis of what we now call ADHD predominantly hyperactive-impulsive type.

Unfortunately, no one knew what to do or tried to help my brother to diminish his hyperactivity so he could focus more efficiently. My brother's hyperactive behavior led other children to dislike him, which was detrimental to his self-esteem. That low self-esteem led him into dangerous situations as he got older when he became involved with a very risky group of young adults. I am certain that one of the reasons, among many, that my brother lived a life of social hardship was that no one reached out to help him try to diminish his hyperactive behavior. He was always looked upon as the "bad child." He spent most of his academic life either in the principal's office, in detention, or suspended from school.

Chess (1960), among others, then replaced the term "minimal brain dysfunction" with "hyperactive child syndrome." He described "the hyperactive child as one who carries out activities at a higher rate of speed than the average child, or who is constantly in motion or both" (p. 239).

Ready for another change? Researchers in the 1950s and 1960s questioned the unitary implication of "hyperactive child syndrome." This was important because

> (1) It emphasized activity as the defining feature of the disorder . . . as other scientists of the time would do; (2) it stressed the need to consider objective evidence of the symptom beyond the subjective reports of parents or teachers; (3) it took the blame for the child's problems away from the parents; and it separated the syndrome of hyperactivity from the concept of a brain-damaged syndrome. Other scientists of this era would emphasize similar points (Werry & Sprague, 1970) (Barkley, 1998, p. 9).

Following the logic at the time that this syndrome was more diverse than one definition, in 1966 the National Institute of Neurological Diseases and Blindness delineated at least ninety-nine symptoms of this disorder (Barkley, 1998, p. 8).

> By the early 1970s, the defining features of hyperactivity or hyperkinesis were broadened to include what investigators previously felt to be only associated characteristics, including impulsivity, short attention

span, low frustration tolerance, distractibility, and aggressiveness (Marwitt & Stenner, 1972; Safer & Allen, 1976) (Barkley, 1998, p. 10).

Now we are getting closer to today's definition. In fact, one of the parents in my field research, Bess, spoke to me about her son's short attention span when she said, "He's just really bright and has difficulty shifting his focus from one thing that is interesting to anything else."

Two models of ADHD evolved, one described by Wender (1971) and the other by Douglas (1972). Wender described minimum brain dysfunction as six clusters of symptoms. These were:

- motor behavior
- attention-perceptual cognitive function
- learning difficulties
- impulse control
- interpersonal relations
- emotion (Barkley, 1998, p. 11)

What were the underlying causes of these symptoms? Wender stated that they were caused by three primary deficits. These deficits were a decreased feeling of pleasure and pain; a generally high and poorly modulated level of activation; and extroversion (Barkley, 1998, p. 11). It seemed to follow because if these children had a diminished feeling of pleasure and pain, they might be less responsive to punishments and rewards. That being said, you can see that those children might not have responded well to their teacher's or their parent's attempts at behavior management.

The second model was developed by Douglas in 1972. He found that deficits in sustained attention and impulse control were more likely to account for these children's problems than just hyperactivity. In other words, they could not remain focused for a long period of time. They also could not control their impulses, such as, to hit or kick other children. He found that hyperactive children were not necessarily more reading or learning disabled, did not perseverate on concept learning tasks, did not manifest auditory or right-left discrimination, and had no difficulties with short-term memory (Barkley, 1998, p. 13).

Douglas (1980) then expanded on her original model and described four deficits that could possibly explain the causes of ADHD. These were

(1) the investment, organization, and maintenance of attention and effort; (2) the inhibition of impulsive responding; (3) the modulation of arousal levels to meet situational demands; and (4) an unusually strong inclination to seek immediate reinforcement (Barkley, 1998, p. 13).

"Attention-deficit disorder" became the new term in 1980 due to Douglas's work (1972) in addition to criteria set down by the APA in *Diagnostic and Statistical Manual of Mental Disorders* (DSM-III). Use of the term "attention deficit," or "poor attention span," rather than "hyperactivity," to describe these children's major problem was necessary because of agreement that hyperactivity was not the only symptom of the disorder (Barkley, 1998, p. 20).

DSM-III placed a greater emphasis on inattention and impulsivity than on hyperactivity. Lists of symptoms were included, as were guidelines for the age of onset as well as exclusion of other childhood psychiatric symptoms (which emphasized hyperactivity; Barkley, 1998, p. 21).

Stepping back a bit into a discussion of treatment, the efficacy of the use of medication, specifically Ritalin, to diminish the symptoms of ADHD was researched from 1939 to 1941 by Bradley (1937), among others. The use of similar medications was continued into the 1970s. In fact, in response to later studies that reaffirmed a positive drug response in hyperactive children, various medications were employed in the 1970s to diminish the hyperactive symptoms of children who were of school age. These medications are still used today. During the same time period, Feingold (1975) discussed the possibility that there were environmental causes of hyperactivity such as allergies to food additives. The latest change in terminology, was soon to come.

In 1987, the APA's *Diagnostic and Statistical Manual of Mental Disorders* (DSM-IV) changed the term "attention-deficit disorder" to "attention-deficit/hyperactivity disorder" (ADHD), and this is the term that has remained in use to today. Included in this new revision were single-symptom lists including single cutoff scores for inattention, impulsivity, and hyperactivity. These lists were based on empirically derived dimensions of child behavior along with established symptoms that were developmentally inappropriate for a child's mental age. Research continued, however.

During the 1990s, neuroimaging research proved that there was brain activity specific to children with ADHD in the frontal regions. Further, researchers found that the posterior sections of the brains of children with ADHD were significantly smaller than those of children without ADHD (Barkley, 1998, p. 35; Semrud-Clikeman et al., 1994).

During this time, DSM-IV also reintroduced the term "attention-deficit/hyperactivity disorder, predominantly inattentive type (ADHD-I), which required evidence of symptom pervasiveness across settings and demonstration of impairment in a major domain of life functioning (home, school, work; Barkley, 1998, p. 38). So what determined whether or not a child had ADHD?

The predominant view of the 1990s was that social and environmental factors influenced whether or not a child had ADHD rather than neurological factors. Additionally, it was thought that these children's most apparent deficit was behavioral inhibition or lack of self-regulation (Barkley, 1998, p. 39).

Barkley, among other researchers, felt that "the subtype of ADHD comprising chiefly inattention without impulsive-hyperactive behavior may possibly be a qualitatively distinct disorder entirely from those children who have hyper-active-impulsive behavior" (1998, p. 39).

Brown (2007) described the inner workings of children with ADHD using a model that described four executive functions:

- activation: organizing, prioritizing, and activating for work
- focus: focusing, sustaining, and shifting attention to tasks
- effort: regulating alertness and sustaining effort and processing speed
- emotion: managing frustration and modulating emotions (pp. 13–17).

There have been many descriptions or models of ADHD, some of which have defined ADHD in a similar fashion and others that have offered varied descriptions. In my experience over many years of teaching children with ADHD as well as in my field research, I have found that most children with ADHD do not fit into a specific diagnostic category. Therefore, parents must be cognizant of the specific and unique behavioral characteristics of their own child with ADHD. Even though most children with ADHD are distractible, for example, not all are impulsive. Additionally, they do not all have social skills problems. However, some of these children may exhibit organizational difficulties, among other symptoms.

This outline of the derivation and causes of ADHD would not be complete without mentioning some very exciting, new research, "in consideration of the fact that 'the prevalence of Attention-Deficit/Hyperactivity Disorder has been estimated at 3%–7% in school-age children, approximately 3,290,000 of those children have ADHD" (American Psychiatric Association, 2000, p. 90; cited in Rapoport, 2007a, p. 225). Researchers have questioned whether or not there is a delay in the brain maturation of children with ADHD or whether children with ADHD are characterized by a total difference in typical brain development.

"Since its earliest description, there has been debate as to whether the disorder is a consequence partly of delay in brain maturation or as a complete deviation from the template of typical development" (Shaw et al., 2007, p. 19649). In a study funded by the NIH, Shaw et al. (2007) found, in groundbreaking research, "that in youth with attention-deficit/ hyperactivity disorder brain (ADHD), the brain matures in a normal pattern but is delayed three years in some regions, on average, compared to youths without the disorder."

The areas of the brain that reflect difficulties for children with ADHD are those that control self-regulation in their thinking, attention, and planning. Therefore, the maturation of this child's brain is quite normal and merely delayed, which should assure parents that their child's symptoms will diminish as they mature because at some point their child will have normal brain maturation. This new information should offer parents great optimism concerning the prognosis of their child with ADHD.

NOTE

1. Appendix A taken directly from *ADHD and Social Skills: A Step-by-Step Guide for Teachers and Parents*, Rapoport, 2009, pp. 12–20.

APPENDIX B—ABC CHART

ABC CHART

Date/Start & end time	A=Antecedent: Location, activity, people, etc.	B=Behavior What did the child do?	C=Consequence What happened after the behavior

Retrieved from http://schools.nyc.gov/NR/rdonlyres/3CBEB620-5B0B-4824-B79A=
6.09F0731B2C/166366/ABCChartAllinOneVersion1Instructions.docx

BIBLIOGRAPHY AND SUGGESTED RESOURCES

This list includes the references used in this book as well as those that will be helpful for parents to investigate. Additionally, other resources are included that parents might find helpful in the search for techniques that will help them to manage the behavior that their preschool child with ADHD may exhibit.

ADDitude. (2018). In this house, we don't tolerate bullying. Retrieved from https://www.additudemag.com/slideshows/no-more-bullying-strategies-for-adhd-kids/.

Agassi, M. (2002). *Hands are not for hitting*. Minneapolis, MN: Free Spirit Publishing.

Alexander, C. (2008). *Lucy and the bully*. Park Ride, IL: Albert Whitman and Company.

American Academy of Pediatrics. (2011). ADHD: Clinical practice guideline for the diagnosis, evaluation, and treatment of attention-deficit/hyperactivity disorder in children and adolescents. Retrieved from http://pediatrics.aappublications.org/content/pediatrics/early/2011/10/14/peds.2011-2654.full.pdf.

American Academy of Pediatrics. (2016a). Family media plan. Retrieved from https://www.healthychildren.org/English/media/Pages/default.aspx.

American Academy of Pediatrics. (2016b). Media and young minds. Retrieved from http://pediatrics.aappublications.org/content/pediatrics/138/5/e20162591.full.pdf.

American Psychiatric Association. (2013). *Diagnostic and statistical manual of mental disorders, 5th edition*. Arlington, VA: American Psychiatric Association.

Armstrong, T. (2018). A kinder "time-out" that really works. *ADDitude*. Retrieved from https://www.additudemag.com/do-time-outs-really-work-adhd-children/.

Baker, J. (2003). *The social skills picture book*. Arlington, TX: Future Horizons.

Bang, M. (1999). *When Sophie gets angry—Really, really angry*. New York: Scholastic.

Barkley, R. A. (1998). *Attention-deficit hyperactivity disorder: A handbook for diagnosis and treatment*. New York: Guilford.

Barkley, R. A., Grodzinsky, G., and DuPaul, G. (1992). Frontal lobe functions in attention deficit disorder with and without hyperactivity: A review and research report. *Journal of Abnormal Child Psychology, 20*, 163–88.

Barkley, R. A. (2015). *Attention-deficit hyperactivity disorder: A handbook for diagnosis and treatment, 4th edition*. New York: Guilford Press.

Berenstain, S. (1981). *The Berenstain Bears' moving day*. Toronto: Random House Books for Young Readers.

Berenstain, S. (1998). *The Berenstain Bears lend a helping hand*. Toronto: Random House Books for Young Readers.

Best, C. (2001). *Shrinking violet*. New York: Farrar, Straus & Giroux.

Bilton, N. (2014). Steve Jobs was a low-tech parent. Retrieved from https://www.nytimes.com/2014/09/11/fashion/steve-jobs-apple-was-a-low-tech-parent.html.

Bowles, N. (2018). Your kid's apps are crammed with ads. Retrieved from https://www.nytimes.com/2018/10/30/style/kids-study-apps-advertising.html.

Bradley, W. (1937). The behavior of children receiving benzedrine. *American Journal of Psychiatry, 94*, 577–85.

Brown, T. E. (2000). *Attention-deficit disorders and comorbidities in children and adults*. Washington, DC: American Psychiatric Press.

Brown, T. E. (2005). *The unfocused mind in children and adults*. New Haven, CT: Yale University Press.

Brown, T. E. (2007). A new approach to attention deficit disorder. *Educational Leadership, 64*(5), 22–27.

Carpenter, D. (2017). How to handle preschool bullies. Retrieved from https://www.parenting.com/toddler/how-to-handle-preschool-bullies/.

Carlson, N. L. (2012). *My best friend moved away (Nancy's neighborhood)*. Minneapolis, MN: Carolrhoda Books.

CHADD. (2019). Frequently asked questions. Retrieved from https://chadd.org/about-adhd/frequently-asked-questions/.

Chess, S. (1960). Diagnosis and treatment of the hyperactive child. *New York State Journal of Medicine, 60*, 2379–85.

Christakis, E. (2016). *The importance of being little: What preschoolers really need from grownups*. New York: Viking.

Clements, S. D. (1966). *Task force one: Minimal brain dysfunction in children*. National Institute of Neurological Diseases and Blindness, Monograph, 3. Rockville, MD: U.S. Department of Health, Education and Welfare.

Coloroso, B. (2008). *The bully, the bullied and the bystander*. New York: HarperCollins.

Cooper, S. (2005). *Speak up and get along*. Minneapolis, MN: Free Spirit Publishing.

Curtis, J. L. (1998). *Today I feel silly & other MOODS that make my day*. New York: HarperCollins.

Cuyers, K., de Ridder, K., and Strandheim, A. (2011). The effect of therapeutic horseback riding on 5 children with attention deficit hyperactivity disorder: A pilot study. *The Journal of Complementary Medicine, 17*(10), 901–908.

Davies, L. (1998). *Kelly Bear behavior*. New York: Kelly Bear Press.

Davies, L. (2005). *24 ideas for instilling manners in children*. Retrieved from http://www.kellybear.com/TeacherArticles/TeacherTip62.html.

Diesen, D., and Hannah, D. (2017). *The pout-pout fish and the bully-bully shark*. New York: Farrar, Straus & Giroux.

Douglas, V. I. (1972). Stop, look and listen: The problem of sustained attention and impulse control in hyperactive and normal children. *Canadian Journal of Behavioral Science, 4*, 259–82.

Douglas, V. I. (1980a). Higher mental processes in hyperactive children: Implications for training. In R. Knights and D. Bakker (eds.), *Treatment of hyperactive and learning disordered children*. Baltimore, MD: University Park Press.

Douglas, V. I. (1980b). Treatment and training approaches to hyperactivity: Establishing internal or external control. In C. Whalen and B. Henker (eds.), *Hyperactive children: The social ecology of identification and treatment*. New York: Academic Press.

DuPaul, G. J., and Kern, L. (2011). *Young children with ADHD: Early identification and intervention*. Washington, DC: American Psychological Corporation.

DuPaul, G. J., McGoey, K. E., Eckert, T. L., and VanBrackle, J. (2001). Preschool children with attention-deficit/hyperactivity disorder: Impairments in behavioral, social and school functioning. *Journal of the American Academy of Child and Adolescent Psychiatry, 40*(5), 508–15.

Early Childhood News. (2007).

Elliott, S. N., and Gresham, F. M. (1991). *Social skills intervention guide*. Circle Pines, MN: American Guidance Service.

Elliott, S. N., and Gresham, F. M. (1993). Social skills interventions for children. *Behavior Modification, 17*, 287–313.

Farone, S. V., and Antshel, K. M. (2014). ADHD: Non-pharmacologic interventions. *Child and Adolescent Psychiatric Clinics of North America, 23*(4), 687–981.

Feingold, B. (1975). *Why your child is hyperactive*. New York: Random House.

Flippin, R. (2005). What is ADHD hyperfocus? In *ADDitude*, https://www.additudemag.com/understanding-adhd-hyperfocus/.

Frye, D. (2017). AAP: Parents should make screen time interactive—Or cut back. *ADDitude*. Retrieved from https://www.additudemag.com/aap-screen-time-guidelines-quality-over-quantity/.

Ghuman, J. K., and Ghuman, H. S. (2014). *ADHD in preschool children: Assessment and treatment*. New York: Oxford University Press.

Graves, S. (2011). *Not fair, won't share*. Minneapolis, MN: Free Spirit Publishing.

Gray, Carol. (2010). *The new social story book*. Arlington, TX: Future Horizons.

Greenhill, L. L., Posner, K., Vaughn, B. S., and Kratochvil, C. J. (2008). Attention deficit hyperactivity disorder in preschool children. *Child and Adolescent Psychiatric Clinics of North America*, 347–66.

Gresham, F. M. (1981). Assessment of children's social skills. *Journal of School Psychology, 19*(2), 120–33.

Gresham, F. M., Sugai, G., and Horner, R. H. (2001). Interpreting outcomes of social skills training for students with high-incidence disabilities. *Exceptional Children, 67*(3), 331–44.

Harvey, E. A., Herbert, S. D., and Stowe, R. M. (2015). *Parenting hyperactive preschoolers*. New York: Oxford University Press.

Henkes, K. (2008). *Chrysanthemum*. New York: HarperCollins Publishers, L.L.C.

Hensley, M., Dillon, J. C., Pratt, D., Ford, J., and Burke, R. (2005). *Tools for teaching social skills in school*. Boys Town, NE: Boys Town Press.

Hoff, E. (2003). The specificity of environmental influence: Socioeconomic status affects early vocabulary development via maternal speech. *Child Development, 74*(5), 1368–78.

Holmberg, K., and Hjern, A. (2008). Bullying and attention-deficit-hyperactivity disorder in 10-year-olds in a Swedish community. *Developmental Medicine and Child Neurology, 50*, 134–38. Retrieved from https://www.kennedykrieger.org/stories/Is-it-adhd-or-typical-toddler-behavior-ten-early-signs-adhd-risk-preschool-age-children.

Klass, P. (2016). *Why parents and doctors should think about ADHD in preschool*. Retrieved from https://www.nytimes.com/2016/12/05/well/family/why-parents-and-doctors-should-think-about-adhd-in-preschool.html.

Krensky, S. (2016). *We just had a baby*. North Mankato, MN: Capstone Young Readers.

Kucirkova, N., and Falloon, G. (2017). *Apps, technology and young learners: International evidence for teaching*. London: Routledge.

Laufer, M., and Denhoff, E. (1957). Hyperkinetic behavior syndrome in children. *Journal of Pediatrics, 50*, 463–54.

Lester, H. (1988). *Tacky the penguin*. New York: Houghton Mifflin Company.

Lougy, R., DeRuvo, S., and Rosenthal, D. (2007). *Teaching young children with ADHD: Successful strategies and practical interventions for PreK-3*. Thousand Oaks, CA: Corwin Press.

Manushkin, F. (2016). *Big boy underpants*. New York: Random House Children's Books.

Meiners, C. J. (2004). *Accept and value each person*. Minneapolis, MN: Free Spirit Publishing.

Meiners, C. J. (2004). *Be honest and tell the truth*. Minneapolis, MN: Free Spirit Publishing.

Meiners, C. J. (2004). *Be polite and kind*. Minneapolis, MN: Free Spirit Publishing.

Meiners, C. J. (2004). *Join in and play*. Minneapolis, MN: Free Spirit Publishing.

Meiners, C. J. (2004). *Know and follow the rules*. Minneapolis, MN: Free Spirit Publishing.

Meiners, C. J. (2004). *Listen and learn*. Minneapolis, MN: Free Spirit Publishing.

Meiners, C. J. (2004). *Respect and take care of things*. Minneapolis, MN: Free Spirit Publishing.

Meiners, C. J. (2004). *Share and take turns*. Minneapolis, MN: Free Spirit Publishing.

Meiners, C. J. (2004). *Talk and work it out*. Minneapolis, MN: Free Spirit Publishing.

Meiners, C. J. (2004). *Understand and care*. Minneapolis, MN: Free Spirit Publishing.

Meng, C. (2016). *Always remember*. New York: Philomel Books.

Mercer, M. (2002). *Helping Mom*. Columbus, OH: McGraw Hill.

Meyen, E. L., Vergason, G., and Whelan, R. (Eds.). (1993a). *Challenges facing special education*. Denver, CO: Love Publishing Company.

Meyen, E. L., Vergason, G., and Whelan, R. (Eds.). (1993b). *Educating children with mild disabilities*. Denver, CO: Love Publishing Company.

Model Me Kids. *I can do it*. Rockville, MD: http://www.modelmekids.com/.

Model Me Kids. *Time for a playdate*. Rockville, MD: http://www.modelmekids.com/.

Naylor, P. R. (1994). *King of the playground*. New York: Simon & Schuster.

NEA.org. (2012). Nation's educators combine push for safe, bully-free environments. Retrieved from http://www.nea.org/home/53298.htm.

Olweus, D., Limber, S. (1999). Bully prevention programme. In *Bluprints for Violence Prevention, Vol 9*. Golden, CO: Venture Publishing.

Olweus, D. (1994). Bullying at school: Basic facts and effects of a school-based intervention program. *Journal of Child Psychology and Psychiatry, 35*(7), 1171–90.

Otoshi, K. (2008). *One*. Novato, CA: KO Kids Books.

Overgaard, K. R., Aase, H., Torgersen, S., and Zeiner, P. Co-occurrence of ADHD and anxiety in preschool children. *Journal of Attention Disorders, 20*(7), 573–80.

Parton, M. B. (1932). Social participation among school children. *The Journal of Adnormal and Social Psychology, 27*(3), 243–69.

Pearson, T. C. (2004). *Myrtle*. New York: Farrar, Straus & Giroux.

Perren, S., and Alsaker, F. D. (2006). Social behavior and peer relationships of victims, bully victims and bullies in kindergarten. *Journal of Child Psychology and Psychiatry, 47*(1), 45–57.

Pfiffner, L. J., and McBurnett, K. (1997). Social skills training with parent generalization: Treatment effects for children with attention deficit disorder. *Journal of Consulting and Clinical Psychology, 65*(5), 749–57.

Pfister, M. (1996). *The rainbow fish*. New York: NorthSouth Books.

Radesky, J. S., and Christakis, D. A. (2016). *Pediatric Clinic of North America, 63*, 827–39.

Radesky, J. S., Schumacher, J., and Zuckerman, B. (2015). Mobile and interactive media use by young children: The good, the bad, and the unknown. *Pediatrics, 135*(1). doi:10.1542/peds.2014-2251.

Rapoport, E. M. (2007a). Homeschool parents teaching social skills to their children with ADHD. *Private School Monitor, 28*(4), 1–14.

Rapoport, E. M. (2007b). Seizing opportunity: Homeschool parents teaching social skills to their children with ADHD. Dissertation, Ann Arbor, MI.

Rapoport, E. M. (2009). *ADHD and social skills: A step-by-step guide for teachers and parents*. Lanham, MD: Rowman & Littlefield.

Ratey, J. J. (2008). *Spark: The revolutionary science of exercise and the brain*. New York: Little Brown & Company.

Reif, S. F. (2005). *How to reach and teach children with ADD/ADHD*. San Francisco, CA: Jossey Bass.

Reimers, C., and Bruger, B. A. (1999). *ADHD in the young child*. Plantation, FL: Specialty Press.

Sandall, S. R., Hemmeter, M. L., McLean, M., and Smith, B. J. (2005). *DEC recommended practices: A comprehensive guide for practical application in early intervention/early childhood special education*. Longmont, CO: Sopris West.

Schuck, S. E. B., Emmerson, N. A., Fine, A. H., and Lakes, K. D. (2015). Canine-Assisted Therapy for children with ADHD: Preliminary findings from the positive assertive cooperative kids study. *Journal of Attention Disorders, 19*(2), 125–37.

Schusteff, A. (2007). Is preschool too early to diagnose ADHD? *ADDitude*. Retrieved from https://www.additudemag.com/preschoolers-adhd/.

Semrud-Clikeman, M., Filipek, P. A., Biederman, J., Steingard, R., Kennedy, D., Renshaw, P., and Bekken, K. (1994). Attention deficit hyperactivity disorder: Magnetic resonance imaging morphometric analysis of the corpus callosum. *Journal of the American Academy of Child and Adolescent Psychiatry, 33*, 875–81.

Seskin, S., and Shamblin, A. (2002). *Don't laugh at me*. Berkeley, CA: Tricycle Press.

Shapiro, L. E. (2008). *It's time to sit still in your own chair*, Oakland, CA: New Harbinger Publications.

Shaw, P., Eckstrand, K., Sharp, W., Blumenthal, J., Lerch, J. P., Greenstein, D., Clasen, L., and Evans, A. (2007). Attention-deficit/hyperactivity disorder is characterized by cortical maturation. *Proceedings of the National Academy of Sciences of the United States of America, 104*, 19649–54. Retrieved from https://www.ncbi.nlm.nih.gov/pubmed/18024590.

Still, G. F. (1902). Some abnormal psychical conditions in children. *Lancet, 1*, 1008–12, 1077–82, 1163–68.

Strauss, A. A., and Lehtinen, L. E. (1947). *Psychopathology and education of the brain-injured child*. New York: Grune and Stratton.

Thomas, P., and Harker, L. (2000). *Stop picking on me*. Hauppauge, NY: Barron's Educational Series.

Time Timer. https://www.timetimer.com/.

Vaughn, S., Kim, A. H., Sloan, C. V. M., Hughes, M. T., Elbaum, B., and Sridhar, D. (2003). Social skills interventions for young children with disabilities. *Remedial and Special Education, 24*(1), 2–15.

Vlachou, M., Andreou, E., Botsoglou, K., and Didaskalou, E. (2011). Bully/victim problems among preschool children: A review of current research evidence. *Educational Psychology Review, 23*, 329–58.

Wartella, E., Rideout, V., and Lauricella, A., et al. (2014). *Parenting in the age of digital technology: A national survey*. Report of the Center on Media and Human Development, School of Communication, Northwestern University.

Wax, W. (2008). *Even firefighters go to the potty: A potty training lift-the-flap story*. New York: Little Simon Publishing.

Wender, P. (1971). *Minimal brain dysfunction*. New York: Wiley.

Werner, H., and Strauss, A. A. (1941). Pathology of figure-background relation in the child. *Journal of Abnormal and Social Psychology, 36*(2), 236–48.

Woodbury, P. (2007). Recognizing difficult behavior in the preschool child. Retrieved from http://www.earlychildhoodnews.com/.

Woods, E. J. (2017). *Rex the dinosaur and a new bike*. Seattle, WA: CreateSpace Independent Publishing Platform.

http://adhdanswers.blogspot.com/.

https://chadd.org/.

https://www.stopbullying.gov/.

www.understood.org. (2018). ADHD and coping with grief: What you need to know. Retrieved from https://www.understood.org/en/learning-attention-issues/child-learning-disabilities/add-adhd/adhd-and-coping-with-grief-what-you-need-to-know.

Zentall, S. S. (2006). *ADHD and education: Foundations, characteristics, methods and collaboration*. Upper Saddle River, NJ: Pearson Education.

ABOUT THE AUTHOR

Esta M. Rapoport received her doctorate in special education from Boston University upon writing her dissertation, which focused on home-school parents teaching social skills to their children with ADHD. She does social skills training with children who have ADHD. Dr. Rapoport is a graduate of New York University and Teachers College of Columbia University. She and her husband, Fred, have three children, Mimi, Ian, and Jake; three grandchildren, Max, Jude, and Mac; and a Dalmatian, Ruby, as well as their Brittany, Rocky.